PERFORMING CULTURE

Theory, Culture & Society

Theory, Culture & Society caters for the resurgence of interest in culture within contemporary social science and the humanities. Building on the heritage of classical social theory, the book series examines ways in which this tradition has been reshaped by a new generation of theorists. It also publishes theoretically informed analyses of everyday life, popular culture, and new intellectual movements.

EDITOR: Mike Featherstone, *Nottingham Trent University*

THE TCS CENTRE
The Theory, Culture & Society book series, the journals *Theory, Culture & Society* and *Body & Society*, and related conference, seminar and post-graduate programmes operate from the TCS Centre at Nottingham Trent University. For further details of the TCS Centre's activities please contact:

Centre Administrator
The TCS Centre, Room 175
Faculty of Humanities
Nottingham Trent University
Clifton Lane, Nottingham, NG11 8NS, UK
e-mail: tcs@ntu.ac.uk
web: http//tcs@ntu.ac.uk

Recent volumes include:

Deleuze and Guattari
An Introduction to the Politics of Desire
Philip Goodchild

Undoing Aesthetics
Wolfgang Welsch

The Consumer Society
Myths and Structures
Jean Baudrillard

Culture as Praxis
Zygmunt Bauman

Spaces of Culture
City, Nation, World
Mike Featherstone and Scott Lash

Love and Eroticism
edited by Mike Featherstone

Sociology of Giving
Helmuth Berking

PERFORMING CULTURE

Stories of Expertise and the Everyday

John Tulloch

SAGE Publications
London • Thousand Oaks • New Delhi

John Tulloch 1999

First published 1999

Published in association with *Theory, Culture & Society*,
Nottingham Trent University

SAGE Publications Ltd
6 Bonhill Street
London EC2A 4PU

SAGE Publications Inc.
2455 Teller Road
Thousand Oaks, California 91320

SAGE Publications India Pvt Ltd
32, M-Block Market
Greater Kailash – I
New Delhi 110 048

British Library Cataloguing in Publication data

A catalogue record for this book is available from
the British Library

ISBN 0 7619 5607 7
ISBN 0 7619 5608 5 (pbk)

Library of Congress catalog card number available

Typeset by Photoprint, Torquay, Devon
Printed and bound in Great Britain by Athenaeum Press,
Gateshead

CONTENTS

Introduction: Performing Culture   1
1 Cultural Theory   20
2 Cultural Policy   39
3 (High-) Cultural Framing   70
4 (High-) Cultural Re-Framing   85
5 Cultural Reading   106
6 Cultural Methods   138
7 Conclusion: Understanding Situated Performance   159

References   178
Index   183

[T]he metaphor of performativity has emerged to focus attention on the subject's (compulsory) performance of gender and the possibilities for performing gender differently. . . . The source of textual meaning has been relocated in negotiations between readers, writers and texts. That has necessitated a theorisation of the subjects who read and write, first a deconstruction of the humanist knowing subject . . . then a gendering and sexing of the subject, and finally a recognition of the importance of her colour. . . . It is now both a feminist and a poststructuralist/postmodernist catchcry, in some places, that one does not analyse texts, one rewrites them, one does not have an objective metalanguage, one does not use a theory, one *performs* one's critique. . . . [But] I want to suggest that there are also seductions involved in allowing oneself to be positioned totally by the discourses and genres of rewriting and refusal of metalanguages, the seductions of an anti-science metaphysics. (Threadgold, 1997: 2, 1)

[Raymond] Williams' conviction [is] that people in society are their own cultural agents, transforming those situations by acting *on* and acting *in* them, in short, by performing them. . . . The significance and even the audience's *perception* of cultural practice *as* culture arises out of the place and occasion, rather than the form, of its performance. This emphasis on performance and participation in diverse cultural practices rather than 'extension' of cultural property allows us to review drama as cultural practice. No small-scale form (such as drama) belongs inevitably to a dominant minority, anymore than mass-mediated culture is 'popular' by virtue of large-scale consumption. By stressing the historical and social specificity . . . of cultural practice . . . it challenges the very commonplace that has excluded drama: the *essential* dichotomy between a 'high' culture of special works and a 'low' culture of leisure consumption [which t]o a remarkable degree . . . still underpins canonical literary criticism and contemporary cultural studies, even though they may take opposite sides. (Kruger, 1993: 56–7)

This contemporary cultural condition – postcolonial, postindustrial, post-modern, postcommunist – forms the historical backdrop for the urgency of rethinking the significance of ethnography, away from its status as realist knowledge in the direction of its quality as a form of storytelling, as narrative. This does not mean that descriptions cease to be more or less true; criteria such as accurate data gathering and careful inference making remain applicable. . . . It does mean that our deeply partial position as storytellers . . . should be . . . seriously confronted. . . . The point is not to see this as a regrettable short-coming to be eradicated as much as possible, but as an inevitable state of affairs which circumscribes the . . . responsibility of the researcher/writer as a producer of descriptions which, as soon as they enter the uneven, power-laden field of social discourse, play their political roles as particular ways of seeing and organising an ever-elusive reality. (Ang, 1996: 75–6)

INTRODUCTION: PERFORMING CULTURE

The opening quotations of this book are about performing one's critique, performing one's everyday situations, and researchers as storytellers. These are matching notions of the poststructuralist domain. Beside them, in part composed by them, are the so-called crises of representation and legitimation that Threadgold and Ang target. Here doubt is thrown on the possibility that (academic or bureaucratic) 'experts' can hope to capture what Williams calls 'lived experience', since such experience is created in the social text that the expert writes.

We are now, said Clifford Geertz, telling stories in an era of blurred genres; and in a recent book on qualitative methodology Denzin and Lincoln spell out some of the implications of this for 'performing one's critique'. Since the early 1980s genre dispersion has been occurring: 'documentaries that read like fiction (Mailer), parables posing as ethnographies (Castaneda), theoretical treatises that look like travelogues (Lévi-Strauss)' (1998: 18). On the other hand, poststructuralism (Barthes), micro-macro descriptivism (Geertz), liminality theories of drama and culture (Turner), and deconstruction (Derrida) have been challenging the familiar 'expert' genres and narratives at their epistemological foundations.

This book is about the 'performing' of culture; and the part played in that performance by 'stories of expertise and the everyday'. Ien Ang's and Terry Threadgold's emphasis on reflexive storytelling and performance – and *yet at the same time* their insistence on 'descriptions that are more or less true' and their warnings against 'the seductions of an anti-science metaphysics' – provide my initial theoretical frame. My substantive frame is also Loren Kruger's, when she invokes Raymond Williams to go beyond the dichotomy between the 'selective traditon' of 'high-cultural' drama and the 'ordinary processes of human societies' as we 'perform our critique'.

The book's agenda comes on the one hand from my own developing research interests in media, theatre and cultural studies – thinking about the performance of 'culture' across its various fields of communication: of popular culture (where most cultural studies work is done); cultural policy (where increasingly – and particularly in Australia – cultural studies has become institutionally significant); and high culture (which has been almost abandoned by mainstream cultural studies, except as dichotomy and polemic). On the other hand, the different chapters and sections of the book also reflect new agendas in anthropology and in theatre studies which situate performance/audience analysis '*both in formal performances and in every-day life*' (Schieffelin, 1998: 204, my italics).

It is that relationship of 'formal' and 'everyday' performance – paralleling in some degree tales of 'expertise' and the 'everyday' – that is my interest here. This needs to be seen, I emphasize, as a theoretical *relationship* rather than the dichotomizing polemic of 'high' and 'popular' culture that is much more familiar within cultural studies. In other words, this is *not* a book about performance theory itself (for a particularly valuable and readable overview from the perspective of theatre studies, see Marvin Carlson's *Performance: a Critical Introduction*, 1996). This *is* a book wherein notions of 'performativ-ity' that come from disciplines dealing centrally with formal performance (theatre studies) and everyday performance (anthropology) are allowed to 'blur genres' with stories of expertise and the everyday.

Performance in theory: some theatre studies accounts

A brief summary of some of the main issues that Carlson raises may help explain why I am drawing on notions of 'performance' and 'performativity' here in the context of cultural studies, and how my choices (which I will then elaborate) fit within the wider 'performance' picture. Carlson usefully describes the development of 'performance' within anthropology, linguistics, sociology and psychology, as well as theatre studies, pointing to some of the parallels and distinctions.

● Within anthropology there has been a shift from the notion of 'perform-ing culture' as a 'whole way of life' (for example, Singer's cultural performances as the events of theatre, religious festivals, weddings etc, where a culture is 'set apart' and thus exhibited to itself). A newer interest has been performance as 'liminal' or 'liminoid' border territory (Turner/ Schechner). Here formal performance is not so much 'set apart' but rather a site of transgressive 'negotiation'. Turner's distinction between 'liminal' and 'liminoid', like the cultural studies debate over Bakhtin's 'carnival', is between performance that may invert the established order but never subvert it (liminal), and the more playful, joyful, contingent and subversive trans-gressions of the liminoid.
● Within sociology and psychology there is the continuing importance of Goffman's work, which brings performance back to everyday life, though within theatrical 'frames' which constitute the everyday as a performance before an 'audience'. Carlson emphasizes also the social constructionism of Berger, Luckmann, Schutz, Garfinkel et al. around 'objective' scripts and their 'subjective' re-working as a pragmatic process of 'bricolage'; and de Certeau's extension of this via his dichotomy of cultural 'strategies' (institu-tionalized frameworks, narratives and scripts for behaviour) and 'tactics'

(improvisatory performances which, while never formally opposing conventional strategies offer a performative ground for change, and for the formation of new, alternative strategies).
● Within linguistics, a central concept has been Austin's notion of the performative (an 'illocutionary' utterance that performs an action as it speaks, as in naming a ship or taking a marriage vow). This has been reworked by Derrida to emphasize 'citation' (or 'iterability') as central to successful performativity (for example a marriage vow, or naming a baby as 'girl' only have power because they 'cite' a long history of vows and namings). Influential, too, has been Bakhtin's emphasis (as an alternative to Saussure's langue/parole) on utterance as a situated, historically contextualized performance.

As Carlson says, each of these sets of distinctions (liminal/liminoid; strategy/tactic; script/bricolage; language/utterance, etc) demonstrates 'the essentially contested essence of the term "performance", with some theorists viewing it as reinforcing cultural givens, others seeing it as at least potentially subversive' (1996: 24).

A strong example of Carlson's point, within theatre studies, is Parker and Sedgwick's book *Performativity and Performance* (1995). There we have Joseph Roach arguing for performance as *transformative* practice (as, in his analysis of circum-Atlantic performance, a collective, often colonized 'memory' challenges the official 'history' of the colonists). But within the same set of covers, Judith Butler (following Austin and Derrida) argues that the performative succeeds only because it is *ritualized* practice, echoing prior speech actions and therefore 'citing' prior authoritative practices (in a manner similar to Althusser's notion of the subject being 'interpellated' by ideological state apparatuses). Meanwhile, in the same book Cindy Patton constructs a complex argument around the distinction *between* 'performance' and 'performativity'. For her, performance, like de Certeau's 'tactics', is never more than an accretion on, or a defacement of, the 'space-oriented, capital-oriented domain of the proper' (1995: 183). The performance discourse is parasitic or is (at its most subversive) the discourse of graffiti. In contrast, performativity is more than 'tactic'. It directs new 'strategies' and policies in so far as it constitutes and reproduces its own citational chains.

Thus, in Patton's argument, tropical medicine is a discourse of performance because it is 'reliant upon stable signs (the marks of coloniality, with their geography of race presupposed by the certainty about the centrality of Europe)'; while modern epidemiology has been a performative discourse both constituting its 'bodies' (HIV 'victims' as 'risk groups') and being reconstituted by them (as gay activists within health agencies have reworked these names to: 'people living with AIDS', and 'risk practices').

Roach's, Butler's and Patton's arguments are far too complex – and richly empirical as well – for me to pretend to summarize them here. In any case, my main point at this moment is to use them illustratively: just to begin to indicate the 'structure/agency' tension that circulates around the concept of performance (with sometimes, as in Patton, the terms 'performance' and 'performativity' themselves representing this 'binary' tension). We see this tension in Terry Threadgold's comments above 'on the subject's (compulsory) performance of gender and the possibilities for performing gender differently'. And we see it, too, within recent anthropology where (though the terms 'performance' and 'performativity' tend to be synonymous, as in the following comments from Schieffelin) the 'tension' of structure/agency is still central.

> The ponderous social institutions and mighty political and economic forces of late capitalism which weigh so heavily upon us are, like illusions of maya, without any reality except in so far as they or their effects are actually and continually engaged and emergent in human discourse, practice and activity in the world: generated in what human beings say and do. It is because human sociality continues in moment-by-moment existence only as human purposes and practices are performatively articulated in the world that performance is (or should be) of fundamental interest to anthropology. (Schieffelin, 1998: 195–6)

Here we are closer to Tony Giddens' notion of 'structuration'. But within this broader poststructuralist reconfiguration of 'structure' and 'agency', it is particularly the relationship between performance understood as the agency of a 'theatrical event' and performance as a 'daily practice' that has brought anthropology and theatre studies closer together. Even though each discipline has its own emphases, both focus on 'the expressive processes of strategic impression management and structured improvisation' (Schieffelin, 1998: 195) of performance.

Within theatre studies, as Joseph Roach argues, there has been a widening distinction between 'theatre' as 'a limiting term for a certain kind of spectatorial participation in a certain kind of event', and 'performance', which,

> though it frequently makes reference to theatricality as the most fecund metaphor for the social dimension of cultural production, embraces a much wider range of human behaviours. Such behaviours may include what Michel de Certeau calls 'the practice of everyday life' in which the role of the spectator expands into that of the participant. De Certeau's 'practice' has itself enlarged into an open-ended category marked 'performative' . . . 'a critical category. . . . The performative . . . is a cultural act, a critical perspective, a political intervention'. (Roach, 1995: 46)

At the same time, Loren Kruger has challenged cultural studies' reifying of both traditional and local theatre as a residual 'high culture', arguing for 'an emphasis on performance and participation in diverse cultural practices' rather than as an "extension" of cultural property' (1993: 56). Hegemony, she reminds us (following Williams and Gramsci) is *lived* as consent.

> While we can certainly track the evidence of hegemony in the historical exclusion of the majority from 'high culture', we cannot assume that the association of certain forms [like theatre] with a privileged audience is categorically fixed, nor

can we presume the shape of a 'popular' alternative. In each case, we must investigate the historical emergence of particular forms, the occasion and place of their legitimate performance, and challenges to that legitimacy. (Kruger, 1993: 62)

These tendencies in theatre studies are parelleled, as Conquergood emphasizes, by the wider 'ethnographic' shift from viewing 'the world as text' to 'the world as performance', which opens up a new set of questions.

- The question of cultural process: What are the consequences of thinking about culture as 'an unfolding performative invention instead of reified system'?
- The research question: What are the consequences of viewing fieldwork as 'an enabling fiction between observer and observed'?
- The hermeneutic question: 'What kinds of knowledge are privileged or displaced when performed experience becomes a way of knowing, a method of critical inquiry, a mode of understanding?'
- The epistemological (*and* 'performance indicator') question: 'What are the rhetorical [or institutional] problematics of performance as a complementary or alternative form of "publishing" research?'
- The political question: 'How does performance reproduce, enable, sustain, challenge, subvert, critique, and naturalize ideology?' (Conquergood, 1985, cited in Carlson, 1996: 192)

Yet even as this 'performative' thrust takes theatre studies further into everyday life, so its theorists pause to take stock of its specific and situated 'expressive processes'. Carlson argues that although the importance of emphasizing the performative aspect of agency and identity in a wide range of everyday social and cultural practices is undoubted, what is often missing in these other areas of activity is 'the specific blending of occasion and reflexivity that characterizes "theatrical" performance. . . . Performers and audience alike accept that a primary function of this activity is precisely cultural and social metacommentary, the world of self and other, of the world as experienced, and of alternative possibilities' (1996: 97). Loren Kruger says that at 'a time and place where centralized and rationalized power make large-scale appropriation of the media difficult, the intermediate technology of small-scale actions may provide an effective stage for alternative "strategies for encompassing social situations" ' (1993: 66). Jill Dolan has argued for theatre studies' distinct contribution as 'a place to experiment with the production of cultural meanings on bodies willing to try a range of different significations for spectators willing to read them' (cited in Carlson, 1996: 197); and Carlson argues that this is true for traditional theatre as well as for 'performance art'. He thus gestures to the amazing omission in mainstream cultural studies of both this particular 'formal performance' site (the theatre) and its process (of performing bodies differently).

Theatre, Carlson concludes,

> is a specific event with its liminoid nature foregrounded, almost invariably clearly
> separated from the rest of life, presented by performers and attended by audiences
> both of whom regard the experience as made up of material to be interpreted, to
> be reflected upon, to be engaged in – emotionally, mentally, and perhaps even
> physically. This particular sense of occasion and focus as well as the overarching
> social envelope combine to make it one of the most powerful and efficacious
> procedures that human society has developed for the endlessly fascinating process
> of cultural and social self-reflection and experimentation. (1996: 198–9)

And Kruger argues that the occasion of theatre (but not media) performance
'creates a *liminoid* space in which alternative or *virtual* public spheres can
be performed, tested, *entertained*' (1993: 68).

Performance in theory: some recent anthropological accounts

Just as in theatre studies the relation (or opposition) of 'theatre'/'performance'
has been central, so an important direction in anthropology has been the
focus on the need to explore ritual and performance as relational rather than
essential terms. In a recent edited collection, Felicia Hughes-Freeland speaks
of this relationship as situated social practice which, far from being part of
an exoticizing anthropology, is all about 'how anthropologists and social
actors frame reality, and what the relationship is between the ordinary and
the non-ordinary in terms of social action' (1998: 2). Hughes-Freeland and
her contributors argue on the one hand that both ritualization and performance are social action forms that *stand out* as 'more than the everyday'. But
on the other hand their emphasis that performance is 'not understood as the
replication of a given script or text' but as 'techniques and technologies of
the self/selves' (Hughes-Freeland, 1998: 3) leads also (as in Dolan and
Carlson) to a focus on the *daily, processual relationship* between them
as 'living human bodily expressivity, conversation and social presence'
(Schieffelin, in Hughes-Freeland, 1998: 13).
    Thus performance:

> cannot be explained anthropologically without reference to the specific context
> which frames the action and/or performances. The agency of situations is one
> which is constituted by a range of participants. The focus on performance allows
> us to understand situations interactively, not in terms of communication models,
> but in terms of participatory ones. (Hughes-Freeland, 1998: 15)

The emphasis on performance, in anthropology as in theatre studies, then
leads away from a textualist account of meaning to an emphasis on the
embodied and rhetorical 'argumentative context' (Billig, 1987: 91; Shotter,
1993: 8) – to the 'dialogic' (Bakhtin, 1986), focusing 'upon the actual
"formative" or "form giving" moment in speech communication' and emphasizing the unique, social, relational (and intrapersonal) functions of situated
language use' (Shotter, 1993: 40). The understanding of performance as

'technologies of the self/selves' thus focuses on 'words in their speaking' (Shotter, 1993:43) as embodied *situationally* in both 'formal' and 'everyday' performance. We are reminded again of Dolan, emphasizing that theatre studies is 'a material location, organized by technologies of design and embodiment . . . a pedagogically inflected field of play at which culture is liminal and liminoid and available for intervention' (cited in Carlson, 1996: 197).

Within anthropology, Hughes-Freeland argues, recurring key themes underpin this debate about performativity as situational interaction: agency and intentionality; creativity and constraint; the participatory nature of spectatorship; and the implications of different framings of relationships between reality and illusion.

• Concerning *agency and intentionality* in ritual and performance, Schieffelin argues that it is because performativity is the expressive dimension of the strategic articulation of practice that the distinction breaks down between a Baumann-style definition of performance as *a particular aesthetic event evoking an imaginative reality among spectators* and Goffmann's sense of human culture and social reality as articulated in the world of *everyday performative activity*. Though anthropologists vary here as to the emphasis that they place on the intentionality of performativity – Schieffelin for example argues that it is 'the expressivity (and hence performativity) inherent in any human activity in everyday life which renders our actions communicative and effective to others in our situations whether we mean them to be or not' (1998: 197), whereas Rostas speaks of ritual as 'way of acting that is non-intentional . . . that has become part of the habitus' and performativity as entailing 'the deployment of consciously formulated strategies' (1998: 89, 90) – there is agreement that ritual and performativity must be understood relationally, where the actor (both on and off the stage) is a 'double agent' (Hastrup, 1998), performing 'between identities . . . which makes it possible to work on "being" and "becoming" simultaneously' (Rostas, 1998: 92). Above all, the emphasis on the 'never-ending reflexivity' of this double-agency means a move beyond the 'linguistic turn' of cultural studies: ' "Performance" deals with actions more than text: with habits of the body more than structures of symbols, with illocutionary rather than propositional force, with the social construction of reality rather than its representations' (Schieffelin, 1998: 194).

• Concerning *creativity and constraint*, performative agency is 'not unfettered agency but creativity contingent on a structure or a field of preconditions which constitutes a set of references . . . a liturgical script' (Hughes-Freeland, 1998: 7). Thus Coleman and Elsner in their analysis of 'performing pilgrimage' to the Anglo- and Roman-Catholic shrines in Walsingham, England, describe both 'canonical' performance (embodying an interactive intensification of collective belonging to forms of religious liturgical authority and stability not found in one's 'home' church) and

performance (involving either a self-parodying and ludic 'excess' of
practice or through more communal forms of liturgical transforma-
he point is that in both cases performativity requires 'the presence of
cal forms as symbols and actions against which to define themselves'
7). Clearly this creativity/constraint relationship between 'ritual' and
'performativity' can be extended not only to other pilgrimage or 'heritage'
sites, like the museum, as Coleman and Elsner suggest, but also to the
full range of popular cultural (for example soap opera, Ang, 1985) and
'canonical' high-cultural sites. As Coleman and Elsner argue, 'Along with
other contemporary ritual forms . . . pilgrimages to Walsingham are partially
supported and revived by the practices of a modernity shading into postmodernity, such as the cultivation of leisure, consumption and the commer-
cialized "staging" of culture, and are thereby sometimes transformed into
objects of play, displaced from conventional temporal or liturgical frames'
(1998: 62–3).

● Concerning *spectatorship as participation*, it is here that anthropologists
of ritual and performance have perhaps drawn most on media and cultural
studies, arguing that 'Agency does not reside in a specific group of
performers who are separate from an audience of passive spectators. . . . If
the degrees of technological intervention differ between media events and
live ones, this is not an intervention which negates the agency of viewers or
audiences' (Hughes-Freeland, 1998: 8, 10). Thus whether comparing the
television viewing practices of a London middle-class family with the New
Guinean participants in a Fuyuge gab ritual (Hirsch, 1998), or analysing
the growing role for women in bullfighting as television supplements the
masculinist *ambiente* of the actual Spanish bullring (Pink, 1998), or describing the performative role of television in relation to the historically and
politically evolving rituals of the Welsh National Eisteddfod (Davies, 1998),
or discussing the embedding of new video practices in initiation rituals at
urban shrines in Benin City, Nigeria (Gore, 1998), all of these anthropologists emphasize a conceptual framework of agency, locality, strategy
and skilled daily practice in understanding their 'spectators'. Thus the
'diversity of experiences within a fixed site in media becomes subject to
the variables of time and space: the media event is decontextualized, disconnected, diffused, re-diffused, and raises questions about methodological
procedures for understanding it' (Hughes-Freeland, 1998: 10). It is here that
anthropologists of ritual and performance are also most critical of media and
cultural studies: for a too limited notion of ethnography, and for an over-
privileging of the reifying powers of the media (Hirsch, 1998). While
supporting Ang's emphasis on telling stories situated between the local and
the global, Hirsch warns that her understanding of anthropology's 'local' is
outdated and simplistic. Thus, 'in all the talk of local and global relations it
has to be remembered that one never actually leaves the local. . . . Rather it
is the system of local contexts, their distributions and linkages, that creates a
global field (such as IBM or Hollywood)' (Hirsch, 1998: 223). An underlying emphasis of all of these anthropologists' accounts is thus on the

relationship between performativity and local knowledge: where, as Rapport argues, whatever the degree of globalized commoditization and structural power, 'It is through narrational performance that we maintain conscious selves; through the performance of narratives, we continue to write and rewrite the story of our selves' (Rapport, 1998: 20).

• Concerning the *framing of reality and illusion*, Schieffelin critiques the high-cultural *western dramaturgical* (Roach's 'theatrical') framing of socio-logical models of performance. 'Fundamental to this image is the division between (relatively active) performers and (relatively passive, but emotion-ally responsive) audiences. In Euro-American (basically Aristotelian) tra-dition this divide is also a metaphysical, even ontological, one between a world of spectators which is real and a world conjured up by performers which is not, or more precisely, which has another kind of reality: a virtual or imaginary one. . . . What I am concerned with here is that this set of ideas about the relationship entailed in performance carries hidden moral and epistemological judgments, when transported into anthropology, that tend to undermine our ethnographic intent.' (Schieffelin, 1998: 200) In Schieffelin's and Hughes-Freeland's accounts, the emphasis on 'illusion' in performative models in the social sciences is 'endemic'. 'Is social life merely a tissue of illusions skilfully woven by us all? Where are the truth and efficacy in ritual located? The fact of the matter is that these issues are in large part an artefact of the way the relation between performers and audience is conventionally (if naively) conceived' (Schieffelin, 1998: 202). Rather than move into a radically postmodernist celebration of the fake, the illusion, the simulacrum, Schieffelin and other anthropologists of performance move further into the local and the ethnographic. 'The simplest lesson for anthropology is that the exact nature of the performative relationship between the central performers and the other participants (including spectators) in a cultural event cannot be sustained analytically, but must be investigated ethnographically. . . . [F]or anthropology, these relationships need careful investigation – both in formal performances and in everyday life – because it is within these relationships that the fundamental epistemological and ontological relations of any society are likely to be implicated and worked out: because this is the creative edge where reality is socially constructed' (Schieffelin, 1998: 202, 204). As 'creative edge', performativity thus becomes central to ethnographic analysis. 'The central issue of performativity, whether in ritual performance, theatrical entertainment or the social articulation of ordinary human situ-ations, is the imaginative creation of a human world . . . and these need to be explored ethnographically rather than a priori assumed' (Schieffelin, 1998: 205).

The move we need to make, all these scholars in anthropology and theatre studies are telling us, is away from a reifying textualism or a determinant globalism, towards the localized, situated 'performing of one's critique'. But performance is never agentive in a voluntaristic way. It *is* situated in historical time, geographical and conceptual space.

Thus it is in the context of both anthropological and theatre studies' emphasis on **performativity as embedded in 'liturgy' but also as 'ludic' excess, as limited by 'canonical theatre' but also as 'political intervention', as 'citation' but also as transformative practice** that this book tells its stories. It is on behalf of that particular focus that it makes its selection of 'performance' debate within theatre studies and anthropology. I am not trying to be 'representative' or to present an archival 'survey' in my discussion of 'performance' in either theatre studies or anthropology. Inevitably, I perform the texts I have chosen from these disciplines too.

So, perhaps unusually, the book tells in one place 'ethnographic' stories of expertise and the everyday that focus on performing Chekhov as parodic 'excess' and political intervention side by side with others about designing HIV/AIDS campaigns within the daily leisure performances of Australian Builders' Labourers (and against the grain of 'canonical' government campaigns). My point is not to take further the blurrings and distinctions between 'ritual' and 'performance' within anthropology, or between 'performance' and 'performativity' (which exists in some parts of theatre studies, but not in others). For this reason there will be no attempt here to 'put right' the slippage between 'performance' and 'performativity' that occurs in some of my key intertexts, like Hughes-Freeland's *Ritual, Performance, Media* (see, for example, the beginning of Chapter 4).

Rather, my point is to try to address in one place the different 'popular' (and expansive) and 'high' (but effaced) terrains of cultural studies *via* the kinds of theoretical and practical performativity discussed here. Thus just as Brian Wynne has drawn on the 'local knowledgeability' of Cumbrian farmers in challenging the 'liturgical' expertise of the British scientific institution, so I have drawn on Cumbrian teenagers in their spectating of the canonical, high-cultural 'Chekhov'; and also on Sydney building workers in co-designing an Australian HIV/AIDS campaign.

To try to engage conversationally and rhetorically with the academics' (or health policy makers') 'others' is, as Shotter says, a different matter from the familiar, top-down 'disciplining' of our audiences.

> And this is why – when claiming to represent the needs of others unlike ourselves, the poor and the oppressed, those 'outside' our language games – we fail to grasp why our representations of them are demeaning. We exclude their voices; they can play no part in those fleeting, extraordinary moments of indeterminacy, undecidability and ambivalence, when we determine each other's being, each other's identities. Our conversational politics excludes them. . . . [N]o matter how concerned with 'their' liberation, with 'their' betterment, with preventing 'their' victimisation, etc – the fact is that 'we' do not make sense of 'their' lives in 'their' terms. 'We' do not even make sense of 'their' lives 'with them', thus to arrive at a version upon a common 'ground' between 'us'. (Shotter, 1993: 48)

It is because I have not wanted my 'conversational politics' to 'exclude their voices' that I have adopted a case study format to this book. For example, the Sydney building workers' voices are given space in this way (and I wish there was space for this in other case studies). On the other hand, I do not want to fall into the romanticizing discourse of seeing the local, situated voice as simply 'authentic' representation of the 'disadvantaged' (Silverman, 1993: 6). The Sydney building workers are men, and their voices engage interactively in our interviews with other men, reworking gender alibis, mythologies and various 'liturgical' stories of their own; similarly, the Cumbrian teenagers' voices are also interactive within a cultural 'micropolitics' of constraint, in this case as 'A-level' students in English or Russian studies. Those 'forms of order' need to be understood as conversational activities too; as must the 'reading formations' of the researchers/interviewers in the same interactive process. These 'experts' tell their own stories in their own words, often 'dense' or 'difficult' words, as my opening pages have represented. And so the words and languages of 'expertise' and the 'everyday' also blur as genres in this book.

Performance on the street

All of this sounds very theoretical for a book which emphasizes stories of both 'expertise' and the 'everyday'. So, I want to move straight into every-day 'story telling', to try to flesh out some of these more abstract 'disciplinary' points. My first narratives come from 'Julie', a respondent in a recent Fear of Crime consultancy that I conducted in New South Wales with colleagues at the Centre for Cultural Risk Research, Charles Sturt University.

Julie was one of the parents of teenagers (one of three generational cohorts in our research) whom we interviewed by focus-group and long interview methods. The two-hour interview with Julie about fear of crime and the media generated many stories, conveyed as a series of biographical memories. Together these helped constitute Julie's understanding of any one of her current performances.

Julie remembered, for example:

- how as a child she had been brought up in a communist/anarchist household; where, for all his libertarian ideals, her father when drunk 'beat her to the wall and back';
- how later, in her twenties she had joined a radical feminist group where she learned that 'there is no safety anywhere, anytime, so you may as well live your life and not let the fear control you';
- how when she was a women's refuge co-ordinator and protester, she had drawn on this feminist confidence to physically swing away a 'rogue male' policeman who had seriously injured her female colleague by throwing her down the steps of Parliament House in Canberra;
- how even today, she uses this feminist consciousness to walk through the trains at night when passing through 'scary' suburbs, talking with nervous women travelling by themselves; and

- how recently she, her female partner, and her teenage daughter had seen off a group of men and youths intent on robbing a drunken older woman on the train.

Yet, despite her confidence in her partner who boxes, her daughter who at least twice has assaulted a male harassing her, and her own physical profile that 'gives out "Don't mess with me" ', Julie is reflexively aware of the potential power of the globalizing media over her. She will not watch movies on TV where women are stalked because, from her experience in childhood, she feels she has become especially sensitive to the signs of male threat. The global, as Hirsch would say, is created in the local. It is because of the range of signs of male violence which her father taught her that she thinks these media texts disempower her now, reducing her self-confidence. For example, having watched the first episode of *Millennium*, she gave it up.

> I don't watch things that are too close to home. And the fact that in the very first episode the fellow's wife and child were threatened and there was an implied threat that may come true in the future – That made me think I don't want to watch that any more.

On the other hand, she loves watching popular TV series like *The X-Files* and *The Pretender*, enjoying a 'resistance to US authority' reading. Her Left politics convinces her that the 'government cover up' emphasis of these series is an accurate representation of the relationship between the US government and her Australian one, and between her government and herself (as with the policeman on the steps of Parliament House, Canberra).

> I really like the government conspiracy ones. . . . I especially like *The Pretender* – nasty government agency doing all sorts of funny experiments on children. . . . One of them grows up and escapes and is being chased by the agency. . . . It's the fear of authority getting at you, but the fear more of what they're doing out there than what they're doing to me; and I like the aspect of escaping from authority and getting even with them. I really, *really* like that aspect of *The Pretender*.

The particular story that I want to focus on (to work through Hirsch's and Rapport's discussion of the global and local, and Roach's emphasis on the performative as a critical category) is one when Julie left behind her familiar 'mental maps of the city' (Taylor et al., 1996: 313), and went to the USA, where one night she was walking through the streets of Seattle.

> I was very aware, say late at night in inner-city Seattle, of being much, much more fearful. And what I did, as I walked, doing my usual thing of eyes up and walking straight ahead, was to think 'is my fear justified or not?' . . . And nothing 'bad' came at me. . . . But in fact the portrayals of race violence in America did affect me. . . . I was very conscious that it had gone into my head. So when I was walking through an area that had a lot of black people in it I was much more conscious of the fear then. But thankfully I *was* conscious of it and thinking about it and *judging* it all the time.

Julie is a white, middle-class, lesbian woman who, in this particular story, focused on her brief encounter with two black men in American city streets at night. She is far from being racist; indeed, she tells the story of how a particular anti-racist text has helped her work through her own fears.

> I *know* about violence, it can't scare me. I've just been reading a wonderful book about a white woman in the southern states of America who . . . said 'I have been there. I have experienced the fear that the racists can make me feel. I have lost sleep, sat up all night with a gun in my hand. . . . I know what they can do. They may hurt me. They may kill me. They will never make me fear again.' . . . For me it has taken more processing than that, a lot of ingrained fear that I had to learn about in order to get past it so I could say 'I will never fear again'. . . . Mine was a long-term project to get there. But that feeling at the end . . . is very real for me.

Yet Julie's story indicated the way in which both her own 'long-term project' and her 'globalized' view have to be *reflexively renegotiated* and performed in each new, fine-grained, localized experience. At a strategic moment Julie performed, and at the same time, to use de Certeau's terms, her role as globalized spectator expanded into that of participant.

> A black man was walking towards me. He had a piece of paper wrapping up something in his hand. As he got fairly close to me he crumpled it up and threw it at my feet. He was *directing* it at my feet, at the ground right in front of me. I didn't look at him but I stepped around it, sort of slightly bowed my head in his direction, and kept him in sight as I walked past him. I didn't turn my back on him until I knew he was past me, and continuing on his way; and *then* I turned around and kept walking. At this point I brought my eyes up again to assess the crowd around me, and the next black man who was maybe twenty feet behind the first one, looked at me and met my eyes and smiled. . . . I have no idea how my reaction was perceived by either man. It was a completely instant reaction. . . . I was in a way acknowledging the first man's presence by half-nodding my head, stepping around the paper. . . . It was an unusual situation. I didn't know the ground rules. I was very conscious of the media's portrayal of race violence, and I didn't *know* how much of it was true, how much wasn't. . . . My conditioning was a very, very big factor there. . . . And the second man's smile – I was trying to read so much into two seconds. But I would say I saw a slight humour in it, I would say I saw a slight appreciation of my tactics, I would say I saw a slight reassurance 'I'm not going to do the same thing'. Who knows how much of that was real, but I looked up, and I met his eye, and he smiled, and I gave a half-smile, and I nodded again, and kept going – and thought 'whew, calm down now'.

In Julie's perception the first black man, the second, and Julie herself are all engaging in what de Certeau calls 'tactics' – the sequences of 'advances and retreats, tactics and games played with the text' (1984: 175) called 'race riot'. Whatever the strategies of the US government in this regard, and whatever the strategies of the media in globalizing popular meanings about 'black city race riots', the first black man in Julie's story has his moment – in Roach's sense – not of theatre, but of the performative as 'a cultural act, a critical perspective, a political intervention'. In turn, Julie's acknowledgment by way of her body's very particular response to his challenge – her sidestep, her slight bowing of her head, her cautious eyeline – are performative too, in Rapport's sense where her 'performance (voiced and unvoiced) is the currency of ongoing individual consciousness' (1998: 179). And further, in her reflexive reading of this embodied, interactive 'text', the second black man is both spectator, showing 'a slight appreciation of my tactics', and performer too, as his smile indicates yet another way to perform this text of 'race riot/race relations'.

In this particular incident, there was no overt conversation, and yet what Bakhtin calls 'living utterance' was embodied, where each 'utterance refutes, affirms, supplements and relies upon the others, presupposes them to be known, and somehow takes them into account' (Bakhtin, 1986: 91). The 'responsive reaction' of Julie and each of the black men she constructs here did indeed refute, affirm, supplement and presuppose the 'city race riot' voice. They were 'primarily a *response* to preceding utterances in a given sphere' (Bakhtin, 1986: 91).

Julie's story embeds and embodies 'citations' (Derrida). It also illustrates Rapport's point about performance: that narrative is 'the "form" of consciousness, the form of our experience through time' (1998: 180); and also that narratives are constructed in exchanges of power within everyday situations.

> If power, après Foucault (après Nietzsche), is properly devolved to the micro-socialities of every exchange in every relationship, then contra Foucault, I argue that such power cannot be understood without the interpreting person; without those individuals who partake of the relationship and partake of the exchange. (Rapport, 1998: 180)

Julie's narrative – as an interpreting person – is one of the 'stories of the everyday' that give a title to this book. But the title is also about 'stories of expertise', and that brings me back to the heart of Ien Ang's and Terry Threadgold's own emphasis on power and reflexivity (as well as Schieffelin's point about the 'epistemological stumbling block' inherent in performance/spectator models in the social sciences). Despite the relevance (in Julie's Seattle story) of Hirsch's critique of Ang that 'the local can never be left for a larger entity known as the global' (1998: 223), he does not resolve Ang's primary question about what our own political role as researchers is in 'seeing and organizing' the elusive reality of this street performer/spectator encounter between white and black, between two men and a woman. Both Ang and Threadgold are aware of the difficulties of celebrating 'local'/ 'resistance' discourses (Julie, for example, reads the second black man's smile as a complex text in part *because* of the power of globalized 'race riot' TV genres). Both theorists also know the power of globalized discourses of 'expertise' (whether of the American media or indeed of their own) to contain and control the 'performing of gender differently', as Julie is trying to do in this encounter.

Julie's story in fact exemplifies each part of Threadgold's opening statement about performativity: Julie locates the 'textual meaning' of US television's representation of 'race riots' (and the second black man's smile) in a very situated 'negotiation between reader, writer and text'; Julie's long-term project as a lesbian feminist is about 'a gendering and sexing of the subject'; and her embodied action in this encounter does focus reflexively on the issue of her colour which severely influences 'the subject's (compulsory) performance of gender and the possibilities for performing gender differently'. Also, like Ien Ang, Julie is reflexively aware of the way in which her own storytelling as a producer of descriptions – 'Eyes up, walk straight ahead. . . . "Don't mess with me" ' – enters here 'the uneven, power-laden field of social discourse'.

Julie is, in other words, perfectly aware of how her body and her feminist theory *together* perform her critique and yet also betray her in the streets of Seattle when she meets one, then another, black man at night. Without ever knowing her stories, Terry Threadgold describes both this 'multiply positioned' Julie and my necessary project here, when she says:

> for every individual, these multiple positionings and constructions must be seen as forms of identity and experience which frame and constitute the sexed, classed and raced human subject's life history, which gives it both its narrative coherence and its discursive and narrative multiplicity. To understand even some of these complexities is to provide the scope for much more acute empirical and theoretical accounts of the intersections through which what used to be called the categories of class, race and gender – or of ethnicity and age – might actually be produced as changing and constantly processual forms of subjectivity, subjects who are both synchronically and diachronically in process. (Threadgold, 1997: 7)

It is towards this very particular project of 'empirical and theoretical accounts' that this book is working via its stories of expertise and the everyday. Above all – and here we focus on the politics of our 'expert' accounts – the book accepts the view of both Ang and Threadgold that many powerful analyses (including feminist ones) of agency and 'performativity' are both too 'metatheoretical, failing to engage with the specificities of . . . semiotic labours and material practices that might actually be involved in "power as resignification" ' (Threadgold, 1997: 83); and too embedded in a white, middle-class 'expert knowledgeability'. This, Ang argues, is to invent a *new* 'master discourse', and disguise 'the fundamental structural divisions created by historical processes such as colonialism, imperialism and nationalism' (Ang, 1996: 73).

Julie meets those historical processes head on in the streets of Seattle. As Threadgold says (quoting Ang), unless we focus on 'the material and institutional constraints on real bodies' in a neocolonialist space where (like Julie's body translated from a *situated* neocolonialism in Australia to the uncertainty of globalized 'race riots' in the USA) 'even the *nature*, the materiality of bodies, is constructed against their will', current theories

of performativity may not constitute an adequate model of agency. 'The
material realities are more complex and it may well be that it is only those
with a certain level of cultural and economic capital and the right colour skin
whose lives as discursive practices are really open to any intervention or
resignification of this theoretical kind' (Threadgold, 1997: 84).

Threadgold engages sympathetically but critically here with Judith Butler's
notion of discourse as performativity. As Butler argues,

> Performativity describes the relations of being implicated in that which one
> opposes. . . . The effects of performatives, understood as discursive production, do
> not conclude at the terminus of a given statement or utterance, the passing of
> legislation, the announcement of a birth. The reach of their significability cannot
> be controlled by the one who utters or writes, since such productions are not
> owned by the one who utters them. They continue to signify in spite of their
> authors, and sometimes against their authors' most precious intentions. (Butler,
> 1993: 240–1)

It is here that Threadgold's concern with Butler's 'metatheoretical' approach
to performativity makes its point for the context of this book. It is not only
those with the power of strategies to interpellate ('performativity requires a
power to effect or enact what one names', Butler, 1995: 203) who lose
control of what they utter. So, too, did Julie in night-time Seattle. Here the
iterability, the 'citations' of gender and race conveyed in body language and
thought were, as Butler would have it, 'mobilized by that long string of
injurious interpellations' (Butler, 1995: 203) which are the sedimented
'community and history' of 'It's a girl' and 'It's a black'. But – and this is
my main point, as it is of Hirsch and of Rapport – it is not the case *simply*
that Julie was 'temporarily produced as the belated and fictive origin of the
performative itself' (Butler, 1995: 203). Butler argues that the 'subject
achieves a temporary status in the citing of that utterance, in performing
itself as the origin of that utterance. That subject-effect, however, is the
consequence of that very citation; it is derivative' (Butler, 1995: 203).

But clearly Julie's performance in Seattle is not simply derivative, a
'subject-effect' of iterability. To understand how that citation is *reflexively*
contextualized, narrativized, made rhetorical, embodied and changed in that
momentary performance on a city street at night, we need to know also
about her embodiment over years of *her* feminism, how she perhaps partially
loses control of that 'citation' too as a result of sedimented 'black race riot'
representations on American TV; but then not that entirely either, since the
person she meets is *male* as well as black.

And we need to know how she brings her memory of her father's
violence, and her self-perception of her sensitivity to the cues of male
violence (trailed through her own choice of what TV she will and will not
watch) to her embodied performance in that momentary encounter. It is,
as Threadgold says in critiquing Butler, necessary to 'engage with the
specificities of genres, contexts, semiotic labours and material practices'
here, rather than write off her situated response as simply a derivative

'subject-effect' – which is to repeat in other words the performance 'themes' of Hughes-Freeland et al.: of agency and intentionality; creativity and constraint; the participatory nature of spectatorship; and the implications of different framings of relationships between reality and illusion.

Now to the chapters that follow.

The chapters

In Chapter 1 I examine the issues of 'which stories do I tell?' and 'for whom do I write?' in terms of cultural theory. Taking three pieces of writing (each about one decade apart, from the late 1970s to the late 1990s) which have been influential in my own academic development as researcher and teacher, I look at three different ways of approaching the 'participatory nature of spectatorship' (Hughes-Freeland). By mapping this process across a diachronically shifting set of 'resistance' theories in cultural studies, and comparing it with the scientific-instrumentalist 'master narrative' against which culturalist risk theory sets itself, I draw attention to the issue of reflexivity within our own 'expert knowledgeability'.

In Chapter 2 I look at cultural policy, mapping the 'creativity and constraint' relations of Hughes-Freeland et al. across Grahame Murdock's own dichotomy of 'citizenship or consumption'. By way of a case study of a low-cost, low-tech, HIV/AIDS campaign designed collaboratively with Sydney building workers, I explore the relationship between the men's narratives, our stories as researchers and interviewers, and other 'expert' bodies such as advertising agencies. This chapter directly addresses Ang's question about the politics of our own representational orders.

In Chapter 3 I move from a focus on 'the performance of everyday life' to 'formal performance' analysis. My argument here is that cultural studies ignores high-cultural sites of performance – whether in the 'regimes of value' of academia, the theatre or the media – at its own cost, because these are all important places where 'modernism' and 'modernity' are constructed; and these high-cultural sites and high-cultural definitions have deeply influenced cultural theory itself. By examining three academic 'frames' for constructing history and modernism/modernity around one of high culture's key players, Chekhov – the canonical artist above all others who is (symptomatically) performed 'above' ideology or economics – I examine what Raymond Williams and John Frow call the 'ideology' and the 'fantasy' of modernism. In the concluding case study of the chapter I explore this 'fixing of the modern' in a key high-cultural location outside academia, the Royal Shakespeare Company.

While cultural studies of text, performance and audience have been slow to turn to systematic analyses of high culture (despite the example of Bourdieu), the 'turn to theory' in literary studies – especially in Shakespeare studies – has been developing strongly. In Chapter 4 I elaborate on those

theoretical developments in literary studies which bear directly on my theme
of 'stories of expertise and the everyday', particularly in new historicism and
cultural materialism. It is my view that the large number of courses in
cultural studies which do not present students to these 'high-cultural'
theories (as well as associated developments in postcolonial and feminist
theory) are much the poorer for not doing so; and so this chapter is a
deliberate intervention in that respect. As in Chapter 3, I am interested in
examining the working of these 'expert' narratives (and their attempts to
release 'voices of the everyday') in different high-cultural sites. In the case
studies of this chapter I examine examples of a *transformative* performing
(Roach) of the 'canonical' and 'liturgical' that have recently been occurring
in situated places within the academic, theatrical and televisual frames of
high culture. In doing this I am arguing for a new performativity within
cultural studies itself in relation to the rhetorical sites of high culture.

In Chapter 5 I draw on perhaps the defining parameter of the concept of
performance – that it relies, whether in 'formal' or 'everyday' events, on an
interactive and dialogic relationship with a spectator – to begin to draw
together some of the key performance themes of the book. I point to my own
'provisional closure' (in 'third generation' audience theory's emphasis on
spectators as discursive constructs located within multiple interpretative
frames) to examine issues of research reflexivity, high-cultural commoditization and 'expert' ('A-level') framing of audiences, in relation to Chapter 3's
and 4's analysis of Chekhov performance. These discursive constructions of
the audience are examined via two 'offstage performance' case studies (the
marketing of high culture; and the academic institution) and two 'onstage
performances' (which explore actor/audience interaction).

In Chapter 6 I turn to cultural methodology since, despite its general
effacing by 'theory' in much cultural studies discourse, without it neither our
theory nor our practice (as 'experts' in cultural policy) can proceed very far.
Between postmodernism's rejection of 'innocent' observation and 'impartial'
methods of analysis (as rhetorical moves of modernism), and a bureaucratic-
technological society's opposite demand that 'numbers talk', I argue for a
'metamethodological' approach which does, still, combine qualitative and
quantitative methods, but which embeds these in the dialogic exchanges we
have as we 'socially construct' the subject matter of our investigations 'in
concert with our fellow investigators'. These fellow investigators – whether
they are the 'formal' performance professionals of theatre and television or
'everyday' performers like our building workers and school students –
become a warrant for our methods as we situate our research in its various
performative sites.

In the concluding chapter, I return to cultural performance in relation to
the various theoretical and methodological frames of this book. Reversing
the direction of Chapter 6, I endeavour to show that methodological rigour,
the testing of hypotheses, and the explanation of 'deviant cases' can work
from the quantitatively imprecise to the qualitatively precise and situated. At
the same time, I review the overall trend of this book: which is performativity

as it has emerged as a concept focusing attention on both the subject's (compulsory) performance of gender, age, race, class etc, and the possibilities for performing them differently. Performing culture, this chapter tries to show, is always going to be a matter of stories told – dialogically – of expertise *and* the everyday.

1

CULTURAL THEORY

In the face of nuclear, chemical and biotechnical dangers it is no longer possible for authoritative decisions to be made by groups of experts. Because of this epistemic authority no longer rests with particular groups of scientists, politicians and industrialists, but has fragmented across a huge range of social groups, the incessant interaction of which is potentially raising society to a qualitatively new level of self-critique. . . . [C]ritique is endemic to the risk society, and does not have to be introduced from outside by the sociologist. (Lash, Szerszynski and Wynne, 1996: 6)

The question, then, is what kind of representational order we should establish in our stories about media consumption. (Ang, 1996: 77)

This chapter will focus on the issue of 'stories of expertise and the everyday' at the level of *theory*. As Ang is arguing, the foundational theoretical questions are not only 'which stories to tell', but also 'who the "I" is who writes'. What are my (changing) kinds of representational order?

I begin here from the notion that any culture (including an 'expert' culture like cultural studies) is both an archive (in Foucault's sense) as well as being agentive (within the constraints discussed earlier). In other words, as archive, our term 'culture' is not an empirical given. Rather, it is a shifting problematic in which sets of rules that establish (as Foucault puts it) the limits and forms of expressibility, conservation, memory and reactivation are (in a given period, in a specific historical context) repositioned – that is to say, *agentively* performed and resignified. However, that performance of theory is always under certain conditions, contextually and intertextually. We are, as Shotter says, 'even when all alone, writing down our "thoughts" on paper . . . interacting with an "other" . . . from within an inner conversation' (1993: 4, 7). That, as he says, is how my 'knowledge emerges, and is made available to me – not from within my own "mind" but from within the words I use' (1993: 7). In so far as the words we use are always (and already) uttered elsewhere, our identity as writers is inevitably both fragmented and yet also (in the very process of that dialogic exchange) our own project, our own theoretical narrative. That is how I (we) 'perform' cultural studies.

Foucault's cultural archive consists of the 'problematic' of what can and cannot be said, of both 'expert' and 'lay' knowledges, of 'canonical' writings and 'resistant' rewritings, of some 'stories' that are remembered and others that are neither expressed nor conserved. 'Cultural Studies' (as 'expert' theory) itself inevitably pertains to these conditions of 'said' and 'unsaid', 'expert' and 'lay', 'canonical' and 'resistant' writing, 'agency' and 'structure'; and in this chapter I take three examples, two from Australian film theory and one from risk media analysis, which focus on this problematic centrally for me as a writer. I have chosen them because I have been centrally involved with them – directly or indirectly – as a researcher and teacher of, first, Australian film theory and, secondly, of media audience theory. As such these texts have helped establish my archive, its limits at one time, and its new performances at another.

So I am choosing 'which stories to tell' here for two reasons. The first is because, at the time of writing, I had been for 25 years an Australian academic; and that element of reflexivity – of what my contextual and intertextual constraints are in telling this tale – is important. The three case studies in this chapter represent different moments (roughly each a decade apart) in that period. The second reason is because theory itself should not be seen as immune from the concepts it describes. Australian cultural studies (like other daily textual negotiations) has itself been positioned in the 'postcolonial' which Ang and Threadgold emphasize (for example, the dominance in the 1970s of British screen theory and British texts which seep through in the first of my theoretical case studies). But the Empire, we hear, has struck back, with many leading cultural theorists internationally now being 'Australian'.

This chapter is not trying to tell this as an heroic and celebratory tale: it is not – in a simplistic structure/agency sense – about 'cultural imperialism' opposed by the 'resistance' of an Australian 'Caliban's Revenge' (we can leave that, as we will see from Meaghan Morris, to *Crocodile Dundee*). Rather, the chapter is about an historically positioned theoretical archive, and about how at certain times, under particular kinds of contextual and intertextual conditions, certain analytical stories begin to be told, retold, performed again. For me, this is 'the "I" that writes'.

The contextual and intertextual conditions of teaching cultural studies in Britain and Australia have been similar in some ways, different in others. Raymond Williams has written lucidly about the history of British cultural studies in a narrative which emphasizes the 'lost voices' that helped construct its origins in adult education. Here some of the better-known latter-day 'experts' (like Edward Thompson, Richard Hoggart, and Raymond Williams himself), but also 'many others whose names are not known' (Williams, 1989: 154) talked about 'imaginative literature' with people who insisted that it should be brought into 'their own situation, their own experience' (hence the shift from 'high-cultural' to localized knowledgeability). Williams describes how it then was taken back into the universities as part of the Liberal Studies movement, in response to a 'cultural distrust of science and technology' (Williams, 1989: 156); and how, after the 'linguistic turn' in cultural studies, 'the revival of formalism, and the simpler kinds (including Marxist kinds) of structuralism', there was a further shift away from theories related to the 'practical encounters of people in society

. . . since the main inherent forces of that society were [seen to be] deep in its structures' (Williams, 1989: 157).

For Williams, the university management and bureaucratization of cultural studies was the result of its constitution as a 'defensible discipline' (with a defensible size of student uptake!). Thus 'the people's questions are not answered by the existing distribution of the educational curriculum' (Williams, 1989: 160). The 'project and formation' of cultural studies has been 'brutally interrupted' by, first, university bureaucratization, second, the 'very conscious counter-revolution' of the 'linguistic turn' (Williams, 1989: 159).

The 'project and formation' of cultural studies in Australia was in some ways a different one, emerging first *in* the universities, and at roughly the same time as the new Labor nationalism of the Whitlam government. In my own case, cultural and media studies were an inflection of the film and media 'sociology' that I could establish in a 'General Studies' context for the same reasons that Williams says innovation was possible in the new Liberal Studies departments in Britain: because the university's 'disciplinary' project here was 'so vague', embedded in a suspicion of science and technology, and concerned that students 'should discover certain of the finer things of life' (Williams, 1989: 156).

Yet in my institution this 'general studies' was to be compulsory education for the students of science and technology. In that enforced situation, what Williams describes as the 'very conscious counter-revolution' of more formalist British versions of cultural and screen studies often seemed, in their abstraction and in what Williams calls their structuralist 'idealism', very far from the 'life-situations' of the students.

Film theory, in that decade of the 1970s, was at the leading edge of British (and Australian) cultural studies; and so it is not a coincidence that our *'expert'-led* turn to the 'local' included the development (in these particular Whitlam and post-Whitlam years) of courses (and the writing of books and articles to serve those courses) in Australian film. This was to be Australian film as embedded in its own 'local' industry; and again it is no coincidence that the editor of the first series of academic books which brought cultural studies and the Australian film industry together was someone who had herself performed (as writer and critic) in the development of the new Australian film industry, Sylvia Lawson.

The two articles on 'Australian film' that are the subject for my first two case studies around 'theory' were in fact both written by cultural theorists who have also been practising film critics (spanning two kinds, then, of 'expert knowledgeability'). And between them they also span the moment of the 'new Australian cinema', from the early (Whitlamesque) 1970s to the late (post 10BA tax-concession) 1980s, representing the tendencies towards an Australian nationalist contextualism on the one hand and a 'post' (postindustrial, poststructural) theoretical formulation on the other hand. As such – as diachronically shifting dominant 'expert' voices within Australian film theory – they engage just as much with the risks of inventing a new 'master discourse' (as Ang puts it) in cultural studies, as with the 'scientific' instrumentalist paradigm that is the reference for my third case study in this chapter.

Sylvia Lawson's 'Towards decolonizing film history in Australia' (1979)

The theme of each of the three case studies in this chapter is the way in which cultural theory (in different decades) accesses the voices of 'the local'. Lawson's project of decolonizing Australian film (and its local history) was itself a 'resistance' to the early 1970s 'linguistic turn' in cultural (including British screen) theory. Starting her teaching in Australian universities at that time, Lawson found there were no theoretical texts focused on Australian film or media. Rather, there were available combinations of theory: Saussurian linguistics, Lacanian psychoanalysis, and the mix of these theories with feminism and Marxism in British screen theory. Together these replaced the French film theory of the late 1960s in finding readings 'against the grain' *within* formal textual manoeuvres. This was difficult and decontextualized terrain for local Australian students. Lawson's sense was that a new 'turn', or *return*, to history was needed if 'everyday' Australian narratives (that is the 'lost voices' of local film-makers' and historical audiences) were to be restored (via our own 'expert knowledgeability' as academic film theorists) to the 'local' voices of our students.

For Lawson there were two other 'limits and forms of expressibility', in addition to this pedagogic one. First, there was her position as a long-term practitioner (film critic and writer) in an embryonic Australian film industry, embedded in the Whitlam and immediately pre-Whitlam years of nationalistic government. Secondly, there was the combined governmental and academic focus on 'cultural imperialism' as the target of discourse – the conceptualization of 'Hollywood' as representing the 'official' discourse of cinema against which the new Australian film-makers needed to 'perform their critique'.

Memory and reactivation were important to this new, Australian performance of history. For Lawson, if film-makers, film critics and film teachers were to understand the conditions in which they were struggling for production funds, for aesthetic space and for audience response in the 1970s, they needed to look to the past – to silent cinema – as the only other period of serious 'Australian film'. Her article therefore engaged with the history of the Australian film industry in order to understand its earlier conditions of local success and popularity (Lawson was about to celebrate this particular memory of Australian film history with a new series of academic books, and the first book in this series focused – symptomatically – on that early period of local cinema: Tulloch, 1981).

As Lawson put it in her 1979 article, those

> films of fifty and sixty years ago, opening on to social worlds which are so far past and yet still our own, may seem no less foreign than those out of Glauber

Rocha's Brazil, at the same time they are no less problematic, no less alive. Their vitality, the strength of their communicative links to both sources and audiences, holds clues to the puzzles of the present (31).

The comparison with Glauber Rocha was symptomatic of Lawson's 'limits of expressibility' – he, too, was challenging film imperialism (and we all taught Rocha's Cinema Nuovo at this time). Further, Lawson's emphasis on 'communicative links to both sources and audiences' fed off both her academic and her industry expertise. As an academic, Lawson was positioned in the post-auteurist (post-Barthes) period of cultural and media studies; yet she celebrated Raymond Longford as the foundational auteur of early Australian cinema. Her way round this impasse was to focus less on Longford himself than on the 'conditions of production and reception' of his time, arguing for a transparency of communication between those silent film-makers and their publics which, as an 'industry' person, Lawson argued was important to fill cinemas.

Her experience of the 'new Australian cinema' in the 1970s – as an academic/film-maker committed to working within one of a number of colonial societies 'which cannot easily shed their colonizations' – was frustrating. She criticized the films of the early 1970s that she had so far seen (*Picnic at Hanging Rock*, *Sunday Too Far Away*, and *Caddie*) because they began to explore a colonial society's conflicts – between colonial culture and the uncolonizable bush, between men's mateship and the exported system of capitalism, between women and patriarchy, between poverty and wealth – but then failed to work through those conflicts as 'visible narrative indices'.

> And the failure is like the nervousness of a speaker who was never sure of the audience and who, in midstream, senses that they might be bored, might even be leaving. The confusion, the conceptual blurrings, make the films illegible, unless due account is taken of the inheritance of silence, and the consequent groping for the lost audience: where did they go when the lights went out on the old Australian picture show? (Lawson, 1979: 27)

It was to reach *that* ('lost audience' of) local knowledge that Lawson reinvented her history. It was all the more necessary to examine the films *as* history because there was no way to get access directly anymore to the narrative voices of that 'lost audience'. She could not reach them via the current methodologies of audience analysis (focus groups, long interviews, surveys) that I use in my third case study of this chapter. Other than the rare oral histories that were being taped with surviving workers in that early film industry, there could be little of Ang's 'ethnography of storytelling' here – *except* through the eyes of the film-maker. Elsewhere Lawson described Longford and Ordell as Italian neo-realists before their time, drawing, on the one hand, on the 'living concentrations of social history' conveyed by early socialist and/or republican newspapers, and on the other, on 'a whole group of film workers who knew, intimately, the sort of life they were transmitting to the screen' (Tulloch, 1977: 206).

Thus, says Lawson, 'methodology cannot replace history, no matter how true it is that each should inform the other' (1979: 25–6). And thus, to *reach* those 'lost audience' voices, Lawson turned to the silent film-makers and their actors, reading off through their texts the specific historical conditions, of reception as well as production. So the films of Raymond Longford and Tal Ordell acknowledged 'certain intractable conflicts . . . arguably imaging both the struggles of the urban working-class as the Depression loomed up, and the situation of those lone local film-makers up against the giants' (Lawson, 1979: 29–30).

The then dominant thesis (in Labor government and cultural studies academia) of media imperialism became the 'expert' discourse that Lawson drew on to get access to local and 'lay' knowledge. She found in these early films a mythical tension between the 'un-English, anti-English' pioneer-mateship national dreams 'mapped on to those intractable inland spaces' and a spreading 'modern, Anglo-American, urban–suburban' globalization of domesticity and leisure. Within this local/global tension, the films' 'patterns (as distinct from the plots) communicate conflicts within the community, which included both film-makers and audience' (Lawson, 1979: 29).

As well as Lévi-Strauss's notion of myth, there was something in Lawson's theory here of Raymond Williams's concept of 'structure of feeling', whereby artists articulated intuitions of unease, anxiety and change 'which could give a sense of a generation or a period' (Williams, 1977: 131). In Lawson's theory, conditions of production *spoke back* to conditions of reception, and thus early film-makers and the (now lost) picture-show audience engaged in a mutual reciprocity of locally voiced understanding. Film-makers 'could be confident in their address, and so rendered the myths back to their owners' (Lawson, 1979: 30). This was not a simple naturalist 'transparency' theory, of the kind critiqued by Colin MacCabe in British screen theory at this time. Lawson adopted a materialist position which recognized that all film histories (including her own) are

> narratives produced in contexts. . . . The critic-historian, no less than the film-maker, is a storyteller, reworking material from the near and further past (choosing, indeed, which past shall be of service), projecting the home society's unacknowledged conflicts, exposing, rejecting and denouncing for and on behalf of readership and audience. (Lawson, 1979: 20)

Lawson is well aware that she is one of Ien Ang's 'expert' storytellers, 'the researcher/writer as a producer of descriptions' in the 'uneven, power-laden field of social discourse' (Ang, 1996: 75–6). In Lawson's case – as a critic and film-maker who had worked against the 'double colonization' of Australia and its films (first by Britain and then by the USA) – a particular political story had to be told *at the moment of reinvention of the 'new Australian cinema'*. It was 'the story of Hollywood as a global force, with styles and structures [in local cinema] which demonstrated not only colonial capitulation but also some significant colonial resistance' (Lawson, 1979: 25).

Sylvia Lawson was very aware of 'who the "I" is who writes'; but also of 'which stories to tell, in which form, to whom, where and when'. Her history was a diachronic one – relating 'lay knowledgeability' *then* (1920s) to 'semiotic labours and material practices' (Threadgold, 1997: 83) *now* (1970s). And in a very important sense, those 'lost audience' voices were not 'then', but 'now'.

Meaghan Morris, 'Tooth and claw: tales of survival, and *Crocodile Dundee*' (1988)

The story of colonial 'resistance' to Hollywood as a global force was also Meaghan Morris's theme around *Crocodile Dundee*. But here, a decade later, was an important difference, signified by Lawson's choice of an 'auteur' in Longford, and Morris's selection of the popular cultural textual hero, Mick Dundee. Sylvia Lawson was seeking the lost voices of the '*lay*' (audience) understanding of historical time and local context through Longford and Ordell. Meaghan Morris, in contrast, was engaging with the '*expert*' (academic) voices – including Lawson – which told those tales, berating them for their own nostalgia-*in*-history.

Symptomatically, Morris's theoretical and intertextual archive was very different from Lawson's. It was poststructuralist: Deleuze, Lyotard, Jameson, Baudrillard and Huyssen. Lawson, on the other hand, though briefly mentioning theorists like Gramsci and Foucault, constructed her intertextual register primarily of 'auteur' film-makers (D.W. Griffiths, Eisenstein, Vertov, Renoir, Ford, Welles, de Sica, Rossellini, Rocha) and 'classic' film critics (Bazin, Roth, Sarris). Whereas the stories Lawson remembered – her reactivation of the 'unsaid' – were those of past producers and 'lost' audiences, Morris's '*cannot be said*' were the certainties behind the apocalypse of all grand narratives – including the kind of feminist socialism underpinning Lawson's own stories.

Indeed, Lawson's narrative is one of the three kinds of colonial 'survival' tale which Morris engages with early in her article. This first type of survival story, relating to popular, US-oriented films like *Crocodile Dundee*,

> assumes that unoriginality is a Bad Thing, a byproduct of 'cultural imperialism' ... like the standing down of the great director Raymond Longford to make way for an American hack on the 1927 blockbuster-flop, *For The Term of His Natural Life*.... Not surprisingly, an argument with these reference-points often combines a call for collective originality with a realist aesthetic ('cultural exactitude'), an essentialist model of audience (the eye of the beholder as site of national perception) and a politics of primary anti-Americanism. (Morris, 1988: 246)

As well as a second survival narrative (which is: as film is an industry in a Western mega-culture, any ideals of originality, Australian independent identity and authenticity become inappropriate anachronisms), Morris spots a third 'expert' voice. This kind of survival story

> rejects both hostility to Hollywood . . . and base denials of Australian context. It takes the 'eye of the beholder' as a figure for seeing double: survival and specificity can both be ensured by the revision of American codes by Australian texts, in a play which can be beheld quite differently by various audiences, and individual eyes therein. Furthermore, it has a tradition: parody (like the in-joke) has always been a favourite ploy of Australian colonial culture. As Stuart Cunningham points out, a characteristic example would be the 'extremely successful appropriation' of the road-movie genre by the Kennedy-Miller *Mad Max* films. (Morris, 1988: 247)

'Resistance' and 'appropriation' become key terms in this third type of survival strategy. Morris herself positions the *'export-drive allegory'* *Crocodile Dundee* within its own specific moment of history as a '10BA' film (a government-run tax avoidance scheme designed to stimulate Australian film-making between 1980 and 1986). But few cultural studies academics reading (then or later) her main title theme of 'Tooth and Claw Survival' in a 'market economy' can have failed to see the relevance of her point (and of the parodic 'appropriation/resistance' strategy that she challenged) to their own industry of academia as, post-1987, neo-conservatism, economic rationalism and managerialism bit deeper with their own version of 'consumer choice'.

In the 'contemporary cultural condition – postcolonial, postindustrial, postmodern, postcommunist' that Ien Ang describes as the historical backdrop to our new thinking about the stories we tell – 'parody' and 'appropriation' have been familiar 'expert' strategies in a cultural studies discourse seeking desperately (like Australian film-makers) to put 'bums on seats', or else go under. During the late 1980s and 1990s, as students enjoyed cultural and media studies, but increasingly chose courses that would give them entry into the Australian media industries, 'parody' was a much safer spin on media theory than the old, 1970s emphasis on 'ownership and control'. Some of the shift came with postmodernist critiques of modernism; but the question of how current academic theory articulated with economic rationalist directions within universities did not worry Raymond Williams alone.

The 'resistance' or 'appropriation' via parody device has been central in establishing cultural studies' own 'expert' representational order, especially after the 'linguistic turn' that Raymond Williams critiques; and Morris's own narrative *finale* in her article is to interrogate this.

Like Lawson, Morris's story embraces both textual 'resistance' and systemic British/US imperialism. For instance, she describes *Crocodile Dundee* early in her narrative as a 'post-*colonial* comedy of survival, with remnants of the British, land-taking, appropriative regime (bushmen, Aborigines, Darwinian "natural" perils) emerging into the "multinational" cultural space of American-made modernity' (1988: 244). But, centrally, Morris implicitly interrogates Lawson's realist wager of a lost lay/public voice as one of 'nostalgic returns to a theory of cause and effect' (1988: 269).

In contrast, 'appropriation' in *Crocodile Dundee* is a *series* of theoretical stories told by Morris, in terms of multiple causes and effects. Thus, there is indeed the 'appropriation/resistance' *Crocodile Dundee* of '*positive* un-originality' where 'the privileged metaphors of postmodernism can come in to play – image-scavenging, borrowing, stealing, plundering and . . . recoding, rewriting, reworking' (Morris, 1988: 247). Thus the film plays with three 'signs of appropriation' of American bush-hero mission: '*Davy Crockett*', '*Jungle Jim*' and '*Tarzan*'.

> Each of these reiterates frontier codes, and also reconciles, for Australian con-sumption, the old bush mythos with the imported media culture of the 1950s. So their function is initially confirmatory, and sentimental. But in each case, an imbalance is created by a failure to fit the model. . . . In this context, appropriation is a competitive activity: a seizing not only of comic advantage, but mythic power (capital). (Morris, 1988: 247–9)

Morris speaks here of

- the appropriation in the film's final New York subway scene of 'dense American space' via 'an Australian, rural medium of communication over vast distances: an echoing cooee-call. . . . The New York subway has become another setting for an Australian country practice' (1988: 250). Thus the 10BA spawned *Crocodile Dundee* becomes a '*takeover* fantasy of breaking into the circuit of media power, to invade the place of control . . . [A]ppropriation as positive unoriginality figures as a means of resolving the practical problems of a peripheral cinema, while reconciling conflicting desires for power and independence: symbolic nationalist victory is declared, but on internationalist (American) grounds' (1988: 250).

However, theoretically-speaking, there are also other kinds of 'appropri-ation' voiced in Morris's narrative of fragmentation:

- The appropriation of Aboriginal land, and the devaluation of a 'land-rights' resistance to this via Dundee when he in turn appropriates Aboriginal speech – here Dundee as 'cultural poacher' *effaces* the politics that opposes land-appropriation.
- The film's overall rhetorical work in defusing the hostility to land rights as 'a function of the pressure of mining companies' (1988: 260). So, in Sue's discourse, 'land rights' and 'arms race' are *alternative* tools of liberal discourse, separated and then reduced in turn by Dundee: the first by cultural poaching (Dundee's 'the Aborigines don't own land, they belong to it'); the second via sexist reduction, as Sue's 'protestant liberalism' is pinned down to her vulnerability as a woman, unable to survive in the 'tooth and claw terrain of "real" [outback] struggle' without Mick (1988: 261). Thus, Morris argues, there is '[N]othing in the comedy that . . . allows a hint to emerge that the outback – primal

space of land appropriation and cultural exchange – might now also provide the raw materials for global nuclear threat' (1988: 260).

Then there is also, Morris emphasizes, the *style* (the plenitudinous promise to all of us as *audience*) of appropriation.

● This is appropriation as 'Caliban's *Revenge*', appropriation as a 'lexical mini-myth of power, a promise, if not of freedom, then of survival. All energies become seizures, and we all get a piece of the action' (1988: 267). There is, fundamentally, a 'corporate raider chic' quality to this 'appropriation'. Morris notes the sense of abundance and plenitude this connotes, for both conservative and left postmodernists. 'Appropriation's' profile here displays the cultural logic of affluence.

Thus it is, Morris argues, that 'postmodernised radical criticism has mostly ceased to talk about "impoverishment" by culture, preferring the wealth released in proliferant appropriation. As Geeta Kapur points out, it is a term implying not only aggression, but abundance' (1988: 268). The 'cleverness' of *Crocodile Dundee* is in establishing a consensual representational order quite different from the critical spirit normally associated with de Certeau's 'tactics' of *bricolage*-appropriation. Rather, the film displays

a zestful entrepreneurial optimism that differs (at least in its shameless *avowal* of competitive ambition) from the lugubrious celebration of a lost past predicated so often for, or by, the conservative post- (or anti-) modernism with which it nevertheless shares many racial, sexual and political hostilities. (Morris, 1988: 268)

Lawson's story is also a 'celebration of a lost past', though it is neither a politically conservative nor a lugubrious one. And her key 'loss' is indeed the sense of filmic impoverishment since the days of Longford and Ordell. The impoverishment is of 'lay' (audience) knowledgeability, and its mutuality with film-makers who recognize and articulate its voices. This is the focus of her 'conditions of production/reception' emphasis.

In contrast, Morris calls for a new venture into 'the gap between the politics of production and the regimes of consumption, or rather, since that distinction is now engulfed, between the politics of culture and the politics of politics' (Morris, 1988: 268). As 'the distance between cultural politics and political politics has become so great' in current cultural theory, Morris argues that how to *invent* (rather than remember or retrieve) 'some connections is now a major ethical and imaginative . . . problem for radical politics. It isn't a matter of nostalgia for fundamentals' (1988: 268).

In appropriating the appropriations of popular culture, criticism doesn't so much abandon old terrains of 'genuine' struggle as Jameson might say, but more seriously, loses credibility: it ceases to be able to say why it thinks that cultural 'struggle' should be so necessary, or rather – it keeps on sleepily assuming *that it knows*. (Morris, 1988: 268–9)

Like Ang and Threadgold, then, Morris emphasizes that a textual 'politics of poetics' must not replace a dialogic 'politics of politics'. It is not at all surprising, she says, that

> the figure of the colonial should now so insistently reappear from all sides not as deprived and dispossessed, but as the naive spirit of plenitude, innocence, optimism – and effective critical 'distance'. Primitivism for art is (like Dundee for action-cinema, the outback for tourism) only an obvious conservative version of this figure. Resistant postmodernism has had its equivalents in popular culture on the one hand, and idealized enclaves of colonized Others (women, blacks, etc . . .) on the other. That the latter may sometimes prove slow to seize their place in post-modernity suggests a problem with the premise of surfeit. (Morris, 1988: 268)

Like Ien Ang, Meaghan Morris argues that there is no way back – *either* to the lost 'lay' voices of Sylvia Lawson, *or* to the expert 'apocalyptic guarantees of historical determinism' (1988: 265), which is a story that fundamentally marked Lawson's project. And also like Ang (and Threadgold), Morris emphasizes 'a major ethical and imaginative action' which requires a reflexive investigation of how our own 'expert' discourses have in fact colonized Others.

Her 'Tooth and Claw' article is an emphatically reflexive look at cultural theory as 'expert knowledgeability', and at the kinds of representational order we have established in our stories about media consumption – where, as Morris puts it, ' "appropriation" has become as commodified a catch-phrase as Paul Hogan's "*G'day*" ' (1988: 268).

Morris argues that the 'corporate-raider chic' of 'appropriation' is 'no doubt better adapted to the mood of the times than the industrious term "production" – which was overworked in much the same way by criticism in the 1970s' (1988: 267). Other cultural theorists still emphasize 'production', of course – as in Terry Threadgold's comment on the 'effects of perform-atives, understood as discursive productions' (1997: 82). But this is also a poststructuralist and interactive sense of *performative* production, where Threadgold, like Morris, emphasizes that the failure of theories of perform-ative 'resistance', 'poaching', 'appropriation' and 'power as resignification' are *at* the level of politics.

> [T]he politics of the performative speech act, its iterability, its unforeseen effects, its productivity, cannot be substituted for social and political theory, for under-standings of the materiality of corporeal alienation. . . . What I am suggesting here is that it may be unwise to accept these metaphors as empirical tools. The material realities are more complex and it may well be that it is only those with a certain level of cultural and economic capital and the right colour skin whose lives as discursive practices are really open to any intervention or resignification of this theoretical kind. (Threadgold, 1997: 83–4)

We need, following Threadgold and Morris, a new approach to 'the materiality of corporeal alienation' which does not slide instantly into a textualist 'premise of surfeit'. It needs to discover its 'lost voices' neither in the 'nostalgia' of 'master narratives', nor in the 'commodified catchphrases' of postmodernist 'corporate-raider chic'.

To prepare for my third case study, I want to turn to one of the books I have most enjoyed in recent years. In a very different field from film theory, but in a similar (political and epistemological) vein to what Threadgold and others have been saying, Ian Taylor, Karen Evans and Penny Fraser redirect our attention to 'impoverishment' rather than theories of 'corporate-raider chic' in their study of the postindustrial cities of Manchester and Sheffield. They point to 'a certain lack of reflexivity' whereby 'certain kinds of cultural studies literature, caught in an admiring circle with leading figures in the cultural industries themselves' (1996: 293) theorize the postmodern city as a place of *flâneur*, excess and flexible pleasure-seeking rather than rising unemployment and crime.

They argue that while the construction of a flexible life project amidst a range of diversions and pleasures in the face of the collapse of modernist meta-narratives may be the world of some members of the new, globalized professional class, this is not 'in any sense equivalent to the exploration of "structures of feeling" and social behaviours across the social formation as a whole' (1996: 293). Rather than universalize (and essentialize) the post-modern city *flâneur*, Taylor et al. look for the voices of 'different folks'. They explore 'the way in which memories and myths may work differently in different places – either as part of a process of acquiescence and surrender to fate and destiny, or as part of an active appropriation of a local culture' (1996: 35).

So we have that word 'appropriation' again, but situated neither in Hollywood's (and Australia's) past, nor within a 'premise of surfeit'. Now, at last, Sylvia Lawson's 'lost voices' can re-emerge – these ones, like her 1920s Australian voices, trapped in a tension between different representational orders. But in the case of these northern English voices, what is being lost is the very same industrial order – the British home base of wool, cotton, steel, cutlery – on which the colonial connection was built. Once there was a masculinist working class employed at the centre of these industrial cities' connection to an Empire. Its mental maps reached out to that wider colonized landscape. But now instead, the authors note, the postindustrial city is a more inward-looking place. Instead of pleasurable surfeit we have many local 'landscapes of fear'.

A major emphasis of Taylor et al.'s important book is on ethnographic and qualitative research which recognizes how, in this context of a fear of crime, local women adopt 'different forms of resistance or adaptive practice . . . the construction of a "women's city" within the larger urban configuration', and how 'the elderly, children and young people, the new poor and different ethnic minority peoples try to negotiate a space within these essentially male-dominated old industrial cities' (1996: 312) where both unemployment and crime rates are high and rising.

Here, then, we have the concept of 'resistance' too. But it is a resistance within a new, post-1970s impoverishment, and often it is locked in the memories of a 'residual' culture, as well as in a new awareness of risk.

[I]n both these northern cities, the patterns of avoidance of city space by women clearly derived from a close knowledge of certain streets or locales as having been colonised by threatening groups of young men. . . . So also did members of different ethnic minorities have an indicative map of the cities in which they lived, identifying particular streets and territories as places of avoidance. The elderly of these two cities, occupying a rather different 'risk' position, focused on the different dangers of particular street corners, bus stations or streetscapes, so modifying in later life their own emotional feelings for the city. (Taylor et al., 1996: 314)

And so, a decade on from Meaghan Morris's piece on *Crocodile Dundee*, the call for the local 'lost audience' is embedded in a claim for 'critical empirical work on cities by sociology, especially in giving some practical grounding to an area of social theory which threatens at present . . . to become an abstract and second-order celebration of consumer and enterprise cultures themselves' (Taylor et al., 1996: 314). The new representational order of the 'risk society' is these authors' antidote to the 'corporate-raider chic' of certain versions of postmodern 'appropriation' theory. There are indeed impoverished voices who do not have 'the right colour skin' (Threadgold) still outside 'second-order celebration of consumer and enterprise cultures' – both in Britain and Australia. Hence to the 'local voices' of my third Australian case study.

Risk, fear of crime and the media: a story of 'lay knowledge'

Anyone even slightly acquainted with the current 'Risk Society' debate will know where my terms 'stories of expertise and the everyday' primarily come from; and also the terms 'expert' and 'lay knowledgeability' that I have been using in this chapter. The issue of 'expert' and 'lay' reflexivity has been central in risk theory recently. Indeed, Ulrich Beck and Anthony Giddens focus on the issue of reflexivity as the *defining* aspect of the risk society. Beck, who originated the term 'risk society', argued that the environmental hazards produced by modernity could no longer be contained within its own 'expert' systems of prediction and control.

But despite his talk of emergent social groups, there is a tendency in Beck's work to think of reflexive modernization as a 'self-refuting', non-agentive and systemic effect of 'real' physical risks generated by the 'expertise' of large-scale nuclear and chemical technologies. Giddens, on the other hand, has taken the issue of *non*-expert anxieties and responses to expert systems further, to include the public contestation of expertise. But, as Wynne argues, this 'lay' process of reflexivity about scientific expertise has tended to be conceived by Giddens in terms of *rational choice*. 'In the face of contestation of expert claims, publics invest active trust in expert systems – that is, trust is invested in particular systems via deliberate choice between recognised alternatives' (Wynne, 1996: 47).

Scott Lash has criticized the genuine reflexivity of 'Risk Society' experts themselves, as a failure at the level of politics.

Beck's and Giddens' virtual neglect of the cultural/hermeneutic sources of the late modern self entails at the same time a neglect of this crucial dimension of politics and everyday life. It means further that their conceptions of sub-politics or life-politics focus on the experts with relative neglect of the grass roots. (Beck et al., 1994: 200)

Brian Wynne has also challenged Beck's and Giddens's notions of reflexivity, arguing that 'expert' scientific knowledge of risk is no less indeterminate and hermeneutic than 'lay' knowledge (without the latter's often more local-specialist, multi-dimensional and adaptive practical under-standings). In Wynne's view, public anxiety and insecurity in areas of risk are the result of being made to be *dependent* on the voices of experts, while on the other hand having a basic mistrust of them. As Lash, Szerszynski and Wynne put it, 'This anxiety is, often, only exacerbated by social-scientific surveys of public perceptions of risk, surveys that share the epistemological assumptions of the natural scientists, effectively joining them, along with government and various business interests, in an actor-network of literally overwhelming proportions and power' (1996: 8). In this context, all of us as lay people are impoverished by science's representational order.

The culturalist critique of risk theory has a crucial policy focus in relation to management, media and communication (which I will develop further in the next chapter). International approaches to the management of risk perception are seen as still predominantly empiricist. Both Handmer and Wynne argue that much 'top-down' risk communication has been neither genuinely reflexive (challenging the normative boundaries of intellectual paradigms) nor about 'partnership between experts and public', but 'more about persuading people to tolerate something that they would rather do without' via imposing 'one view such as a probabilistic assessment on another group and trying to push them into accepting it' (Handmer, 1996: 88). Lash, Szerszynski and Wynne (among many other culturalist risk theorists) accuse 'authoritative scientific and policy vocabularies' of being 'epistemologically "realist", positivistic, disembedded, technological and cognitivist', thus masking significant cultural, social and personal dimensions of the contemporary 'environmental crisis'. 'As modern science has expanded its social authority and its social reach, its formalised and reductionist vocabularies have delegitimated and displaced many of the more situated understandings that people have of the world and their place in it.' (Lash, Szerszynski and Wynne, 1996: 13)

They argue that by the late 1980s, environmentalist narratives had been adopted as an 'official' agenda by big business, government and inter-national institutions such as the OECD (Organization for Economic Co-operation and Development) and the EC (European Community), creating conditions for a paradigm shift in environmental discourse, from the notion of 'balance' and 'equilibrium' in an environment under threat, to the master frame of 'economic sustainability'. 'Growth' has thus replaced 'equilibrium' in an 'environmental discourse proffering optimistic technological solutions' (Lash, Szerszynski and Wynne, 1996: 19).

These 'top-down', empiricist-rationalist positions assume that objective risk needs *first* to be calculated by science and *then* is mediated, perceived and responded to in various ways via social, cultural and political processes. Consequently, a guiding assumption of this paradigm of risk research is that the best public function the media can achieve is *neutrality*, obtained by conveying the scientists' calculations to the public 'appropriately' but 'objectively'.

This, of course, also assumes a somewhat passive, over-emotional audience (to be 'filled up' with the rational data of scientific empiricism). 'Top-down' risk research thus usually ignores the role of the media itself in engaging with an *active audience*'s daily leisure and work-time pleasures and fantasies. It also ignores, in Wynne's view, the fact that 'expert systems are typically importing dense but inadequate meanings' (Wynne, 1996: 60).

In an alternative ('below-up') perspective, the media are not (and cannot ever be) simply 'responsibly' neutral vehicles for the top-down facts of empiricism, but rather, as Sparks (1992) and others argue, are inevitably engaged with audiences who are skilfully situating the symbolic within everyday social routines and practices. It is this approach to the *situated narratives* of 'lay knowledgeability' which we can readily accommodate with Ien Ang's call for a poststructuralist 'ethnography of storytelling'.

Our own Fear of Crime research was a consultancy tendered by major state agencies which were seeking research-based policy guidelines in key areas of crime and violence in Australia. In particular, in our media sub-study we wanted, within a major policy intervention (funded by the National Campaign Against Violence and Crime, the National Anti-Crime Strategy, and the Criminology Research Council), to go beyond a textualist 'politics of poetics'. We saw this as an opportunity to adopt a 'below-up' and culturally situated approach to 'lay' voices about contemporary risk and fear of crime. The stories told by Julie – one white lesbian mother faced by two black men – were part of a deliberate research attempt to 'avoid the objectification of "audience" ' (Ang, 1996: 77). Other very different stories, for example, were told by gay teenagers in a refuge in inner-city Sydney, by a group of 'Leftie' retired unionists in Sydney, and, in the case we will look at next, by a group of seven working-class teenagers (four Aboriginal, two Pacific Islander, one white) 'near Redfern', also in inner-city Sydney.

We chose Redfern because this inner-city Sydney suburb – together with the Sydney red-light district of Kings Cross, and Cabramatta ('known' for its Asian gangs and drugs) – were strongly indicated in our quantitative survey as Australian 'landscapes of fear'. Redfern was feared because of what were seen to be high rates of mugging and theft there, particularly related to its Aboriginal population. In our overall survey, we elicited responses to a closed-ended statement, 'Australia has become a more dangerous society to live in': 80 per cent strongly agreeing or agreeing. In an open-ended follow-up 'why' question, the link between people's addiction to illicit drug use and crimes of violence was frequently made; and this in turn was frequently linked to structural unemployment, to a sense of break down in deep-held values, or to lack of guidance and discipline among young people.

As well as our overall study, we ran a separate 'fear of crime and the media' qualitative research programme. And here we asked the kind of young people who were targeted as the major 'risk' in the overall survey, their own view of the local 'landscape of fear'. Hence our choice of Redfern – which was a place where fear of crime was linked not only to drugs and 'young people', but also to the 'colour of skin' (Threadgold).

The teenagers we talked to were from a state school close to Redfern, and a number of them lived there. They strongly contested the media's stereotyping of

one particular race. . . . There's a lot of drugs here but there's a lot of other suburbs. Like Cabramatta – it's not in the media as Redfern is.

And all those other areas are worse than Redfern.

There is drugs there.

Not all the people in Redfern are dogs, like alcoholics . . .

It's not like people say it is in the media.

They say all the bad points, they don't say the good points.

This group believed that the media do not show enough positive news about Redfern – the community achievements, the university places gained and other successes of young people from the area, and so on.

Redfern's a real strong black community, like they're all helping each other out and that. . . . Besides the drugs and stuff, everybody sticks together. . . . You don't get very many black communities ever like that. There might be drug addicts and that, but there's Aboriginals in Redfern that work hard just as much as other people do.

This is, of course, a 'resistance' reading of one aspect of the media. But it is not a consistent or systematic one. They do not generalize their own critique of the media for racial stereotyping into support for the Vietnamese community in Cabramatta. Furthermore, these teenagers are also often prone to reiterate 'expert' representations and 'citations' – whether from the media or the police.

I'm afraid of break-ins to my house, like police say girls get their throats slit or raped when they're in bed. That's scary . . .

On television they just talk about murders and that's it.

I get scared when I watch *Australia's Most Wanted* when I'm walking about by myself. That's scary, eh. . . . There's heaps of deviates about.

Yes there's a lot of devos, men. . . . who are in late night cars and when they see girls sitting there by themselves they stop.

Media representations (as in the police-supported TV series *Australia's Most Wanted*) *and* their own experience on Redfern streets late at night clearly blended in these last two statements – a typically performative mix of the 'liturgical' and the 'creative' that we have seen elsewhere in perform-ance analysis. But overall, it is the lack of local, situated knowledge that they blamed the media for.

> They don't know what really goes on in Redfern. They don't really have a clue.
>
> They don't know, they haven't lived there.

These students said that 'We know what Redfern's like because we come out of there'. But they felt that the bad media images *stop* other people from coming there to find out for themselves (a majority of people surveyed in all age-groups in our study in fact said exactly that).

These teenagers had plenty of the same fears of crime as the broader Australian public that we surveyed – for example, of drug-related crime, 'of a junkie coming up like to get money trying to stab me with a needle'. But the basic daily reality of these kinds of things are not covered in the media, in their view. A number of their everyday stories did in fact relate to drug addicts. But they argued that the drug cases that get sympathetic publicity and 'expert' treatment in the media are in 'rich' environments (as in case of the upper-middle class, north shore Sydney teenager, Anna Woods, whose death at a rave got huge media coverage).

As well as late-evening encounters with drug addicts and 'devos', these teenagers also had a lot of negative routine experience with police – especially police on the beat ('experience from the gutter').

> When the police pick you up they're all racist . . .
>
> With media they try to make out that police are really caring.
>
> Real heroes!

The one white boy in the group said that when he walks down the street in Waterloo the police don't pull him up because he is white; when his Aboriginal friend walks down the street they do, even though he has done nothing wrong. Two of the students said they had been assaulted by the police; and a girl recalled how her old uncle was choked in jail by a police officer, was vomiting blood, and had red marks around his neck. The group argued that you do not see any of this in the media.

> They don't show the things that we go through.
>
> They show like this court case about murder but they don't show a case about three Aboriginal boys getting threatened by police. But in the media they show like 'this happened *to* police'.

Some of the teenagers said that the police make up stories about what Aboriginal kids are doing; and the group retold stories they said they had witnessed themselves, like a boy assaulted by the police and then charged for supposedly throwing bricks at a train.

So these teenagers commonly rejected the 'heroic white male' police images they saw on TV. In all TV genres, police were

> made out not to be racist, made out to be perfect and help every single person. . . . But in real life it's not like that. One in ten is good. All the rest are racist.

> I know a black person from Redfern police station who wanted to leave because he was sick of the shit that was going on there . . . the racist comment.

The Aboriginal girls in the group, rejecting the 'reality' of mainstream TV violence, preferred to reconstruct their own history.

> You know the Port Arthur massacre? See how that was all big, and all in the media and that. Well, see there's things like the Mile Creek massacre, the Oyster Bay massacre, they're all big massacres but they happened to Aboriginal people and so they don't do those in the media.

Overall, the group's response to the media contained a significant cynicism about 'expert' opinion, especially where it related to their own localized experience.

> Whenever you turn the TV on it's crime.

> But it's crime that ain't really crime – it's not realistic crime like the crime that's really happening.

> It's bodgy crime.

All of the groups we interviewed in the media study were asked specifically about potential crime and terrorism at the Sydney 2000 Olympics. Generally each group of teenagers we talked with (in the city of Sydney, the tourist area of the Blue Mountains, and the rural area around Bathurst, NSW) tended to say the same thing: that there will be no terrorism, but there will be a lot more petty crime and mugging because of 'all those loaded people from overseas' (Blue Mountains teenagers), and the 'thousands of rich tourists, thousands of handbags' (Bathurst teenagers).

The 'Redfern' teenagers agreed with this: 'All the rich people coming here from Asia, from Japan, they'll be robbed.' But they also gave a different inflection. They spoke of these Asians not always as 'Others' ('tourists who can't be told', as one white teenager we interviewed put it) but also as 'brothers'. There was a major emphasis in this group on the likelihood of international Olympic boycotts by colonized people (from South African blacks, from Canadian Native Americans, and from Australian Aboriginals). Perhaps, some said, there might even be bomb threats (in relation to what they see as the racist activities of Pauline Hanson's new political party, 'One Nation'):

> because of the way they've been treating the blackfellas and the Asians. . . . Because of all Pauline Hanson's stuff.

The 'near Redfern' group of teenagers was just one of many that we interviewed. Why choose this particular story to tell here? I have two reasons: one is that it is from this 'postcolonial' context that Julie travelled to meet those other black people in Seattle – they are *her* context, and she was very aware of this; secondly, these 'near Redfern' teenagers told us as well as any others stories about the everyday in the *context* of stories of (and about) expertise.

Ien Ang has argued that

> Which stories to tell, in what form, to whom, where and when, and with what intention, are questions which academic scholars are not used to asking themselves, but they are central to the politics of intellectual work. In this respect I agree with Talal Asad's argument that a 'politics of poetics' should not be pursued at the expense of a 'politics of politics'. (Ang, 1996: 97)

And in her *Feminist Poetics*, Terry Threadgold is really saying the same thing.

> If we want to 'rewrite' in a different sense, not transmission but transformation . . . it seems to me that there has to be a very thorough understanding of the contexts, both material and discursive in which we write, and a very detailed understanding of the materiality of texts (the resistance they offer to the meanings we want to make). . . . We also need to be constantly aware of who the 'I' is who writes. (Threadgold, 1997: 56)

The 'near Redfern' teenagers gave us many stories that related their media 'poetics' to their local (and national – in the case of Pauline Hanson) 'politics of politics'. But they also indicated the powerful 'materiality of texts' (for example, in their ability to extend their notion of 'community' and 'brotherhood' to the Asian tourists but not to the Vietnamese of Cabramatta). In that latter case media 'strategies' (in de Certeau's sense) seemed more powerful than their own local 'tactics'. On the one hand, this group of teenagers did not have that 'distance between cultural politics and political politics' that Meaghan Morris complains of in cultural studies 'experts'. On the other hand, they were 'slow to seize' their place as 'idealized enclaves of colonized Others (women, blacks, etc)', as Morris also observed. Theirs were, as Morris would predict, stories of the everyday with multiple causes and effects. But theirs were, also, voices of the 'impoverished' with which we can perhaps challenge the 'corporate-raider chic' of other theories of 'appropriation'.

This chapter has been about unfolding academic theories of appropriation and resistance – about cultural studies voices seeking 'lost' public voices – which have been (dialogically and diachronically) an important part of my own 'inner conversation': the ' "I" who writes. How then to avoid a futher appropriation – as Shotter says, of 'their' voices for 'our' theory? How to at least try to 'make sense of "their" lives "with them", thus to arrive at a version upon a common "ground" between "us" ' (Shotter, 1993: 48)? I will look at that issue in my case study of the Sydney building workers in the 'cultural policy' chapter that follows.

2

CULTURAL POLICY

First, people must have access to the information, advice, and analysis that will enable them to know what their rights are . . . and allow them to pursue these rights effectively. Second, they must have access to the broadest possible range of information, interpretation, and debate . . . and they must be able to use communications facilities in order to . . . propose alternative courses of action. And third, they must be able to recognise themselves and their aspirations in the range of representations offered within the central communications sectors and be able to contribute to developing those representations (Murdock and Golding, 1989: 183–4)

Instead of a celebrity on television telling you [about STDs and HIV], you know what you need? You need a penis there with sores and a have real full-on syphilis penis . . . and show people, this is what you're going to look like, this is what's going to happen to you. . . . Put it on television, put it on the sides of buses, trains whatever. (Sydney builders' labourer)

This chapter is about public 'creativity and constraint' in relation to the performance of cultural policy. It examines the activation *as* policy of models of communication theory, and in relation to notions of public agency and citizenship. It explores state agendas in the area of HIV/AIDS, and the relationship between expert systems, unofficial narratives ('lay knowledge-ability') and the 'risk society'. In particular, it explores ways in which Ang's 'ethnography of storytelling' can be put to work in the context of health policy. Its case study describes a 'below-up', low-technology media campaign (in which I was involved) which attempted to take seriously the notion of men 'taking responsibility for their own sexuality' by making them 'citizens' (Murdock) rather than consumers of an HIV/AIDS campaign. The chapter's focus on cultural policy will allow me to be both reflexive about this 'storytelling' (Ang) and describe the performativity of 'political intervention' (Roach) as 'expert' and 'lay' knowledgeability are exchanged dialogically at several sites and levels.

'Expert' and 'lay' knowledges

I begin here from Brian Wynne's view (Chapter 1) that 'the fundamental sense of risk in the "risk society" is risk to identity engendered by dependence on expert systems which typically operate with such unreflexive blindness to their own culturally problematic and inadequate models of the human'. The emphasis here is on the way in which 'scientific expert knowledge . . . denigrates specialist lay knowledges' and 'defines lay resistance as based on ignorance or irrationality rather than on substantive if unarticulated objections to those inadequate constructions of lay social identity which the expert discourses unwittingly assume and impose' (1996: 68).

We should note that Wynne tends to refer to *specialist* 'lay knowledges', focusing particularly on farming communities. His rationale for the particular narratives he tells is to challenge the 'dismissive modernistic view of indigenous knowledges' conveyed by powerful scientific knowledges whose main epistemic principles are 'instrumentalism, control and alienation' (Wynne, 1996: 70). Thus Wynne shows that farmer's knowledge

> is indeed systematic theory, even though this is in a syntax linked to the local labour process and does not presuppose a universal and impersonal world. . . . Seen from the farmers' vantage point this variability is a reflection of the conscious purpose of building diversity into practice, and of adaptive coping with multiple dimensions in the same complex area. . . . [I]t should be noted that local or lay knowledges do not celebrate some romantic state of lack of control. They too seek control, and this does not exclude forms of social control . . . but it is of a kind which is radically different from that embodied in normal scientific epistemic commitments. This kind of knowledge is manifestly local and contextual rather than decontextual and 'universal'. (Wynne, 1996: 69–70)

This is a 'kind of adaptive "control" . . . which is exercised with personal agency and overt responsibility' (Wynne, 1996: 70). Wynne goes on to say that it is precisely this personal responsibility which Beck notes is missing from modernity's dominant discourse of scientific control; and 'it is the reintegration of the deleted issues of human agency, responsibility and value which may lead to the democratisation, legitimation and epistemic pluralisation of science' (Wynne, 1996: 70).

As a sociologist of science, Wynne's political/theoretical agenda is open and clear: a greater agency and democratic citizenship in relation to scientific (and therefore social) control. For this reason he emphasizes, on the one hand, the hermeneutic 'imprecision' of science, which is admitted among 'specialists in their esoteric, private and local scientific subcultures' (Wynne, 1996: 69) but seldom in the public domain; and on the other hand, 'specialist lay knowledges' (as in farming). His ultimate critique is of the supposed 'objective boundary between science and the public domain' (Wynne, 1996: 75); a supposition which he continues to find even in 'risk society' theory itself.

> In Giddens' view of reflexive modernity . . . there is no problematising of a boundary between expert and lay domains of knowledge and epistemology – because the most that lay people can do (or are thought to be capable of) is to choose whom to trust, when experts disagree. . . . In Beck's only slightly different view, the . . . 'out-there' risks are identified by counterexperts [hence] the problems of trust and risk are only raised by expert contestation, and as in Giddens' account the public is only represented by different expert factions. The human dimensions of such natural knowledges, whether contested or not by other *experts*, is not recognised or problematised as a public issue. (Wynne, 1996: 76)

It is for this reason that Wynne emphasizes 'specialist lay knowledges'; and indeed he takes to task Van der Ploeg (whose account of Andean potato farmers has been, together with Wynne's own research on Cumbrian sheep farmers, central to his argument) for suggesting that scientific and 'traditional' cultures are mutually exclusive.

> The lay knowledge he describes is complex, reflexive, dynamic and innovative, material and empirical, and yet also theoretical. . . . [But] Van der Ploeg's case-study implies the bleak conclusion that there are categorically distinct epistemological systems, of modern science and indigenous ('cultural') tradition, even if the latter is more dynamic and practically effective than usually seen. (Wynne, 1996: 72, 74)

Wynne is, in effect, arguing for a new kind of public citizenship based on 'collective self-conceptions'.

> The romantic seductions of local knowledges and identities do not come as an *alternative* to modernity's ahuman and alienating universals, but as an inspiration to find the collective self-conceptions which can sustain universals that do not bury the traces of their own human commitment and responsibility. (Wynne, 1996: 78)

Nevertheless, there *is* a kind of 'romantic seduction' about discussing the local knowledge/responsibility of farmers in Cumbria or the Andes in relation to the nuclear pollution of sheep grazing or the modernization patterns around an ideal genotype potato. 'Lay knowledge' may seem very different, and much less 'responsible', when it is the local knowledge of working-class males in relation to sexuality and heterosexual HIV/AIDS campaigns. In this latter case, too, we can talk about the issues of 'personal agency and overt responsibility', of 'highly variable and non-universal knowledge', and of 'adaptive coping with multiple dimensions in the same complex area'. And particularly when we talk, here too, of men aiming 'to seek control, and this does not exclude forms of social control' (Wynne, 1996: 70), a new and potently gendered political dimension thrusts itself into our view. Now it is no longer, somewhat romantically, traditional farmers against government and big corporation scientists, it is men against women.

So, again, this will not be an heroic tale. Rather, it will focus on the power relationship of female 'expert' interviewer and male respondents, on circulating male myths about 'safe sheilas' and risk women, on male potency jokes and alibis about 'when the grog takes over', on sexual narrative questions (as encouraged by our male shop-steward interviewer) and the sites and vehicles of HIV communication that were generated by those questions and became the basis of the media campaign. In other words, I look in this chapter at the dialogic construction of HIV texts within what Patton would call the strategic performativity of cultural policy. And, as *situated* research, the stories I will narrate in my case study will not be those of 'specialised local knowledges . . . linked to the local labour process', as in Wynne, but of (male) lay knowledgeability in leisure time; and in leisure spaces moreover when a primary intention (in addition to 'getting laid') is to let 'the grog take over'.

These will not so obviously convey, then, Wynne's lay knowledge as 'complex, reflexive, dynamic and innovative, material and empirical, and yet also theoretical'. Or not at least in its residually romantic-heroic sense. But it *will* still be all these things – but **outside** what Meaghan Morris calls 'resistant' postmodernism's 'idealised enclaves of colonised Others (women, blacks, etc . . .)'. As Morris says, these latter (and even more so the imperial white males who have done the colonizing) 'may sometimes prove slow to seize their place in postmodernity'. Which is not a reason for excluding them from Wynne's 'view of the construction of knowledge as the construction of hybrid . . . or heterogeneous networks' (Wynne, 1996: 75). These are, after all, perhaps not so far from being Wynne's and Van der Ploeg's farmers on a night out in town.

Policy and citizenship: Australia's 'Grim Reaper'

An opening agenda for this chapter is that as new and contestive definitions of citizenship and equity seep into the meanings and understandings of state agencies, so likewise new possibilities for intervention by academic cultural researchers open up. Take, for example, the 1992 *Access and Equity* report from the Australian Department of the Prime Minister and Cabinet. This emphasizes the need to shift away from the 'concept of universal citizenship, with its assumption that people are equal and homogeneous in their role as citizens and therefore should be treated equally by the state' to an understanding based on 'the reality of difference between various members of society . . . relating to people's social conditions, to possession or lack of power' (Australian Department of the Prime Minister and Cabinet, 1992: 2).

The move here from a formal, universalist definition of citizenship in terms of the rights of individuals to one based on power and the disadvantage 'of groups with specific characteristics and needs' opens up the policy terrain of **cultural** risk – that is 'the fear that those who are already disadvantaged will suffer more' (Douglas, 1992: 34) – and therefore for analysis of citizenship and equity from a cultural perspective. As Mary Douglas says:

> If marginal groups and poor inhabitants of inner cities are specially at risk from sexually transmitted diseases, is there a tendency to forget about them? The answer is emphatically yes, if the culture is individualist. . . . An individualist culture finds ways of making its disadvantaged members sink from sight. . . . Cultural analysis is a countervailing vision which warns which categories in each kind of culture are most likely to be at risk, who will be sinned against, and who will be counted as the sinner exposing others to risk. (Douglas, 1992: 34–6)

In recent years widely read journals in the sciences and health professions have begun to question 'top-down' risk communication. For example, in *Scientific American*, M. Granger Morgan has argued that 'risk management is, fundamentally, a question of values. In a democratic society, there is no acceptable way to make these choices without involving the citizens who will be affected by them.' And he goes on to argue that 'risk analysts and managers will have to . . . adopt new communication styles and learn from the populace rather than simply trying to force information on it' (July 1993, pp. 24–5). In the health field, the lead article in the World Health Organization (WHO)-supported Dutch magazine *AIDS Health Promotion Exchange* have regularly argued that training for health promoters must emphasize how to 'employ a participatory approach rather than the more common teacher–student relationship with members of their target audiences' so that 'community members are partners in HIV/AIDS and STD prevention and care' (Editorial, 1994: 1–2). The emphasis here is on using community members' own language about sexuality and STDs.

As the rhetorics within state agencies change from individualist to cultural risk definitions of citizenship, clearly spaces for new kinds of consultancy develop for academics working in the field of cultural studies. But because cultural boundaries – between state bureaucracies, commercial agencies, academia and a wide range of other cultural groups – *are* being crossed here, the communication is fraught with theoretical, methodological and political (rhetorical) problems. First, there is the residual power of old paradigms. Thus, although the *Access and Equity* definition of citizenship quoted above does emphasize 'mechanisms to ensure participation of disadvantaged groups in decision-making' (Australian Department of the Prime Minister and Cabinet, 1992: 6), its stronger emphasis on equity as an '*outcome*', on 'how to compensate for difference' (1992: 6) leaves it open in its practice to the critique of a pluralist theory of citizenship: that it constructs identity as a 'lack' (the 'Other' needs to be given something that we have) rather than in cultural difference and diversity. Equity and citizenship, in this argument, too frequently become matters which top-down policy experts should 'fix', because the potential citizen as 'Other' is still 'lacking'. This is the policy positioning of outgroups as 'needy' recipients of concessions, as 'target groups' rather than the '*alternative* . . . collective self-conceptions' of a more human commitment to citizenship and responsibility that Wynne speaks about.

To achieve *that* would mean changing the mainstream paradigms underpinning 'risk'. Mary Douglas describes these as a discursive mix of nineteenth-century economic theories of risk-taking and twentieth-century developments in risk psychology. Fundamental to the individualistic probability concept of risk which Douglas criticizes is the Enlightenment/ Utilitarian notion of humans 'as hedonic calculators calmly seeking to pursue private interests. We are said to be risk-aversive, but, alas, so inefficient in handling information that we are unintentional risk-takers; basically we are fools' (Douglas, 1992: 13).

Yet how different the reality of risk *performance* can be was indicated to me by a working-class, Koori female teenager in Sydney who, having seen the first Australian HIV/AIDS television advertisement, 'The Grim Reaper', went to Sydney's red light district to get pregnant. She told me that using condoms was 'chicken'. This was not 'rational' risk-aversive behaviour. But nor was it 'pathological', since within her particular subculture taking risks was a matter of everyday consensus. Stealing and driving fast cars was 'fun', and knocking over old ladies for their handbags was an essential part of their economy. The gap between this group's embodied pleasure in risk performance and the doleful (male) voice liturgically intoning 'Always use condoms, always' at the end of the government's 'Grim Reaper' advertisement could hardly have been greater.

But public service advertisements (PSAs) like the 'Grim Reaper' are the 'canonical' official 'fix it' response to the 'basically we are fools' notion of risk-taking: which is to provide better education via health campaigns. The top-down 'scientific' risk communication paradigm which critiques the media for being too 'sensational' also produces its ideal media vehicle in the PSA, which supposedly avoids the 'commercial' and the 'sensational' by leaving risk information campaigns safely in the hands of public health experts. The world-wide, above-down 'expert'-led media campaigns in HIV/ AIDS education are examples of this tendency. Elsewhere (Tulloch and Lupton, 1997: 79–93) I have examined the first five years of the Australian government's PSA campaigns against HIV/AIDS, where I tried to show that central to the various advertising agencies' final performance of televising PSAs was the way in which concepts and rhetorics of cultural difference, which were circulating both among state bureaucrats and in advertising agencies, were rearticulated (sometimes to the point of occlusion) by more dominant risk-aversive assumptions, by predominantly linear 'effects' communication models, and by state legitimating strategies. It was the rather complex combination of these which constructed the 'implied readers' of the AIDS PSAs as *consumers* of the government HIV education campaigns.

Although there is no space here to elaborate on this dialogic performance – as 'conversational realities' were played out between two different 'expert' voices: of health bureaucrats and of advertising agencies (which drew on 'ordinary voices' through focus-group interviews) – I can emphasize that these were not (in any serious and systematic way) sharing the 'common argumentative forms' (Billig, 1987: 196) of their 'target' audiences. We can begin to map more precisely the extent to which the 'target population' of young people were constructed as 'Other' in these campaigns, by referring to Graham Murdock and Peter Golding's paper on 'Citizenship in the Age of Privatised Communications', in which they identify three main kinds of relation between communications and citizenship (see header quotation). The early Australian national HIV/AIDS campaigns failed significantly in all three of Murdock and Golding's requirements for citizenship.

First, as regards the information to pursue rights effectively, while young people were told to 'always use condoms, always', no advice was given at any stage of the media (or indeed school education) campaigns about how to 'pursue rights effectively' – no 'information, advice, and analysis' to teenagers, for example, or on how to negotiate condom use in the context of male/female power relations, on how to deal with embarrassment (expressed especially strongly by our respondents in small town and country areas) when buying condoms from local chemists, or (as a number of our respondents commented) on how to find the money to *pay* for 'always using condoms, always'.

Secondly, as regards 'access to the broadest possible range of information, interpretation and debate', and thirdly, to communications facilities to propose alternative courses of action and alternative representations, it goes without saying that young people were not given any access as user-participants at the level of production of the HIV media campaigns – except as 'targets' of market researchers. And as 'consumers', they were offered the narrowest possible range of debate, with little or no information about links between STDs and AIDS, and with the concept 'safe sex' being confined to condoms, and therefore to the apparent normalcy of penetrative sex. As Sue Kippax and June Crawford have said:

> This focus on condoms is a sensible one *if* sex is equated with intercourse. And it is clear that in most of the campaign material that is exactly what was assumed. The two unwritten assumptions of most of the campaign material accord with the male sex drive discourse: sex *is* penetration by the man. Condoms make sex safe. (Crawford et al., 1992: 53)

At the levels, then, of information to effectively pursue their rights, of a broad range of information and debate, and of being able to contribute to developing the range of representations within which they could recognize themselves and their aspirations, the young people of Australia were consumers not citizens by Murdock and Golding's definition. In the field of AIDS and cultural risk, this meant the freedom to pursue one's individual interests within the choices provided (primarily relating to penetrative sex and the purchase of different kinds of condom), rather than achieving the degree of collective and self-representing activity that Murdock and Golding define as citizenship.

The Heterosexual Men's Campaign

Turning from consumers to the strategy of citizens (in Murdock and Golding's sense) as *performers* in health-risk campaigns, I will describe my involvement with the NSW Department of Family Planning's Heterosexual Men's Project (Venables and Tulloch, 1993). This campaign, as initially set out in its brief to me as consultant by its project officer, Sue Venables, had a number of aims which distinguished it from the earlier PSA campaigns. It was seen as important to:

- move away from the medical experts' 'Three Waves of HIV' media preoccupation to the notion of heterosexual men taking responsibility for their own sexual behaviour;

- move away from the moralistic, bogey-man type campaigning of the 'Grim Reaper', since research indicated that though this raised aware- ness in the general population, it did not translate into significant safer- sex behaviour change in the heterosexual population;
- adjust the more recent campaign concept of women taking responsibility for safe sex (the 'If it's not on, it's not on' campaigns). As a feminist, Sue Venables noted behind the tendency to position women as guardians of socially responsible sex, a number of problematic assumptions, including 'the commonly held belief in the male sex drive discourse (Hollway, 1984) which renders the male sex drive as somehow uncon- trollable' (Venables and Tulloch, 1993: 4);
- avoid using representations of women designed to titillate heterosexual men and instead find alternative vehicles to attract their attention;
- personalize the risks of HIV/AIDS for heterosexually active men by linking both the behavioural and biological risk factors of STD infection with HIV;
- 'move away from the top-down trend of previous large-scale campaigns, and adopt community development approaches, successfully used in Australian gay campaigns. This meant involving heterosexual men throughout the process in determining the messages, vehicles and direction of the campaign' (Venables and Tulloch, 1993: 9).

From the beginning Venables knew that the campaign would be minimally funded ($110,000). Consequently, she rejected the notion of 'surveying heterosexual men in New South Wales', and chose instead a more situated, 'local knowledgeability' approach. Building workers were chosen as the group to work with, not because they were representative of 'heterosexual men', but because there had already been a successful series of HIV/AIDS theatrical performances titled 'No Condom, No Start' by the Sidetrack Theatre Company on building sites in Sydney. The Heterosexual Men's Project was conceived as a follow-up, *low-tech*, communication project which would take advantage of this normally hard-to-get entrée to a particular male, working-class group as a result of the support of the Building Workers' Industrial Union. It would also be able to extend the theatre group's 'formal performance' (in Joseph Roach's sense of perform- ativity as a cultural and critical act) to the building workers' own 'creativity' in designing a health campaign. In other words, the primary focus was an HIV/AIDS *campaign performance* (not simply 'research'), and the Sidetrack intervention was seen as a valuable launchpad for this, given the rather minimal funding that was available.

The BWIU organizer who had co-ordinated the 'No Condom, No Start' theatre performances (and was known and trusted by the men), Jeff Ashby, was used as a co-interviewer with Sue Venables in the ten focus groups that we ran at work sites in different parts of Sydney. A total of 118 men were interviewed in these focus groups, with ages ranging from 17 to 60 years, and including men from a variety of non-English-speaking backgrounds, including Italy, Greece, Lebanon, Portugal, Russia and Yugoslavia. The groups included single men, men in long-term relationships, divorced and separated men, and fathers. All the men interviewed were volunteers, though participation depended on the men's ability to leave their work task for about one hour. Each group was tape recorded with the consent of the men in the group.

In these interviews, the project emphasis on men taking responsibility for their own sexual behaviour was both clear, and presented in different discursive forms by Sue Venables, as female sexual health counsellor, and Jeff Ashby as heterosexual male and workmate. In other words, the *choice* of interviewers – Sue Venables with her 'scientific' narratives as a practising sexual health counsellor, and Jeff Ashby constructing working men's sexual 'scenarios' out of his knowledgeability *as* 'one of the men' – related to an important principle of the research/campaign strategy: that these men were not simply to be treated as 'exotic' research objects in these interviews.

It is clear that a number of 'expert' discourses – scientific, feminist, etc – already underpinned a campaign which claimed it wanted to avoid the 'top-down trend' in HIV campaigns. Here the role of Jeff Ashby was seen as important from the start: to collaborate 'on the development of the interview format and questions, translating them into culturally appropriate language. This included, for example, exchanging the term heterosexual for "straight", HIV for "the AIDS virus", and using colloquial rather than medicalised terms for description of sexual practice' (Venables and Tulloch, 1993: 11).

In fact, the different kinds of 'story' told by each of the two interviewers were integral to the campaign performance that followed.

The interviewers: the expert's narrative

By combining a working (female) expert in the 'science' of STDs with a working male with considerable local and 'lay' knowledge, we were doing a number of things. First, we were avoiding the 'expert contestation' (risks as identified by counter-experts) which Wynne complains weakens both Giddens's and Beck's interest in lay knowledgeability. Secondly, by having an 'expert' and a 'lay' interviewer in the health field, we were attempting not to erect a boundary between, as Wynne puts it, on the one hand 'a mono-lithic culture of rationality and scientific modernity', and on the other a 'defensive and non-innovative, epistemically closed realm of indigenous "tra-ditional" cultures' (Wynne, 1996: 72). Rather, we were hoping (to use Wynne's words) that 'collective self-conceptions' would arise out of the dif-ferent discursive moves, the different modes of 'storytelling' of the inter-viewers. Thirdly, by having a *female* as well as a male interviewer – and moreover a female who used without embarrassment the men's language – we were posing the issue of both female and feminist (via Sue's non-moralistic questioning) negotiation directly to the men. Fourthly, we were encouraging the men's 'own human commitment and responsibility' (Wynne, 1996: 78) as *part* of a campaign performance aimed *at* men's sexual responsibility.

Some extracts from one of our long focus-group interviews will illustrate these points, and particularly the different 'storytelling' roles of Sue and Jeff as interviewers. All the interviews began as follows, with the men being asked (by Jeff),

Jeff: 'So what are some of the sexual health problems we've heard of?'
   :   'Herpes.'
   :   'Syphilis, gonorrhoea.'
   :   'AIDS.'
   :   'How come yous know all of them!' (men laugh)
   :   'NSU.'
Sue: 'You're the first person in these groups to mention NSU, actually.'
   :   'Do you win an award?' (men laugh)
Sue: 'You get a gold star.' (laughs)
   :   'What's MSU?'
   :   'NSU, non-specific uteralitis, or something.'
Sue: 'Urethritis, yeah.'
   :   'Is it contagious like the others?'
   :   'It's like a flu in the old fella.'
Sue: 'It is basically.' (men laugh) 'It's a bit like having a throat infection in the old fella.' (men laugh) 'People say it's like pissing razorblades.'
   :   'That could be taken as stones, then, would that?'
   :   'Yeah, same.'
Sue: 'You'd probably get the same symptoms, yeah – maybe a discharge as well with NSU.'
   :   'And is that on the level as a transmittable . . .?'
Sue: 'It is an STD, yeah.'
   :   'NSU – girls get thrush, don't they?'
Sue: 'That's a yeast infection, which isn't really sexually transmitted. Chlamydia, that's very similar to NSU and it's something that – have you heard of chlamydia?'
   :   'No, can't say we have.'
Sue: 'Again it's a bacterial infection like a throat infection, but a bit more serious because if it's left untreated it can leave you infertile, sterile. . . . Women don't have symptoms at all, and also some men don't have symptoms. You can have a bacteria sitting there and not know.'
   :   'And be a transmitter.'
Sue: 'Yes.'
   :   'Well, if not a lot of people know, and they consider that they have stones in the kidneys because they think they're pissing razorblades, how would the distinction come about? Say the person didn't get it examined, would it just rot his brain away and die like syphilis?'
Sue: 'No, it doesn't get into your system the same way that syphilis does – syphilis is one of those that can travel to your brain. But with NSU it's going to travel further up into your urethra and can leave you sterile, if it's left untreated – and the only way you're going to find out is to have a test.'

This extract illustrates the relaxed and humorous interview style, using the men's language. Nevertheless, Sue's interventions as interviewer/expert set her principle from the start: that is, that it is unethical, anywhere, anytime –

but *particularly* in relation to her own profession as sexual health counsellor – to simply plunder 'respondents' for research information as the 'exotic Others' of qualitative or ethnographic research. So, as well as being relaxed, Sue was also 'expert' in her role as interviewer.

Still, as this opening extract also indicates, though Sue did draw on standard discursive conventions of 'teacher-talk' (specifying the topic, checking, summarizing and defining understanding, correcting, editing, and monitoring the flow of talk), it was important to try to avoid the assymetrical us/them communicative relationship that is symptomatic of teacher-talk. From the beginning we were trying as far as possible also to avoid Foucault's sexual confessional where the agency of domination does not reside in the one who speaks, but in the one who questions (Foucault, 1978). Sue was not constructing her interviewing role as that of the objective anthropologist discovering the 'secrets' of the men's culture. Nevertheless, she did, at appropriate moments, speak as 'health expert'.

This policy had a practical as well as an ethical dimension. Both in this research/campaign programme with working-class men and in a different research project on teenage students and school-based HIV/AIDS programmes (where Sue Venables was again the interviewer), we found that the respondents, as the men say later in this particular interview, 'relax and open up', feeling that they are gaining something from the discussion. In the school-based interviews, students, when asked what kind of HIV education they would prefer, tended to say 'from a person like you' (this focus-group impression was strongly confirmed by quantitative survey research with 1,000 NSW students; Tulloch and Lupton, 1997: ch. 11).

Moreover, Sue was careful to draw on the knowledge of the men themselves, and extend their own language, metaphors and rhetorical moves – as in the 'throat infection in the old fella' example. These heterosexual men were very preoccupied with their 'old fellas', as the continuing interview indicated. Just like the school students we interviewed – who strongly indicated (at 95 per cent level in the survey) that they were 'sick and tired about hearing about how you get AIDS; we want to know more about what STDs do to your body' – these men were concerned about bodily health and bodily performance, and so very quickly responded comfortably and openly to this line of questioning.

Jeff, at this early point in the interview, began to probe the men's *valuation* of these different STDs.

Jeff: 'Leaving AIDS aside for the minute – all the other STDs, how do we feel about them? Do they worry you at all, or . . .?'
   : 'When we were kids we used to just rip in and never give a damn, and then two weeks later you'd have a sore on your dick, wouldn't yer?' (men laugh) . . . 'What was it called – gonorrhoea?'
   : 'Yeah, gonorrhoea.'

Sue: 'Do you worry about STDs? – you know, if you're having casual sex? Is it something that crosses your mind?'
    : 'Well . . . penicillin come along and . . . where it was a killing thing once upon a time, what it was now was a couple of jabs in the bum and it was all over. I suppose . . . you don't really care as much as you used to care, eh?'
    : 'I think people . . . were worried about something that was going to be permanent, like herpes. . . . Then you'd go "hey, what's going on here". But you'd go down the pub and tell everyone if you'd got the jack, eh?'
    : 'Yeah.'
    : 'You know, "I got the jack mate, rrrh, rrrh!" ' (laughs)
Sue: 'Right, 'cos that can be cured?' [Men agree] 'But things like herpes you don't go down the pub and say . . .?
    : 'No, well you wouldn't tell anyone, would you?'
    : 'Well, there's no cure for it is there? Like AIDS, where you wither away to nothing.'
    : 'Is it a killing thing, herpes?'
Sue: 'No. It's something that may give you recurrent outbreaks. . . . It's not going . . . to kill you or anything like that. But it can be really restricting.'
    : 'It lies dormant, is it?'
Sue: 'Yes, it's the same as . . .'
    : 'Cold sores.'
Sue: '. . . the cold sore virus, when people are under stress. You can get cold sores on your mouth or you can get genital herpes, there's two different sites. But if you go down on a woman and you've got a cold sore on your mouth you can actually pass that on to her on her genitals. So she can get genital herpes. And if *she's* got a cold sore and she goes down on you . . .'
    : 'Look at the men going all funny'. (laughter)
Sue: 'Lots of people don't realize that cold sores are herpes.'
    : 'I've never had a cold sore.'
    : 'I've got one now.' (men laugh)
    : 'Who've you been goin' down on?' (men laugh)
Jeff: 'So . . . just with AIDS, I mean how do we look at that, do we really think . . . that it could affect us?'
    : 'Yes, I do.'
    : 'I don't.'
    : 'Yeah, but you're on the sun roof.'
    : 'That's right, I've been married twenty-five years so it doesn't exist.'
    : 'And you're too ugly to fuckin' clinch one.' (men laugh)
Sue: 'What about the rest of you. Is AIDS something that you think you could get?' . . .
    : 'Me myself, I can't see myself gettin' it.'
    : 'He's with a safe girl.'
    : 'A one-woman man you could call it.'
    : 'Yeah, but you still don't know. Your partner could go out and do something you don't know about.'
    : 'True, well there you go. That's right.'
    : 'What sort of women are you going out with!?' (men laugh)
    : 'I used to go down the Cross [Sydney's red light district] but I don't anymore.'
    : 'Ah, well you may have it anyway – it takes five or six doesn't it, to show? How long does it take to come out?'
Sue: 'It could take five, it could take ten years for people to get symptoms. But you can actually find out by having a blood test – and find out in three months.' . . .

> : 'Everybody should be screened, I think, and you should have a card – you go round and say here you are.'
> : 'Here's me OK card.' (men laugh)
> *Sue*: 'Would you carry around your own card saying you've got AIDS?'
> : 'If I found that Shorty or Bill had it I'd get it tattooed on their forehead' (men laugh). 'But it's open to corruption. They do it in the Philippines – the girls just swap cards.'
> *Sue*: 'The problem . . . if you had a casual fuck last night . . . and you want to find out whether you are infected or not, you have to wait three months to have a test. So basically you would have to have a test done every day to actually find out, if you are having multiple partners.'
> : 'Oh. And then in that three months you could go out and spread it around even further, isn't it?' . . .
> : 'Unless technology advances so much so that you'd say to a sheila "piss in this bowl" and you put your litmus paper in and say "not tonight darling!" '
> *Sue*: 'And yet there is actually something that we can do to protect ourselves.'
> : 'Condoms.'

Jeff's original question draws out a feature of this working man's culture that we found in all the focus-groups: that the men distinguished between curable and non-curable STDs, and boasted about the former 'down the pub'. This was clearly a 'liturgical' performance among the men, played and replayed at routine performance sites (the bar, the workplace) as the local male community established 'standards, ways of judging, to which one must conform if one is to be accounted a member' (Shotter, 1993: 35). In some groups this performance was brought to the research venue, as men joked about 'spraying the old fella with Mortein' (an Australian commercial flyspray) to deal with gonorrhoea – to plenty of mutually supportive laughter. Incurable diseases like herpes and HIV, on the other hand, were something more shameful, something you hid, something you did *not* perform.

Sue's final set of questions in this section of the interview revealed her concern as 'expert' about this hiding of serious STDs; and also her recognition from a number of the other focus-group interviews that many men confuse the time it takes to get test results about one's HIV status and the time it takes for symptoms to show. In another focus group, for example, a man said he was responsible now he was married, both partners taking tests each year – because they had been married only three years, and it 'would take five years for AIDS to show'. Moreover, Sue used her own identities as (feminist/health worker) 'expert' to *challenge* the notion that science and technology would come to men's aid (the 'litmus paper' test), by bringing the discussion back to what the *men* (not the woman-as-object of technology's next test) could do right now: 'condoms'.

Sue's role as interviewer in fact moved (as Wynne would prefer) backwards and forwards across the boundaries between 'scientific' and 'lay' knowledgeability. For example, the *process* of her questioning, leading from discussion of the men's talk about other STDs in the pub to questions about HIV, brought the men back to encountering Sue as 'health expert'. Her experience as a sexual health counsellor had been telling her that many people did not know the potential link between STDs and AIDS. Consequently, the men's standard reply that other STDs were something of an in-group joke, led her to a 'scientific' intervention.

Jeff: 'So, relating to the issue of AIDS and STDs, if you have an STD, or you've had one in the past, do you think that you'd be in a higher risk bracket for getting AIDS?'
: 'I've never had any transmitted disease. . . . There's something about it tells you yeah or nay doesn't it? There's something in your character that says "I like this sheila" and you go for her and not for the sheila sitting over in the corner with her legs apart and wanting to piss in a schooner glass.' (men laugh) . . .
Jeff: 'The answer is yes . . . you do have a much higher chance of getting AIDS if you have got or if you've had in the past an STD.'
Sue: 'The reason for that is that any STD – be it herpes or gonorrhoea or whatever – actually can damage the tissue of your dick, OK. It's almost like leaving a scar that's probably not visible to the naked eye. But it does mean that if you have sex with someone who has the AIDS virus, you've got a higher chance of actually picking it up because of the damaged tissue there.'
: 'It's like an ulcer scar in your stomach?'
Sue: 'Yeah.'
: 'Like for instance when you injure your back, there's always a certain amount of scar tissue that's underlying around the muscle area and that scar tissue will help to make that injury or muscle strain recur because it's weakened the muscle structure, the fibre structure in that area.'
: 'Does that mean if you've never had a sexually transmitted disease, you're still going to get AIDS anyway, aren't you, if you go to bed with someone that's got it?'
Sue: 'Well, if you haven't had an STD and you come into contact with someone with the AIDS virus and have unprotected sex with them you may not be infected after one fuck – it might take several encounters before you get infected. If you've had an STD or you've got an STD it's much more likely to be that first contact that infects you. So it does increase your risk.'
: 'The fact that . . . you pick that girl in the first place leaves you open the same way you got it the first time, which is that you're not a very good fuckin' judge. . . . Doesn't that stand to reason? . . .'
Sue: 'But do you think you can tell in that way, that maybe it's the rougher looking sheilas that've got the STDs?'
: '. . . There must be a clever part the way you go about things to pick 'em up in the first place – they must be attractive for some reason, whether they just say they like opera or something, and the next minute yous are together and it might be the way they talk, smell, you know what I'm saying . . . you should be . . . a high percentage sure that this girl's all right. That's the way I feel, and to justify that. . . . I've never had a transmitted disease, so I suppose I've got something in my favour. Now it's all condoms because I've been in a relationship twelve years, but things happen – things happen. I wouldn't be game. It's like that lady in Sidetrack Theatre who was up the ladder, and the shock value of saying "I love a fuck. But the fact that I'm going to die because you fucked me and never wore a condom" . . . gets across to you in the sense that makes me tick from now on. That's a value that I'll never forget – the sheila sitting up the ladder saying "I love a fuck". I wish every sheila said that!' (Sue and men laugh) "Get a condom and have a fuck!" . . .'

Jeff: 'So, I mean, who should take the responsibility for your sexual health?'
    :   'Both parties.'
    :   'Yeah, both parties.'

This part of the interview is interesting for several reasons. First, there is the sense of shock – very often in these focus groups conveyed by a significant silence (among men who are generally very ready to talk, laugh and perform) – at the recognition that having had an STD, even if apparently cured, makes one more at risk of HIV from unprotected sexual encounters. This was an 'expert' challenge to the men's 'lay knowledgeability' of such potency that, accepting the expert's knowledge, the men went on to argue that the relationship they had just discovered between STDs and HIV should become the central focus of the public communication campaign we were collaboratively designing (hence the 'real full-on penis . . . on the sides of buses' request of our header quotation).

Secondly, there is the fact that once given this 'expert' information, some of the men *immediately* are able to draw rhetorically on their own expertise (perhaps gained through experience playing sport, or from other experiences of sickness) to use analogies and metaphors for understanding this new risk information. Hence the working analogies with back injuries or stomach ulcers are ways in which they make Sue's 'expert' information their own – an example of the adaptive practical understandings that Wynne points to in 'lay' knowledge systems.

Thirdly, there are still some men who respond just as they did *before* Sue's new information about the link between STDs and HIV: with the notion that because they have never had an STD they must have 'a clever part the way you go about things to pick 'em up in the first place'. This is open to further challenge, either by the interviewer or by other men in the group; and in most focus groups this belief that you can intuitively 'spot a risky sheila' was challenged by other respondents – though the general view was that you should be cautious of the woman who had 'her skirt half way up her arse'.

Fourthly, however, it would be to caricature these men to suggest that even the most resistant of them responded simplistically. In fact, in the case above, we can see clearly the way in which (a) Sue's 'expert' opinion, (b) one man's sexist self-confidence *and* (c) the influence of the Sidetrack Theatre's performance all negotiate with each other. In the case of Sidetrack, it is probably very important that it was a *woman* up the ladder performing these things. To see a young female actor saying 'I want a fuck' challenged this over-confident man's own previous perception of promiscuous women. If the young actor could say that, how would his 'clever part' be able to spot *her* in a crowd. The fact that Sue talks openly in this same kind of language also impressed this particular man. Later in the interview there was the following exchange between Sue and him:

Sue: 'Is bringing up the subject of safe sex with a partner difficult? . . .
   :   'Not if it's kept on . . . a level that you can all talk on. If you get the
professor that this [interview] goes back to, and you get him sitting here in a
clinical fuckin' sense and looking at you and fuckin' wanting clinical answers,
then you'd wouldn't be getting the answers you're getting now. . . . But if you
don't lose your sense of humour and have a discussion about it, open forum, on
a working man's level . . . we dropped our guard. . . . Long as you can use your
own language you don't feel out of place. . . . If the professor was here and
we're all sittin' in front of a fuckin' bloke usin' magic words that nobody
understood . . .'
   :   'Bloody bow-tie and bloody . . .'
   :   '. . . you wouldn't get boo out of us . . .'
Sue: 'But is it difficult to talk to *women*, new partners, about safe sex?' . . .
   :   'When it's something you're going to die from, if you can't talk about that,
what can you talk about?'
   :   'It's like the RSL club up here.' (men laugh) 'No, women up there . . .
years ago . . . wouldn't talk about anything. But you can get them out of the
bloody toilets up there for three for a dollar or something.'
   :   'What, the sheilas!?' (Sue and men laugh) 'What are you telling me.'
   :   'Friday night. . . . Years ago sheilas wouldn't have had a bloody condom
and wouldn't ever talk about it. But now, it's just a common factor. They're out
for a good time too.'
Sue: 'Yes.'
   :   'It's the first thing they're prepared for I reckon, "Oh yeah, we're right,
let's go". None in the bag? She'll say "Hey, you go to the toilet, have a piss and
bring back a handful".'
   :   (laughs) '*Handful* Shorty! You deviant!'
   :   'But that's just at that place up there, and if you go to St Mary's Band Club
it's the same thing up there.'
   :   'People just talk about it more openly.'

In another group, the men talked about the difficulty of discussing sex with
a potential partner until something relaxes you.

   :   'You know that anyone who hasn't had a drink – when a woman like
yourself comes in here we're all going a bit shy, and then all of a sudden we're
started talking about pricks and cocks and the barriers broken, right. It's that
initial . . . once that feeling of you know, at ease, right everyone goes for it. But
beforehand it's like there's always this wall.' . . .
   :   'That's when you have one schooner more.'
   :   'Exactly.'

Criticism of 'the professor' with his 'clinical questions . . . wanting
clinical answers', was in contrast with the praise for Sue's use of the men's
language, and the 'sense of humour and . . . open forum, on a working man's
level' that this generated. This is 'lay resistance' to what Wynne (in very
different language) calls scientific expert knowledge that 'embodies assumptions . . . about social relationships, behaviour . . . control and prediction'
(Wynne, 1996: 68). Sue Venables's discourse as both female 'interviewer'
and 'expert' shows very clearly that the boundaries that Wynne critiques

between expert and lay knowledges can be breached both in research and health policy. And, significantly, this 'breaking of the barriers' by way of humour 'on a working man's level' was to lead to the *genre* of health communication vehicle we were co-designing.

The interviewers: 'lay' narratives

Jeff's opening questions (probing the men's knowledge and valuation of different kinds of STDs) was also the first move towards his own highly formulated 'men's story'. This 'scenario', as Jeff described it, led the men not 'outwards' towards Sue's scientific information, but 'inwards' towards their own leisure times and spaces.

Jeff: 'I mean, if you're going out looking for a straight fuck, where would you go?' . . .
   : 'Night clubs where young people are going to be.' . . .
Jeff: 'All right, let's use a scenario. Say you're at the night club or the Rooty Hill or Panthers League Club, and you're getting on the piss, and you're about six to eight scotches into the night . . .'
   : 'And the more you drink, the better they look.' (Sue and the men laugh)
Jeff: 'And you're crackin' on to this bird. You just happen to say the right thing at the right time, and you get up on the dance floor with her and things develop and she's got her tongue shoved half way down your throat, and you've got yours half way down her's, and things develop more and you piss off outside to the car park. Some people say that you wouldn't waste the petrol going down the road, some people do it in the car park, some people drive down the road or go to her place, or whatever. And you're at the point where . . .'
   : 'The old fella takes over.'
   : 'You're listening to the little head.'
Jeff: 'Yeah, I mean, the old bloke stands to attention – well, that happened a long time ago, but I mean like you're ninety-nine per cent sure you're going to get in. Does the thought of safe sex enter your mind? At what stage do you think about it?'
   : 'Well, personally you think about that *before* that, because when you get to that stage you really don't . . .'
Jeff: 'When would you think about it?'
   : 'I don't know about you younger blokes, but I'm 42 and if I go out I've got a condom in my fucking wallet. I went to the State of Origin [Rugby League match between the top players born in Queensland and New South Wales] the other month, and the old woman wanted some money and I tipped the fuckin' wallet out and the condoms fell out, and straight away I said "those mates, they're fuckin' arseholes – they've loaded me" ' (men laugh uproariously) 'She "knew" I wouldn't carry them, so it was O.K. – but I'm telling you that when I go away, when I'm expecting . . .'
   : 'A bit of action.'
   : '. . . the possibility of action, the condoms are there. I think that the message had struck home to me – the fact that I'm 42 and been with a girl twelve years, to think that I'd pass it on to my *partner* through being promiscuous, and her fuckin' going to die because all you needed was an eight bob fuckin' condom, you've really got something to fuckin' answer for haven't you? . . . What would you say to her? "I was up in Brisbane and got this lovely fuck, I got AIDS and you're going to die within four years". . . . So the message has struck home to someone like me at 42, I can tell you that.'

Jeff:　'So, with our scenario, when would it enter your mind, at what stage of the night?'

Sue:　'You said that it would enter earlier on.'

　：　'Yeah, even before you went up to her . . .'

　：　'When you've gone outside and you jump in the car or something like that, then it would probably cross your mind and you would ask her "have you got any?" But you can't really put it on either the male or the female to be responsible. I think you've both got to be responsible.'

　：　'How does that vaginal cream work – that anti-viral stuff? What's that do – will that kill AIDS?'

Sue:　'No. . . . It could be a spermicidal.'

　：　'What's that mean? It kills sperms – you don't have to be on the pill.'

Sue:　'It's not going to protect you against *any* STD, but it might help you stop getting pregnant.'

Jeff:　'So, getting back to the scenario, I mean, so you'd think about it even before you went up to her?'

　：　'No, I'm not saying that.'

　：　'I would.'

Sue:　'Does that mean you'd have one in your back pocket?'

　：　'Not that I'm going to use it much, but you never know.'

　：　'It would get blue mould in your fuckin' pocket.' (men laugh) 'What's the shelf life on them?'

　：　'Not long – I think they last twelve months.'

　：　'Well, silicone's got twelve months' use out of it, so you'd think rubber would be the same.'

Sue:　'They've usually got a couple of years, but if you leave them in the sun or if they get hot then forget it.'

　：　'They break on your dick.'

Sue:　'They should have a use-by date on them anyway.'

Jeff:　'So let's develop the scenario a bit further, all right, you're in the back of the car . . .'

　：　'All right!'

　：　'Look at Rodney get all excited.'

Jeff:　'and you're in the back seat or on the mat or whatever, and you've got her gear off, her legs are open, she's ready to go, and nobody's brought it up, nothing's been said about a condom . . . are you going to bring up the subject, or are you just going to fuck away?'

　：　'. . . I was with a girl last weekend, and we were in the back seat – or actually on the front seat, and we were going for it, all right? And half way through it I stopped, thinking I was an idiot and I didn't use a condom and actually I asked her "shouldn't we use a condom?" And she asked me why.'

　：　'Some women think that if you say "have you got a condom?" . . . that you're putting shit on them. They say "I haven't got AIDS or anything like that".' . . .

Sue:　'What if . . . it had been the woman who stopped and said "have you got a condom"?' . . .

　：　'Initially you probably think . . . "jeez, this girl must have sex all over".'
. . .

Jeff:　'So, would . . . you now, after that, have reservations about bringing up the subject again?'

　：　'I really don't know. . . . It just entered my mind . . . end of story.'

　：　'You're always like that on your first.' (men laugh a lot) . . .

Jeff:　'What if there's no condom, what are you going to do?'

　：　'Mars Bar.' (men laugh)

: 'I heard that a bloke in Africa had no condom so he put a wrapper on.' (men laugh) . . .

Sue: 'But in that situation, would you think of doing something *different*?'

: 'You'd think twice about it, but usually you'd put it in the back of your mind again. . . . You know "have you got a condom?", "no", oh well . . . and you're half-pissed, and you're in the mood for it, and bang.'

: 'That's right, your little head thinking instead of your big head.' . . .

Jeff: 'Does anybody else think of any other alternative methods for sex?'

Sue: 'If you haven't got a condom?'

: 'Blow job.' . . .

: 'It can be transmitted by oral sex though.'

Sue: 'It's much lower risk.'

: 'It has to be something like you've got a cut in your mouth or she's a cut in her mouth.'

This extract from the interview illustrates two things about the interviewers' process. First, it shows the 'lay' and the 'expert' working together, but directing the discussion in different ways: Sue answering the men's sexuality and health questions, Jeff constantly pulling the debate back to his sexual (men's voice) 'scenario'. Secondly, it shows Sue working with different identities at different times: both 'health expert' *and* feminist, as she (not for the first time) draws attention back to the man's responsibility for his own sexuality, and in particular, shifting the questions away from the normative models of 'human behaviour' which suggest that penetrative sex is the only 'real' sex.

This part of the interview also shows various urban myths that circulate among heterosexual men: the 'Mars Bar' example here has a racist connotation, but elsewhere (and frequently across the various focus-groups) 'Mars Bar wrappers' and 'Gladwrap with a rubber band' are used as humorous signifiers of 'rough' sex – storytelling here includes bikies 'in the bush' as well as Africans. As such, they often re-direct Sue's question in the interviews about 'doing something different' into the male 'normalcy' of penetrative sex.

But, these stories also are part of men's 'rough-humour' performance among other men – one of their many potency jokes. This is illustrated in the above extract as friendly put downs *both* of the 'young stud' who has talked about his sex in a car the previous weekend ('You're always like that on your first') *and* the older man who carries condoms even though he doesn't expect much 'action' ('It would get blue mould in your fuckin' pocket'). Sue Venables's response to the 'Mars Bar' story indicates the way in which her particular politics enters the debate without overt moralizing – by asking a question about other, non-penetrative approaches to heterosex.

Different interviewer discourses, then, were in operation in this set of interviews – of sexual health counsellor, of feminist (and female interviewer), of male workmate and elected union official – which we need to take account of in analysing the focus groups. This is not either a theoretical or a methodological 'problem' or a 'regrettable shortcoming' in our process, but as Ien Ang says a necessity of poststructuralist research, indicating the representative orders we are inevitably patterning around 'the otherwise chaotic outlook of the empirical landscape' (Ang, 1996: 77). These are, to quote one of Ang's headings, part of a process of 'Constructing Positioned Truths' as an overt politics.

To take Ang's argument a little further than we did in the Introduction:

> Radical contextualism can then act as a stance governed not by a wish to build an ever more 'comprehensive theory of the audience', which would by definition be an unfinishable task, but by an intellectual commitment to make the stories we end up telling about media consumption as compelling and persuasive as possible in the context of specific problematics which arise from particular branches of cultural politics. This is what Stuart Hall means when he argues that 'potentially discourse is endless: the infinite semiosis of meaning. But to say anything at all in particular, you have to stop talking. . . . The politics of infinite dispersal is no politics at all' (1987: 45). Therefore it is crucial to construct what Hall calls 'arbitrary closures' in our storytelling practice . . . even though 'every full stop is provisional' (ibid.) Anthropologist Marilyn Strathern has succinctly put it this way: 'I must know on whose behalf and to what end I write' (1987: 269). That is, our stories cannot just tell 'partial truths', they are also, consciously or not, 'positioned truths'. (Ang, 1996: 78)

Our 'positioned truths' in the Heterosexual Men's Project were, we hoped, consciously and reflexively about *both* 'expert' and 'lay' knowledgeability – rejecting, as Wynne says, the notion that 'the two cultures are simply mutually incompatible and that it is either one, or the other' (Wynne, 1996: 72, 74). But our 'positioned truths' were *also* about class and gender, and the way in which our 'arbitrary closures' around these matters of political choice were worked through the issues of power and dialogic exchange in the interview situation.

It was not *just* a matter of getting at situated 'lay knowledgeability'. It was also a matter of trying to make overt the various layers of class, gender and (in the case of these men as a multi-generational work group) age which were woven through this campaign which had 'begun' with the young Sidetrack actress up her ladder, and was now continuing its performance under the surveillance of a working-class male unionist and a feminist sexual health counsellor.

Co-designing the campaign

> It was envisaged that a close collaboration between these groups, using material from taped discussions with building workers would facilitate the development of a 'bottom-up' campaign and circumvent issues outlined by Crawford, Kippax and Tulloch (1992) concerning transmission of messages to audiences. This, however, proved to be a difficult process, resulting in the final concepts and design being developed independently by the Media/PR consultancy, by the working party and other Reference Group members. (Venables and Tulloch, 1993: 1)

We were involved, as I have said, not simply in a research process, but also in the co-design of a health campaign. I will describe the 'outcomes' of this under three headings: multiple intertexts; provisional narrative closure; and cross-boundary (inter-'expert') negotiation.

Multiple subjectivities, intertexts and reading formations   Both in her working practice designing the interviews and in her final report, Sue Venables typically quoted (as above) 'expert' research that led the campaign *towards* heterosexual men's ideas about how best to construct a campaign that would make men more responsible for their own bodies. During the interviews, this approach meant that Sue had to negotiate with the men's stereotypes – for example of 'dirty sheilas' that are easy to spot, and of homosexuals being more promiscuous and therefore at the heart of the 'targeting' problem. At these times, she typically brought the campaign issue back to the responsibility of heterosexual men by drawing on her 'expert' knowledge.

> *Sue*:   It seems that gay men have changed their behaviour and by and large are using condoms, straight men aren't, and the AIDS virus is actually on the increase among straight men in the 20–40 year-old age-group, so that's what's partly motivating this campaign – lots of straight men aren't using condoms. . . . So it's how to get those messages across to straight men.

Thus as we examine the transcribed interview material, and look at the discursive relationship between interviewers and interviewees, we can see multiple subjectivities at work as they draw on a range of pre-existing utterances, 'stories', discourses and intertexts. Because we wanted the men's involvement in the campaign itself, part of the interview involved asking them about media responses to HIV/AIDS, so that their positive comments about the 'Grim Reaper', 'Suzi's Story' or the 'Forum' section of *Penthouse* began to circulate among the many other circuits of communication from which they drew stories for the interview.

The pushes and shifts of subjectivity in the interview situation became part of a system of inter-textual co-ordinates. In a single interview, for instance, the building workers depended on a wide variety of inter-textual regimes for 'reading', drawing on

- the Sidetrack Theatre performance;
- forum articles in soft porn magazines;
- newspaper accounts of identity card swapping in the Philippines;
- male 'safe girl' and 'risk-women' myths;
- other urban myths about Gladwrap and Mars Bar wrappers;
- male potency jokes;
- historically sedimented boasts about STDs that you admit to in the pub (and those that you don't);
- 'real life' tales about sex 'last weekend';
- 'horror' stories they had heard of women pick-ups who left 'join the AIDS club' written on the mirror, or a dead rat with its head cut off for the sleeping male after his night of sex;
- memorable television interventions in the HIV field like the Australian documentary 'Suzi's Story' and 'The Grim Reaper';

- male alibis about 'when the piss takes over your little head's thinking instead of your big head';
- medical analogies to explain the links between STDs and HIV;
- medical discourse as circulating through 'Three Waves' causalities;
- stereotypes of gays and bisexuals as 'permissive' conduits of HIV into the heterosexual male community.

The men were thus drawing on a range of inter-textual utterances to engage with the interviewers' own stories, establishing at different times different subject positions, and different social relations of reading.

For instance, both in the case of Sue Venables's own discourse in the interview and the Sidetrack Theatre performance, the men were unaccustomed to young women speaking so explicitly about the sexual body and practices (in the 'formal performance' sites of theatrical event and research interview, at least); and they negotiated with this across a range of routes of identification, from male camaraderie jokes about 'look at the men going all funny' as Sue talked about herpes and women 'going down on your dicks', to reflexive comments about the men being more open with Sue for 'speaking our language' than they would be if 'the fuckin' professor' was here, with his bow-tie and 'clinical fuckin' language', to the claim that female actors talking explicitly about sex and condoms at the Sidetrack performance have changed one's actual sexual practice at the age of 42.

So 'reading formations', in Tony Bennett's sense (Bennett and Woollacott, 1987: 60) of specific inter-textual relations which 'bid and counterbid' in the particular context of the interview, and which configure the relations between respondents, interviewers and the latter's preferred text ('take responsibility for your own sexuality: use condoms'), can be traced as meaning was co-produced within these particular discursive formations. It is in *this* context that the campaign was being developed.

'*Arbitrary closures*'   We were concerned to avoid the poststructuralist 'politics of infinite dispersal' that Stuart Hall critiques. We did want to come out of these interviews with *ideas for a specific campaign* co-designed by these men.

On the one hand, this heterosexual men's project was deliberately challenging familiar campaign patterns – where health bureaucrats, advertising agencies, academics and others act as 'experts' in composing the 'right' message in the 'right' form, thus preferring 'places upon the "podia", in front of "civilized" and "disciplined" audiences' (Shotter, 1993: 48). A particular 'working-man's' culture had been selected as both 'subject' and 'object' of the campaign: 'subject' in the sense of drawing on its tacit and discursive local knowledges and its 'insider's' work-to-leisure values and voices in co-operatively designing the campaign; and 'object' in viewing these men as part of the campaign 'target' of promoting male responsibility for safer-sex behaviour.

On the other hand, we wanted to avoid what some audience theorists have seen as the populism of so-called 'active audience' theory, which has ascribed a voluntaristic power to audiences as the sole source of media messages. This tendency has been augmented by a long history in ethnographic research of exoticizing the audience group as 'Other'. We neither wanted to fetishize our male working-class group, nor construct the men simply as determinants of 'authentic' condom messages.

While, certainly, these men were active definers of 'safer-sex' meanings, they did so

- within an historical and cultural context that shaped their relative access to different discourses and understandings for making sense of HIV/AIDS;
- in the context of institutional powers (of the media, for example) which set agendas for male desire; and
- in the context of many other circulating stories drawn from a wide range of circuits of communication.

All of these contexts need to be considered when we talk about so-called 'below-up' or 'active partner' health campaigns. All of these discursive contexts require as much consideration, in other words, as those associated with 'above-down' government campaigns before we too easily rush off into a new era of 'active partner' health communication research.

For example, without exception, having sex without condoms was ascribed in each interview as a major effect of heavy drinking. It was felt that alcohol reduced a man's resolve to practise safe sex for three reasons: it made you feel invulnerable; it made 'your morals go out of the window'; it reduced your ability to discriminate between a sleaze and a nice girl. The following conversations, taken from a number of focus groups, illustrate both this general view about the link between alcohol and sexuality, and the men's ability to 'prove' this generalized view by way of storytelling.

   : 'I'm single. I know you can get AIDS . . . but when you're out at the club and you got a gut full of grog, and you get on to someone, it all goes out of the windows, you don't really give a shit.'
   : 'You're too worried about running them home, not running to the chemist . . . get them home to bed.'
   : 'If I go and have half a dozen beers, or maybe ten, then I couldn't give a shit. There's going to be no condom jump on my old guy.'
   : 'If you're down the club or the pub, a few drinks and after that the big head has no say in it.'
   : 'The little head takes over.'
   : 'If you're about half drunk I don't think you'd even attempt to pull one out – all you'd think about is trying to get in.'

Three things were particularly noticeable in these men's sexual stories: First, the loss in inhibitions as a result of alcohol were associated with stereotypically sexist representations of women. One typical story was of 'two Kiwi sheilas . . . built like the sides of barns' at a 'little hotel called "The Loaded Dog" ', who a 'dozen schooners later [got] ten out of ten, Bo Dereks, the lot. Full on. . . . Danced with them all night. We were on a killing' (men laugh). Like the heavy drinking (which not one of the 100+ men interviewed saw as a problem in itself), these female images were part of a performed male camaraderie which both reduced condom use and led to a dangerously stereotyped view of 'safe sheilas'.

Secondly, in 'spotting safe sheilas' via their 'manners, dress, morals, smell, what they drink', the men were looking for some way of 'going on' (Giddens, 1984) with daily routines in relative safety. It would be too easy for us in turn to stereotype these men. Even the building worker quoted earlier, who would have preferred a new litmus paper technology to help him 'go on', was aware of the hyperbole in his example. This after all was the same man who having seen the Sidetrack actor up her ladder, said, 'Now it's all condoms . . . the message got home to me.' The qualified comment, 'You can tell – or think you can tell' indicates quite precisely both the men's need for 'going on' *and* their reflexivity about the inadequacy of this procedure.

> Admittedly we all use that. . . . We've got to go on something; we've got to use some policy – but by Jesus it doesn't really work like that, though we all like to think it does. . . . You don't worry until the next day 'cause you were half-tanked when the time came.

This illustrates a 'lay' reflexivity which is also dominated by the fatalistic determinism ascribed to alcohol. Working even more powerfully than gendered, subculturally based stereotypes of women, this particular cultural value (about the irresistibly transformative power of alcohol) is their alibi for justifying unsafe sex.

Thirdly, the men's stories followed a typical pattern where a general principle was asserted followed by a story which legitimated it experientially. The story of the 'two Kiwi sheilas' fleshed out the 'irresistible alcohol' principle. Similarly, in response to Sue's question about use of condoms at the end point of Jeff's scenario ('in the car'), there was the following principle + story asserting the 'male sex drive' narrative closure.

> I think if you've got a condom or something in your wallet, you use it. But if you haven't, and you've got that far, fuck it, you go for it anyway. . . . I was with a girl, we're in the car. Drove over to a nice spot on Woolgover Road. You're ready to do the business. Half your gear off, and all of a sudden she hits you with 'You got a rubber?' . . . and then you say, 'No, I haven't'. But then you don't care and she doesn't care, and then you're into it anyway. . . . And I hit her with, 'If it feels good, just do it', so you just do it.

And maybe, he continues, 'your sexual drive at that point in time' is unstoppable, even without the grog.

'Your sex drive overwhelms your education in other words.'

'It overwhelms everything.'

The male sex-drive myth asserts that 'If you've gone that far, you've got her pants off, and you've got a hard dick . . . you don't say, "Oh shit, put all your clothes back on and we'll go to a chemist or we'll go back inside the pub and then come back and start again".'

All the men's groups insisted that any discussion about condoms must come earlier. So this became an 'arbitrary closure' for our campaign design: how to do this without 'blowing your cover'?

> All your life you're chasing birds. . . . Seven or eight o'clock at night you pick them up. . . . Your first plan is 'at midnight I want to be in bed with her'. Then how many times do you go from 11 to 1 in the morning, and the bird might say, 'Oh, I shouldn't, I've gotta get home' or 'should I?' . . . So you've already got a battle on your hands to get the bird into bed. So there's no way in the world four hours before are you going to say, 'Should I get a condom?' They're going to say straight away, 'Piss off, this bloke's taking me for granted, he thinks I'm just gonna jump into bed with him'. It's impossible, no one's gonna do that.

Rather than sexual negotiation, this is the language of hunt and battle: 'your first plan', 'blowing your cover', 'a battle on your hands'. There seems little sense here that the woman may well be planning for sex too; that the 'battle planning' should stop and a negotiated, interactive performance begin.

So, in the case of many of these building workers, their sexual lives were (as they explained to us in response to Jeff's 'scenario') *embedded in very specific time/space co-ordinates* – and these became our focus for our 'arbitrary closure' in relation to one part of the campaign. At the same time, Sue's input in the course of the interview as 'expert' had added new '*shock*' dimensions to the men's knowledge – most particularly her information about the link between other STDs and higher HIV risk, and also the figure she gave the men of about one-fifth Sydney's population being infected with STDs.

These two 'scenarios' – from Sue's 'expert' stories, and from Jeff's 'local pick-up' script – became the basis for the campaign decisions which flowed from these focus-group interviews. On the one hand, the men were sufficiently struck by Sue's information about STDs to argue for a public information campaign that featured this 'missing' link between STDs and HIV. Large, stark and 'scary' images of 'what your dick looks like with an STD' were (in their preference) to accompany anchoring words about the STD epidemic, and about the links between STDs and HIV, on the sides of buses, freeway hoardings, etc.

On the other hand, Jeff's 'scenario' led to various suggestions about how to raise the issue of condoms *before* the 'back of the car' and *without* 'blowing your cover'. From the very first focus-group on, the issue was raised of somehow opening up an initially de-personalized 'avenue of conversation' as men and women sit around tables at the bar. Perhaps, the first group thought, this could be done by way of condom information on beer bottles, and STD 'epidemic' information on stickers: 'He says "what do you think of that", she goes, "Oh yeah, I think so – I think sex is great", and you're straight into a conversation of condoms.' This was followed by the idea of putting free condoms on the bar tables; and, finally, by the growing consensus on beer mats.

> :   'There's the ashtray and beside it you've got one with condoms in it on each table. The blokes would sit round with the girls having a laugh and blow some of them up. . . . That's only going to encourage people to use them – it takes away any fear of the condom' . . .
> :   'It's like reverse psychology – the girl might think he's cheap, or he might think she's cheap, as soon as you bring it up. And it's all the stigma with sex, it's all that . . . barrier of a condom being like a thing that you get from under the table, not where it's on top of the table. That might lift up the . . . position where you might be able to strike a conversation around it later on in the night' . . .
> :   'It's at arms reach so you can have a joke and say "Well I'm going to take this in case I get lucky tonight". And if you've got it in your hand you can have a joke with everyone' . . .
> :   'Everywhere near the bars. *Something* on display there, because everyone goes to the bar to start with, and from there to the tables and that . . .'
> :   'Coasters.'
> :   'Yes' (general) . . .
> :   'People ought to be able to play with the idea – you can play with the idea of wearing the condom, using it or whatever' . . .
> :   'Last time I went into the chemist I had to get the girl over to help me sort out which were which.'
> :   ' "You got any bigger ones?".' (men and Sue laugh)
> :   'Everyone goes for the bigger ones, mate. Everyone goes for the bigger ones'. (laughter)
> :   ' "Give us a gum boot, that's not big enough".' (men and Sue laugh)

A number of different issues important to the men were coming together as the focus groups developed this notion of 'playing with the idea' of condoms:

- their lived experience that nightclubs and bars are where sexual pick-ups mainly occur;
- their alibi that when 'on the piss' the male sex urge takes over;
- Jeff's time/space 'scenario' from club bar to dance floor to the 'back of the car';
- their concern about ready access to condoms (the men argued particularly strongly for condom-vending machines in schools, because underage students find it harder to get into clubs to buy them there);
- their performance of reflexive potency jokes: that 'everyone goes for the bigger ones';
- their worry about talking 'condoms' with a pick-up because of the 'reverse psychology' and the chance of missing out by 'blowing your cover' too early;

- their jokey camaraderie *as men* about sex (which was now to be transposed so you 'can have a joke with everyone' – including your recent pick-up on the dance floor).

This set of relations (especially between beer drinking, the 'male sex-drive' and 'playing with the idea of condoms') became central to the campaign discussion. The emphasis on 'men's humour' remained central. After the completion of the focus groups, Sue Venables approached Nik Scott, a cartoonist with considerable experience in sexuality and health issues, to design witty cartoons drawing on the men's ideas (size of condoms, timing of condoms, worrying about negotiating condoms with your new pick-up in the bar, etc). Sue then showed these to the men at a barbecue, and the trial beer coaster cartoons were chosen.

Inter-'expert' border crossings We then moved on to the next stage in the campaign, which was to approach Family Planning's advertising agency. It was decided to trial the cartoon coasters and toilet door stickers (which the men also wanted) at one of the major clubs mentioned in the focus groups, the Penrith Panthers League Club. However, when it came to the more public information campaign, problems arose between the researchers and the advertising agency. As Sue Venables described this stage, the

> magazine, bus and billboard concepts and designs proved far more problematic. Conflict arose between desire to use explicit, blunt messages and advertising constraints. The Heterosexual Men's Project media working party was reluctant to compromise by using standard advertising formulae likely to be noticed by women rather than men. It was considered vital to use language appropriate to heterosexual male culture and which accurately reflected the focus-group research. This included using strong, blunt messages addressing the links between STDs and HIV/AIDS, in order to promote a more balanced risk perception amongst heterosexually active men. . . . The complexities and difficulties involved in the process of negotiation between the media working party and media/advertising consultants, combined with the controversial nature of the advertising material resulted in only partial implementation of the PR strategy. (Venables and Tulloch, 1993: 1, 5, 18)

Because of libel considerations, I will not elaborate on this stage of our process, even though I observed it at close hand. In the end, the 'public' billboard, bus and magazine advertising did use the men's language in linking STDs and HIV ('ever had the clap? You've done all it takes to get HIV/AIDS'), but *without* the explicit section of an infected penis that the men wanted. The advertising agency argued that the large pictures of penises with STDs would never be allowed by the State government, and would turn people off anyway. The advertising agency would also have preferred 'hard-edged' safer-sex ads, drawing on John Wayne-style imagery and wording ('ten foot tall and bullet-proof') to emblematize the building workers' more 'macho' focus-group images.

This late 'professional/expert' stage of the process proved to be much more contentious than the earlier collaboration with the building workers.

Here indeed was a case of ' "out-there" risks . . . identified by . . . expert contestation . . . [between] expert factions' (Wynne, 1996: 76). But, to be fair to the advertising agency, they *were* (as in the 'ten foot tall' image) also drawing on the men's talk. It was just that they had very different 'expert' communication models behind their imaging than the more 'active audience' consultancy/research team, and so drew on different aspects of the men's stories.

The inter-'expert' problem was sufficient, in the end, to cause Sue Venables to leave the project. The Penrith Panthers 'trial campaign' did take place, however, and was later evaluated by an independent marketing company. So, bearing these various strictures and late difficulties in mind, it is worth turning back in conclusion to the Murdock/Golding criteria of communication for citizenship to illustrate what we hope was going on in the Heterosexual Men's Project.

Conclusion

To conclude this chapter, I will draw on a distinction between 'canonical' and 'performative' situated stories made in the Introduction to suggest that these are not necessarily incompatible approaches to the analysis of agency and performance. To do so I will compare the discussion above of the Heterosexual Men's Campaign with an article by Cindy Patton that considers a potential shift in the USA from epidemiology to tropical medicine as the master 'expert' discourse determining HIV/AIDS policy.

Patton makes a distinction between tropical medicine's 'performance' of discourse – that is 'reliant upon stable signs (the marks of coloniality, with their geography of race presupposed by the certainty about the centrality of Europe), which it reinscribes but does not own' (Patton, 1995: 183) – and epidemiology's 'performativity' (that is 'as an actant within a place in which the constitution and reproduction of citational chains is constitutive of power', (Patton, 1995: 183)). Like Judith Butler, Patton is working here through a conjuncture of Foucault, Austin and Derrida to define perform-ativity as not only being constitutive of power but at the same time being implicated in that which it opposes.

In Patton's analysis, epidemiology is powerfully constituted. It 'enables itself to declare "disease" from some but not all conjunctures of body/pathogen' (Patton, 1995: 186); it further 'defines the boundaries of a disease by constituting a category of subject ("risk group")' (Patton, 1995: 187); and it constructs a notion of the 'domestic' as 'inarticulate space where disease has not penetrated, the space to be protected by doing work in the "public" space of disease' (Patton, 1995: 188).

But the point as Patton argues it is that, in 'interpellating' a subject called 'risk group' (gays, needle-sharers, etc) epidemiology potentially brings citizen groups into being, makes them performative, and gives them a voice in ways that the 'parasitic' discourse of tropical medicine cannot do, since it is little more than a further performance of colonial expansion (a 'canonical' discourse, in Hughes-Freeland's terms). Epidemiology has confused risk practices with risk identities ('risk groups'); but in doing so it has been 'performative' in *needing* its named 'risk groups' 'in order to declare an epidemic for it to administer' (Patton, 1995: 193). As in Foucault's sense of power, 'risk groups' have become active 'people at risk' with their own voices (as gay men and people living with AIDS), and their own contestation and engagement with epidemiological 'expert knowledge'. Indeed, in many countries, these voices have penetrated the state health agencies. In contrast, tropical medicine, Patton says, accepted an *existing* hierarchy of bodily placement, overlaying colonialist discourse with a 'science' wherein 'natural immunity' was 'the capacity . . . to be the domestic partner of germs – . . . the property of the colonized' (Patton, 1995: 184). For tropical medicine the named 'disease' only affected the *colonist*'s body; and thus 'immunization provides the means of colonial occupation' (Patton, 1985: 184).

However, Patton sees tendencies in the US health and media debate shifting from 'a fundamentally epidemiological understanding of the HIV epidemic, which seeks to understand *who* a body is, to one which is fundamentally related to notions of place – to *where* a body is, a set of ideas closer to those of tropical medicine' (Patton, 1995: 188–9). The *policy* implications of this for Patton are serious. Thus:

> epidemiology can only manage categories it can scientifically produce, but tropical medicine can administer categories already in place through another discourse. If we disliked the necessity, under the performative logic of epidemiology, of responding from the position of 'risk group', then we will find our placement of the already-discounted-native one from which it is even more difficult to engender forms of resistance. (Patton, 1995: 193)

Patton's concern is that

> 'Community' is transformed here from a positive term meant to cover an affiliative grouping seeking legibility in order to make claims for civil rights and their protection on the state and its medical apparatus; community becomes instead a colony. Gay men are not so much other in relation to a self that nominates them, as they are simply self-identical to a space that is already set apart. (Patton, 1995: 190)

'Policy', under the rule of epidemiology, does invoke citizenship; whereas under the rule of tropical medicine the colonized are 'other' to citizenship.

Patton's different usage of 'performance' and 'performativity' here is intriguing because it helps explain the discursive scientific fields in which affiliations between 'expert' and 'lay knowledgeability' have been encouraged, and in which they may be effaced. It is *as* an extension from gay to heterosexual men of epidemiology's *performative declaring* 'disease' as 'a migratory site of pathology' (Patton, 1995: 186) that our attempted health policy of 'going to the public' of the building workers could even be possible. In other words, the heterosexual men we worked with in this campaign were interpellated, in Patton's terms, as 'seeking legibility', not as 'native'.

How far, then, did our 'tactic' (in de Certeau's sense, our 'performative intervention' in Roach's) meet Murdock and Golding's criteria of citizenship?

1   Access to information, advice and analysis which will enable people to pursue their rights effectively.   The builders' labourers were shocked at two pieces of 'expert' information from Sue: the 'scary' STD statistics of a roughly one in five epidemic of genital herpes in Sydney; and the link between STDs and HIV. Their confusion (and sometimes anger) that 'there's not enough information on that . . . that's the first I heard of it', was an indication of information they had not received and had a right to have received. In this case, however, the shock could be turned into performative action, since the focus groups were the basis for a health campaign in the (strongly working-class/migrant) region of Western Sydney. Their suggestion for graphic figures and images of STDs to be carried by bus and billboard posters was an extension (via their own positive experience of the 'shock/horror' 'Grim Reaper') to the public of their own sense of shock at 'expert knowledge' gained during the focus groups.

2   Access to communications facilities in order to propose alternative courses of action.   While the bus and billboard posters ran into similar State legitimacy worries that hampered earlier above-down campaigns – to the extent that the NSW State government allowed only a very modified version of the STD advertisement on buses – another communication vehicle was co-operatively designed which was much more within the men's control. Of course, during the interviews where this happened, all kinds of gender-based assumptions were circulating; for instance, the belief in the male sex-drive which the 'grog' released ('hormones take over – hormones and grog'). But the point of the Project was not to use focus groups to preach a specific morality, but to draw on the discursive patterning of the men's reasoning and experiences to construct jointly a practical intervention. In other words, rather than pointing as 'experts' to theoretical/political problems in their talk (which would obviously have turned the men straight off), planning focused on how the 'blame the grog' alibi, the 'blowing your cover' worry, or the 'biggest condom' male ego-identities might actually be used *performatively* against themselves. The major suggestions were: a series of humorous cartoons on beer coasters which raised the issue of condoms in an unthreatening, de-personalized and non-embarrassing way; and stick-on posters in men's and women's washrooms which challenged the 'blame the grog' alibi, and the 'If he sees I've got condoms he'll think I'm easy' stereotype. So, access of the men in constructing these low-tech vehicles offered the possibility not only of a safer-sex intervention, but also (in Murdock and Golding's words) of 'registering criticism' and 'mobilising opposition' to some of their own most dearly held alibis for irresponsible sex. In that way, in a practical

intervention rather than in metatheoretical discussion, the men were accessing a wider range of information, interpretation and debate.

3   Ability to recognize themselves and their aspirations in the range of representations offered and to be able to contribute to developing those representations. This project focused on a particular male, working-class 'shop-floor' subculture, as defined in terms of its own leisure practices. It focused especially on how these leisure practices, centred round clubs and pubs, were understood by members of the subculture. It was the building workers who suggested the major site for health intervention (clubs and pubs), its communication vehicles (coasters and stickers), its genre (humour), and its specific time/space 'narrative' focus – situated in their *own* performative 'scenario' (between the dance-floor 'pick-up' and later-that-night sex). This was, in their words, 'a tongue-in-cheek level we can all talk on' performative intervention. There is no doubt that these men recognized themselves and their aspirations (*as well as, reflexively, some of their sexual alibis*) in the beer coaster and sticker representations that they helped develop.

3

(HIGH-) CULTURAL FRAMING

> He is like a man who contemplates a perfect work of art; but the work of creation has been his, and has consisted in the gradual adjustment of his vision until he could see the frustration of human destinies and the arbitrary infliction of pain as processes no less inevitable, natural and beautiful than the flowering of a plant. (John Middleton Murry, 'Thoughts on Chekhov', 1920)

> Just as, in order to satisfy his aesthetic tastes, man revolts against the Laws of Nature which creates races of sterile and fragile flowers, so he does not hesitate to defend the weak against the laws of natural selection. (Il'ya Metchnikov, 1921)

I began Chapter 2 with the comment of a building worker who wanted to see syphilitic penis images up on the sides of buses. This chapter starts with a rather different, high-cultural elevation of image, as physical, social and economic pain becomes 'natural and beautiful' in the formal performance of 'Art'. It is perhaps an unusual conjuncture, either in cultural studies or in most other places. But the juxtaposed pain of the 'penis' against the 'flower' does draw attention very immediately to the issue of high-cultural framing.

It is an objective of this book neither to reify high culture as the 'essential' space of performance (as humanist criticism has tended to do), nor to exclude it from situated analysis (as much of the work in cultural studies has done). Rather, as Schieffelin puts it, localized and situated analysis is needed of actor/spectator relationships '*both in formal performance and in everyday life* . . . because this is the creative edge where reality is socially constructed' (1998: 204, my italics). Whereas Chapters 1 and 2 emphasized popular culture and 'everyday life', Chapters 3 and 4 will turn to the framing of high-cultural and 'formal' performance. In particular I will emphasize via case studies in both chapters that the analysis of performativity should focus on actions more than on 'text' (Hughes-Freeland, 1998: 21).

High-cultural framing: tales of humanism, modernism and modernity

As John Frow has described in detail, high-cultural framing is a process of institutional semiosis that establishes 'regimes of value'. He draws attention to the 'sets of interlocking institutions' – such as school curricula; the institutions of theatre, concert hall, museum and art gallery; and quality niches within the media (such as broadsheet newspaper reviewing and certain productions at the BBC) – which between them produce high culture's 'axiological regularities' (1993: 212). These 'regularities' are also produced in everyday life, in the daily, face-to-face conversation of peer and work groups (like our building workers talking about 'clean girls' who like opera), which establish 'particular codes of status-discrimination' (Frow, 1993: 212). But it is especially in the semiotic institutions of high culture that these 'regularities' sediment, and become 'interpretive communities' (Fish) or 'reading formations' (Bennett). What constitutes these high-cultural 'regimes of value'? Frow's own position on this is quite clear.

> High culture is now fully absorbed within commodity production. The relation to the market can therefore not be used as a general principle of differentiation between high-cultural and low-cultural products, nor is it any longer possible to employ the traditional value-laden opposition between the disinterested, organic, original, self-governing work of art and the interested, mechanical, formulaic, and commercial mass cultural text. (1993: 208)

'Chekhov' is no less commoditized than our safer-sex campaign at the advertising agency. Nevertheless, as Frow says, this 'traditional value-laden opposition' has been high culture's most regular and enduring frame, especially in the context of the encroaching 'mass cultural' forces of modernity. Frow notes that one of the significant functions claimed by high culture has been 'to reinforce the discrepancy between aesthetic and economic discourses of value, as a way of designating aesthetic – that is, non-economic – value as a marker of status' (1993: 212). Thus the building workers' 'clean girl' who likes opera; but thus also John Middleton Murry's claim in his 'Thoughts on Chekhov'. Not only is the assumption of 'organic, original, self-governing' art there in Murry's emphasis on Chekhov's 'work of creation' as 'a gradual adjustment of his vision', but so too is the separation of the aesthetic from the economic, as Chekhov's art lifts itself above the economic processes that his stories and plays describe – of class change, peasant hardship and psychological pain in a modernizing Russia – to become instead as 'natural and beautiful' as the flowering of a rose. In this 'theatrical' frame, as Schieffelin has said, 'Art' is understood as a 'performative manipulation', as both an 'illusion', and at the same time as a virtual – or alternative – reality, where the senses may recover from all the 'arbitrary' and 'inevitable' pain of 'being in the world'.

I have juxtaposed the two header quotations of this chapter to emphasize that there was, in fact, nothing either 'natural' or 'illusory' about the flowering of a rose in Chekhov's time any more than now. Rather, its memory is a social event positioned by 'expert' paradigms: whether John Middleton Murry's literary-humanist one or Il'ya Metchnikov's evolutionist-scientific one. Scientific horticulture was, in fact, highly advanced in Russia in the late nineteenth century; Chekhov studied it as part of his medical degree at Moscow University, and pronounced the leading plant physiologist Timiryazev as one of the scientists he admired most. So in my own 'expert' account, which embeds Chekhov in Metchnikov's paradigm rather than in Middleton Murry's, I have suggested elsewhere that Chekhov was a very specific kind of evolutionist doctor/playwright performing in a very particular historical moment of modernization in Russia (Tulloch, 1981).

What are these alternative representational orders? How do they relate to 'canonical' high-cultural framing? I will begin by juxtaposing two very different narratives about 'Art', modernism and modernity.

Liberal humanist tales

Peter Barry's 'ten tenets of liberal humanism' (Barry, 1995) describe fairly typically what many cultural theorists see as the 'archive' of liberal humanist criticism.

1 'Good literature is of timeless significance; it somehow transcends the limitations and peculiarities of the age it was written in, and thereby speaks to what is constant in human nature';

2 The 'literary text contains its own meaning within itself. It doesn't require any elaborate process of placing it within a context, whether this be: (a) *Socio-political* . . .; (b) *Literary-historical* . . . (c) *Auto-biographical* . . . As critics, their adherence to . . . the "words on the page" commits them to . . . "close reading" ';

3 What 'is needed is the close verbal analysis of the text without prior ideological assumptions, or political pre-conditions';

4 'Human nature is essentially unchanging. The same passions, emotions, and even situations are seen again and again throughout human history';

5 'Individuality is something securely possessed within each of us as our unique "essence" ';

6 The 'purpose of literature is essentially the enhancement of life and the propagation of humane values; but not in a programmatic way: if literature, and criticism, become overtly and directly political they necessarily tend towards propaganda';

7 'Form and content in literature must be fused in an organic way, so that the one grows inevitably from the other';

8 'Sincerity (comprising truth-to-experience, honesty towards the self, and the capacity for human empathy and compassion) is a quality which resides *within* the language of literature. It isn't a fact or an intention *behind* the work, which could be gleaned by comparing . . . a poet's view of an event with other more "factual" versions, or from discovering independent, external information about an author's history or context';

9 'What is valued in literature is the "silent" showing and demonstrating of something, rather than the explaining, or saying, of it';

10 The 'job of criticism is to interpret the text, to mediate between it and the reader. A theoretical account of reading . . . isn't useful in criticism, and will simply . . . encumber critics with "preconceived ideas" '. (Barry, 1995: 17–20).

Reflexive *performance* – whether within the literary/theatrical conditions of production or of reception – has little place here. The critic, of course, performs, but supposedly as a skilfully neutral mediator between the 'expert' language of the text and the 'lay' reader.

The liberal humanist's 'Chekhov' matches all of these tenets:

- timeless and transcending the limitations of his age (hence Middleton Murry's Chekhov is above the 'inevitable' world of social exploitation);
- separate from his personal situation within Russian evolutionism and rural medicine;
- 'above ideology';
- portraying the same passions that recur throughout human history: the painful loss of cherished places (*The Cherry Orchard*); the desire for elsewhere (*The Three Sisters*); the infatuations of impossible love (*Uncle Vanya*);
- uniquely an individualist;
- a comically (ironically) 'tragic' propagator of humane values beyond the flux of social change;
- a masterful weaver of polyphonic form via the 'organically'-related non-communicating characters of his 'content';
- with huge sincerity, empathy and compassion for all his 'feckless' people;
- an artist who 'shows' human weakness, not a polemical purveyor of ideas (compared, say, with Gorkii);
- a 'master' writer who is set as an exemplar for students of Russian, theatre and literature alike.

Indeed, so completely does Chekhov match the liberal humanist's pantheon, that one feels if this 'Chekhov' had not existed, he would have to be invented. In particular, we can see the difficulty this high-cultural archive will have with an author who does believe in human and social change.

A 'grand narrative' of modernity

My own 'Chekhov' narrative depends on situating the 'text' in the context of a diachronic sequence of modernizing 'moments' in Russian history.

- The moment when the defeat in the Crimean War was recognized to be the result of Russia's technological and scientific under-development, and a massive shift quickly took place away from the mystical autocratic/bureaucratic regime's traditional suspicion of science. This had immediate effect in the curricula of schools and universities. ('Science . . . is our first need. If our enemies are superior to us, it is only because of the power of their knowledge', Russian Minister of Education, 1855, cited in Tulloch, 1980). Whereas in 1853 only 22 students had graduated in the sciences in all universities in Russia, by 1860 there were over 500. In particular, there was a dramatic growth in both numbers and science expertise in the medical faculty of Moscow University, where Chekhov chose to study in the late 1870s.

- The moment when limited political decentralization had taken place in Russia, where, after the Freedom of the Serfs, the rural *zemstvas* became the new regional administrative units carved as a compromise out of the power struggle between the Tsar and his nobles. Now that the landowners no longer looked after the serfs' health, and with terror of rampant cholera and other epidemics still high among the ruling groups, the new *zemstvas* employed the new-style, scientifically trained doctors coming out of Moscow University. Thus, as in the 1840s and 1860s, so too in the 1880s and 1890s there was a surge of intelligentsia into the Russian countryside; but the difference now was that this latest group were the new, upwardly mobile, materialist professionals who were deeply indebted to science, and particularly to Darwin.

- This was a moment of social evolutionism, however, which was very different from its US counterpart. The Russian doctors' and scientists' evolutionism (as illustrated by Metchnikov) drew on the 'symbiosis within a species' not the 'tooth and claw' edge of Darwin, stressing social change and environmental protection. Chekhov writes in his letters that his models are not literary giants like Tolstoi or Dostoyevskii, but his medical teachers at Moscow University – G.A. Zakhar'in, A.A. Ostroumov and F.F. Erisman, together with leading materialist/evolutionist scientists like I.I. Metchnikov and K. Timiryazev. Each of these emphasized the holistic study of environment as a source of illness and social exploitation. Zakhar'in, for example, lectured to Chekhov that changing a milieu which was unfavourable to an organism's functional strength was the first step in restoring its equilibrium, and he emphasized climate therapy and the rich natural resources of Russia, strong echoes of which are found in Chekhov's letters and plays like *Uncle Vanya* and *The Three Sisters*. In the emerging time and space of the rural *zemstvas*, the new doctors with their grand narrative of evolutionary social change often felt experientially lost in the vast backwardness of the peasantry. This was not only a matter of changing the quality of personal health but of environmental health as well (in *Uncle Vanya*, for example, the *zemstvo* doctor Astrov complains of environmental degeneration as the poverty-stricken peasants strip the land of its trees and its pitch for their fires). This mix of scientific/ideological confidence with experiential angst and exhaustion was a rich source for the comedy and the tragedy of Chekhov's works.

- Whereas the Russian government continued to control primary and secondary teachers very closely (even in the *zemstvo* areas), fearing their potential power to radicalize students, the *zemstvo* doctors enjoyed considerable professional autonomy until the 1917 Revolution. Professional journals, scientific conferences and other institutionalized markers of 'professionalism' within modernity all flourished in the last three decades of the nineteenth century in Russia, and Chekhov took a close interest in all of them. He continued his practice as a *zemstvo* doctor until ill-health forced him to give it up, doing important work as a factory sanitary inspector during the cholera epidemic in the Melikhovo region in the early 1890s. He also conducted (at huge cost to his health) a medical-sociological study of the penal colony on Sakhalin Island in the 1890s. This was designed on social evolutionist lines, and was intended as a doctorate for the medical faculty at Moscow University.

In short, this 'Chekhov' was very much part of a new, modernizing professional elite in Russia; a believer in the grand narrative of science and its potential to contain risk in the Russian early-modern transition (and prior to Beck's 'Risk Society'). He was therefore in broad opposition to the bureaucratic autocracy's continuing efforts to curtail the freedom of speech of other professionals, like teachers (the gap between pedagogical ritual and medical performativity is a frequent theme in his work); and he was also hostile to doctors who were *not* part of the socially reforming *zemstva* movement. A typical trope in Chekhov's short stories and plays throughout his literary career was the doctor who provided only therapy (like valerian drops) for deep-held social or socio-psychological concerns. Even worse was the doctor (as in his long story, *Ward Number 6*), who provided no help at all, on the grounds that 'it will all be the same in a thousand years'.

Chekhov (in my narrative) established quite clear place/time co-ordinates in his works. It is not a coincidence at all that Ragin, the fatalistic doctor in *Ward Number 6*, is not a *zemstvo* doctor; nor that the fatalistic 'degeneration theory' (Max Nordau-style) scientist, Von Koren in *The Duel*, establishes his marine biology research institute on the Black Sea where, as Chekhov knew, research of this kind had already failed because of inadequate resources of fauna. As regards temporal co-ordinates, Chekhov, as a believer in social evolution, neither supported the 'it will be all the same in a thousand years' mystics and conservatives, nor the instant change scenarios of the revolutionists, like Trofimov in *The Cherry Orchard*. For Chekhov there was no 'natural and beautiful' flowering of a rose: it had to be worked for scientifically, as did the 'defence of the weak against natural selection'.

This, then, is my own historically situated narrative of 'Chekhov'. But there are particular reasons why this 'history' does not count as 'expert knowledge' for Middleton Murry – or for many Chekhov academic or theatre critics who have followed him. The paradigms about 'modernity' and 'modernism' which we 'experts' employ are too different, almost incommensurable.

'Fantasies' and 'ideologies' of modernism

John Frow calls the dominant high-cultural paradigm 'the modernist fantasy of self-definition through opposition to a degraded mass culture' (Frow, 1993: 210), and Raymond Williams has described tendencies within 'the ideology of modernism' to create a highly selective, self-perpetuating and historically unreflexive field, frequently framing 'the formerly aristocratic valuation of art as a sacred realm above money and commerce' (Williams, 1989: 34). If we approach Chekhov via the high-cultural frame of Middleton

Murry (and his many descendants) we locate him in this kind of elite and idealist modernism. If, on the other hand, we approach him through Il'ya Metchnikov, we find quite another kind of modernist Chekhov, who, through his plays and particularly his short stories, not only responds to the everyday and its vernacular speech forms, but – far from aestheticizing human pain as 'natural and beautiful' – worked both aesthetically and medically to transform it. In my account, Chekhov, in his *daily performance* – as doctor, as playwright, as writer of letters and short stories – emphasized the 'border crossings' between different kinds of performative event which later critics and interpreters preferred to fetishize as separate specialisms of expertise.

Are there any bridges available between these high-cultural frames? From his cultural materialist standpoint, Raymond Williams describes Chekhov as a modernist Naturalist, a member of an aesthetic movement that had, at its centre, 'the humanist and secular – and, in political terms, liberal and later socialist – proposition that human nature was not . . . unchanging and time-less, but was socially and culturally specific' (Williams, 1989: 84). Williams distinguishes *within* high-cultural modernism. The modernist Naturalists (Ibsen, Chekhov, Strindberg) were 'formed by a new natural history . . . and with an explicit emphasis on the evolutionary process, commonly seen as a struggle for existence, by which a new kind of life tried and as often failed to come through' (Williams, 1989: 84). And though he was surprisingly silent in tracing the differences within naturalist modernism himself (between the varying developments of evolutionism in Ibsen's Norway, Chekhov's Russia, and Strindberg's Sweden, and their different kinds of engagement with the modernizing state), Williams also said that 'each is the work of dissident fractions of the bourgeoisie itself, which became grouped – especially from the 1890s – in new independent and progressive theatres' (Williams, 1989: 85).

Williams found within the chosen form of modernist Naturalism an 'early crisis'.

> Beyond the key site of the living room there were, in opposite directions, crucial areas of experience where the language and behaviour of the living room could not articulate or fully interpret. Social and economic crises in the wider society had their effects back in the living room, but dramatically only as reports from elsewhere, off-stage, or at best as things seen from the window or as shouts from the street. Similarly, crises of subjectivity – the privacies of sexuality, the un-certainties and disturbances of fantasies and dreams – could not be fully articulated within the norms of language and behaviour which, for its central purposes, the form had selected. (1989: 85–6)

It was this contradictory tendency which led, in Williams's view, to the 'fragmented' attempts by authors like Chekhov to find new formal ways of resolving the crisis (especially in *The Cherry Orchard*, as we will see in the next chapter). 'Modernity' in literature and theatre then, in Williams's analysis, saw the bifurcation of these two trends as opposite choices of the avant-garde – for example in Germany, on the one hand, the drama exploring subjectivity, inner consciousness, self-repression and sexuality of Wedekind, Kaiser and early Brecht; on the other hand, the more 'political' theatre affiliating with the working class of Piscator, Toller and the later Brecht.

Williams also distinguishes, separately from the achievements and fragmentation of modernist Naturalism, high culture's more familiar modernists (Apollinaire, Joyce, Beckett, Ionesco), the 'restlessly mobile emigré or exile . . . writers continuously moving to Paris, Vienna and Berlin' (1989: 34). Williams's analysis draws attention to their situated and historical conditions: for example, to:

- the growth at the time of the modernist movement of great imperialist metropolises like Paris, London and Berlin;
- the fact that many of the modernist innovators were migrants to those cities, placed in new relations both to the metropolitan languages and images as well as to their own native ones.

In this *particular* historical space and time, Williams argues, the 'relationships were to the open and complex and dynamic social process itself, and the only accessible form of this practice was an emphasis on the medium: the medium as that which, in an unprecedented way, defined art' (Williams, 1989: 46).

However, what was specifically situated historically in the imperial metropolis was later to become (in the utterances of high culture's 'experts') modernism's fetish, a boundary rhetoric, a paradigm theory, even an epistemology. In key respects, 'Chekhov' is a paradigm case of high culture's negotiation between liberal humanism and what Williams calls the 'ideology of modernism', despite the actual historical differences between Chekhov and Williams's metropolitan modernists. It is, precisely, those historical differences that 'the ideology of modernism' effaced.

There are, then potential continuities between Williams's narrative and my own, especially in his emphasis on different 'dissident fractions' (including evolutionists) among the bourgeoisie with cultural capital. But this is neither the 'modernism' nor the 'Chekhov' that is commonly framed within the sets of interlocking high-cultural institutions that Frow describes. It is precisely the 'timeless' and 'nothing can be done' Chekhov who still dominates university classrooms (as recent research conducted with students and teachers at 17 universities in Britain, the USA and Australia clearly indicated); and by and large it dominates also other institutions of high culture, like newspaper reviewing and the theatre. Further, as literary humanism itself faces assault from 'theory', that effacing of history continues still (which would not have surprised Williams, given his strident critique of the 'new formalism'). Thus Mark Fortier speaks in his book *Theory/Theatre* about Chekhov's time/place co-ordinates in terms of phenomenological abstractions and Derrida's 'deconstruction'.

Visions of human happiness, of life fulfilled, remain compelling, but only through deferral; what endures in life is a radical postponement of living. . . . In as much

> as deconstruction is in part an unravelling of phenomenological assumptions from
> within, Chekhov and Derrida partake of a common project. . . . [T]he new age for
> Derrida or Chekhov is indefinitely postponed. (Fortier, 1997: 36, 42, 47)

It is true that Fortier says that a 'full discussion of Chekhov . . . would need
to examine the historical and social, as well as phenomenological grounds of
disappointment' (1997: 51). But that kind of analysis, too, is 'indefinitely
postponed'.

High culture's *claims* for modernism's superiority over the 'degraded'
everyday (whether of 'mass culture or, for that matter, the Sydney building
workers' grog-filled leisure time) may be 'fantasy', as Frow says. But
undeniably high culture continues to have *rhetorical effect* in powerful ways
which help determine how entire generations of both students and theatre-
goers define not simply artists like Chekhov, but also 'modernism' and
'modernity' themselves. In the institutions of high culture, as Raymond
Williams has shown, there has been a tendency to reduce all modernist
agency to aesthetic challenges to language and form, ignoring the local and
historical conditions in which those cultural breaks were situated.

Williams describes how a *particular* notion of 'modernism' which had
once been primarily situated in the metropolitan 'centres of the new
imperialism' was raised 'to the level of universal myth'. Many of the formal
tropes of this modernist myth – the 'experience of visual and linguistic
strangeness, the broken narrative of the journey and its inevitable encounters
with characters whose self-presentation was bafflingly unfamiliar' (Williams,
1989: 34) – have also become key rhetorical utterances in a 'Chekhov
beyond naturalism' discourse. They have become, as Bakhtin put it, the
utterances that high culture must make as 'a *response* to preceding utterances', the 'Chekhov' that high culture 'presupposes . . . to be known, and
somehow takes . . . into account' (Bakhtin, 1986: 91).

These formalist 'presupposed to be known' tropes have been especially
important in high culture's continuing accounts of Chekhov because he
has also been known as a naturalist – a literary movement all *about* the
economic and social pains of a modernizing society. As Williams says, in
the rhetoric of the avant-garde, 'One word sums up' what it diversely rejects:
'*naturalism*. There is hardly a new dramatic or theatrical movement, down to
our own day, which fails to announce, in manifesto, programme note or press
release, that it is rejecting or moving beyond "naturalism" ' (Williams, 1989:
83). And so, a dialogic Chekhov 'beyond naturalism' has been a dominant
rhetorical move in high-cultural criticism's attempt to fuse 'modernity' with
'Art' for most of this century. Middleton Murry's 'thoughts on Chekhov'
were an early example. A much more recent example is Mark Fortier who
begins his account, 'Chekhov's plays have often been treated as naturalistic
works immersed in the mundane details of Russian provincial life at the end
of the nineteenth century. . . . However . . .' (Fortier, 1997: 34).

This rhetorical fusion of naturalism with an 'abstraction' or 'ambiguity'
beyond naturalism is especially strong in the contemporary high-cultural

theatre, where it has become part of a liturgy of 'formal performance' practice. For example, Sir Peter Hall claimed his 1997 production of *The Seagull* at the Old Vic, London, was liberating Chekhov from naturalism's 'heavy style'.

> The new naturalism has dominated theatre for over a hundred years and we are only now beginning to get free of it. We think of Chekhov and Ibsen as the high priests of this style, but even as they endorsed it, they were trying to go beyond it to something more ambiguous and metaphorical. . . . In our century, naturalism has gradually declined. Even fifty years ago, it was unthinkable to ask an audience to imagine a room without *providing* them with a room. . . . Today, a bare stage with a table and two chairs will suffice – and nobody will mind if a score of spotlights are visible above the set. . . . A century on, the camera has helped the theatre regain its potency. . . . It is therefore perhaps easier to play Shakespeare, Chekhov and Ibsen than it was fifty years ago. (Hall, *The Seagull* programme, 1997: 5)

Similarly, in his 1995/96 Royal Shakespeare Company production of *The Cherry Orchard* at the Swan Theatre, Stratford-upon-Avon, Adrian Noble emphasized the minimalist advantages of the theatre 'house' and set.

> I think what this theatre does wonderfully well is, it enables the inner architecture, the skeleton of the play to reveal itself. . . . We were very keen not to create rooms . . . because it seemed to me that there is a way to the heart of Chekhov that isn't . . . the naturalistic way in. . . . It's very abstract . . . what we eventually came up with, and indeed the way it's played. (Adrian Noble, 1996, public interview with Peter Holland)

Yet, as Peter Hall's comment about a 'century of the camera' indicates, where a specific history is effaced, alternative histories appear. The dramatist Trevor Griffiths has argued that British productions of *The Cherry Orchard* – so often seen as the 'first great play of the twentieth century' and thus as symptomatic of modernity itself – have replaced a situated history with an 'eternalised' class one. For Griffiths, this is what liberal humanism's 'essentially unchanging human nature' is really about, once in the hands of 'class secretaries' and observed by middle-class audiences.

> The play's specific historicity and precise sociological imagination has been bleached of all meanings beyond those required to convey the necessary 'natural' sense that the fine will always be undermined by the crude and that the 'human condition' can for all essential purposes be equated with 'the plight of the middle classes'. (Griffiths, 1978: v)

Similarly, in a recent study (1997) of the Royal Shakespeare Company's *The Cherry Orchard*, Tulloch, Burvill and Hood argued that director Adrian Noble used Stanislavskian rehearsal methods, lighting, choreography of movement, props, set, and the intimate space of the Swan Theatre itself to 'make public the private family grief', enabling the 'loss' of the dispossessed landowners 'to be shared honestly' with (what their questionnaire surveys indicated was) primarily a professional middle-class audience.

I want to end this chapter with a brief account of this study, because it points to ways in which a situated 'high-cultural' studies can work in moving beyond a predominantly textualist focus.

High-cultural performing: fixing the modern

If Trevor Griffiths is right about British theatre's 'fixing' of modernity, how does it work as performance in this semiotic site of the Royal Shakespeare Company? It is never *simply* a matter of 'class secretaries' and middle-class audiences. Indeed, as Frow warns, there is a reductionism involved here in equating 'high culture' directly with the 'dominant social class'. Rather, as Frow elaborates, the implementation of modernity (including high-cultural 'regimes of value' which make modernity into a 'reading practice') is a matter of integrating knowledge into commodity production by 'cultural intellectuals'. Frow is right to define his 'intelligentsia' here as a very broad social formation including 'all those who work in the knowledge industries' (1993: 98), whether 'that knowledge be prestigious or routine, technical or speculative' (1993: 90). This is no less true of a 'critically acclaimed' and highly publicized Chekhov production under the legitimating banner of the Royal Shakespeare Company. Here, at the RSC, we find for example that the very first 'meanings' of this Chekhov production were circulated to over 50,000 potential subscribers by the *marketing* department, well before RSC Artistic Director Noble's first rehearsals. Within Frow's expanded definition of 'intelligentsia' *many* 'histories' are put to work as 'living dialogic threads', each of which, as Bakhtin says, is an 'active participant in social dialogue'. Thus does the performative 'utterance' take its 'meaning and shape in a particular historical moment in a socially specific environment' (Bakhtin, 1981: 276). And thus it is, as I have said, that dialogic social interactions rather than 'text' are the focus of my story.

It is by analysing these 'living dialogic threads' across a wide range of what Worthen calls 'off-stage' and 'on-stage' theatrical sites that the *difference* of formal performance, which Carlson, Kruger and others emphasize, can be approached. In the case of Noble's 'Chekhov', these included:

- A Stanislavskian rehearsal style which encouraged actors to draw on their own biography. So for Alec McCowen, who played the dispossessed Gayev, the rehearsal exercises 'stirred memories for me . . . of my own childhood home and growing up and when we left it. . . . To me the play is really about *my* childhood which was in the 1930s and 1940s and thinking about the values of that time when we had a live-in-maid. . . . Life is so different now. . . . So there is a huge, huge nostalgic element [in it for me].' (McCowen, 1996, personal interview)
- A use of publicity brochures and the programme cover and notes to establish a very specific historical trajectory from 'brutalized' Russian past to the 'liberated-democratic' 1990s. For example, on the theatre programme cover, the 'C' of 'Cherry Orchard' is red, whereas the rest of

the lettering is black. The 'C' is also converted into a toppling sickle which (together with the 'axes . . . ready to swing' contextualization of the 1903/4 play which was conveyed by the first publicity brochures) conveyed to audiences the specific 'then/now' history of this production: 'Revolution 1905/1917→1989'.

- A directorial infantilizing of the Chekhov characters which worked through to his choice of actors. 'There's this curious "We cling to the past": that's Liuba's and Gayev's great sin, they cannot let go. . . . They hang on to the wreckage and they . . . just will not face up to reality. They dance while the house is being sold. . . . And that is to do with an inability to grow up. . . . Then the children they breed . . . can't do that either. Anya has fantasies, as does Trofimov. His form of politics is unreal – there's actually a pamphlet that Lenin wrote called "Left-wing Communism – an infantile disorder" . . .; and you could say that's what Trofimov falls into, it's an infantile disorder' (Adrian Noble, 1996, public interview with Peter Holland). Thus Sean Murray believed he was chosen for the part of the 'emotional' Trofimov after he 'wept' with frustration as an Actors Equity representative in Noble's office in an earlier 'everyday' performance.
- A choreographing of the landowners' 'hanging on to the wreckage' via what most reviewers saw as the high point of the production, the ball scene in Act 3. Here, movement designer Sue Lefton was encouraged by Noble to design a 'manic' dance (in place of Chekhov's waltz) that seemed to make the stage into the Titanic's ballroom, the band playing on. 'Like a ship . . . tipping and everyone slipping down one side, and then tipping and everyone slipping down the other way. . . . I think we achieved the kind of energy of building and building and losing your mind.' (Lefton, 1996, personal interview)
- A use of distorted train sounds (accompanying the raising and lowering of a large gauze box to 'entrap' the actors) to further signify the 'tragic' technological inevitability of modernity. Assistant director Andrew Cooper described how 'Adrian decided that it was very interesting to think of the train as the twentieth-century conveyer of events. The First and Second World War were transmitted around Europe by train. It's the technological revolution which has taken with it everything at various times.' (Cooper, 1995, personal interview)
- A use of dramatically increased lighting in Act 2 to point (in the midst of all this 'tragic' change) to the 'great explosion of life . . . and energy' as the 'house is reinhabited with light, the spirit that Liuba . . . has and brings in to the house' (Noble, 1996, public interview with Peter Holland). Since in Noble's production 'the centre of the play is the house', this lighting elevation of the 'spirit' of the landowner Ranevskaya – in the face of the 'inevitable' change about her – arguably works strongly towards Middleton Murry's sense of Chekhov's 'natural and beautiful' spirit in the face of 'the frustration of human destinies and the arbitrary infliction of pain'.

There has been space here only to list these various dialogic interactions. However, a further theorizing of this situated account of high-cultural performance could then proceed from this point either at the level of 'mediated' or 'face-to-face' symbolic exchange (Thompson, 1995). It could examine performance at the level of mediated narratives via the analysis of newspaper reviews of Noble's production. Most reviewers, for example, picked up Noble's sense of 'mad inevitability' in Act 3.

> Noble is . . . totally aware that the music and the dancing are part of the play's scaffolding. He uses both to drive the scene along at what seems like break-neck speed: there is a feeling of madness and inevitability, and of course, of loss, when the music stops. (Rod Dungate at the Swan, 1995)

Again here, as in Middleton Murry, the defining Chekhov moment is one of 'inevitability'. Modernity is conveyed by technology; and human agency is twice devalued – as infantile illusion, and as 'madness and inevitability'.

Alternatively, a situated analysis opens the way to performance analysis at the level of face-to-face (actor/spectator) interaction. McCowen's negotiation of his performance indicates very clearly the actor as 'double agent' that Hastrup (1998) describes, embedded in the skills and strategies both of the canonical and the (personally) transformative. Bill Worthen has taken this point usefully further in analysing high-cultural theatre perform-ance as he describes an actor's 'trained approach to translating the text into embodied action' (1996: 213).

> Translating the Stanislavskian superobjective into the metaphorical 'journey' involves the actors in a dual engagement with history: with the 'past' traced in the text (the play's given circumstances, the eccentricities of 'character' drawn from an era so removed from our own, their necessary effort to write a motivating personal history for the role) and with the 'present', the moment of performance, which necessarily decentres, occludes, or displaces the authority of the text. (Worthen, 1996: 213)

It is, as Worthen says, possible (but rare) for actors to *occupy* the familiar 'decentred' postmodern position of subjective fragmentation (between 'past' and 'present'). So, for example, a recent production of Shakespeare's *Midsummer Night's Dream*, directed by Mary-Anne Gifford in Penrith (New South Wales), used different time periods (Shakespeare's, the First World War, Scott Fitzgerald's capitalist 1920s as 'one long party') and actors playing several different but thematically related parts. For example, one actor played Hippolyta as the colonized and reluctant bride; Titania as also ravaged of her 'Indian boy' by Oberon; and Peter Quince, director of the 'lower-class' mechanicals. This fragmentation of time and character allowed the production to perform *between* the reinvigorating comedy of Shake-speare's 'playful' pastoral woods and their 'dark' patriarchal and colonist 'Other', as well as *between* the First World War's dark and hidden legacy (a growing Fascism in Germany) and the 'playful' songs of the 1920s' middle-class 'party', without ever being *about* one or the other. However, as Worthen says, Stanislavskian training generally inclines actors to 'understand their interpretive practice less as a mode of self-authorized creation than as a mode of fidelity' to 'Shakespeare' or to 'Chekhov'.

> The actors' use of history to open and sustain their readings of Shakespearian 'character' dramatises these interpretive priorities and situates them in a clear contrast to recent [academic] critical practice. . . . The actors' principal mode of engagement with the past concerns the need to develop a biography for the role, a 'past' to motivate the character's present actions. This act of biographical invention serves the same function as it does for Stanislavski: it enables the actor to produce the illusion of a single whole, coherent 'character' whose behaviour flows from a concrete past into a determined present. (Worthen, 1996: 214)

Whether, then, we examine the mediated performances of 'quality' newspaper reviewing, or the embodied and 'face-to-face' performance interaction of actor and spectator in this RSC Chekhov production, we return to the 'single, whole coherent character' of literary humanism formally performed at the semiotic institution: 'the RSC, Stratford'.

In this brief summary of a case study of high-cultural 'formal' performance, I have tried to indicate the value of situated performance analysis in showing how 'history' is reconstructed as different performance 'utterances' work dialogically within a liberal-humanist frame to establish a technologically determinist reading of modernity. It seems clear that a situated account of high-cultural performance opens the way to a more complex analysis of Williams's 'ideology of modernism' than cultural studies' liturgical tendency to textualist analysis.

Conclusion

My point in this chapter has been that cultural studies (in its mainstream teaching and research enterprises) has been remiss where it has analytically *effaced* high culture as effective 'expert system'; and this is not least because of the imbrication of many of cultural studies' *own* contemporary theories with what Williams has called the 'politics of modernism and the avant-garde'. One of the conventions of *postmodernist* theory and practice is precisely that avant-garde reflexivity and slippage of styles, the bricolage, the 'poaching', the 'mixing texts together', the breaking of linguistic, conceptual and historical frames which, *when unattached* to the situated analysis of history and human agency, concerns Williams so much. 'High' and 'popular' culture thus fuse and confuse in current 'expert' discourse, bid and counter-bid – in theory as in architectural practice.

Yet high culture – as a leisure institution and as a pedagogy of modernism – still has, I have suggested, social (rhetorical) *effect*. High culture may have by and large slipped off the cultural studies agenda (except polemically), but it still frames artistic, educational, government and much commercial discourse. Its habitus (in Bourdieu's sense) still needs tracing as performance and process.

Raymond Williams (clearly one of the 'utterances' that my own narrative in this chapter 'presupposes . . . to be known, and somehow takes . . . into account') has pointed to a disempowering fetishizing of popular culture within cultural studies' disciplinary project (Williams, 1989: 159). And he has also described the top-down textualist tendency – the 'picking over of texts and individuals, from above' (1989: 173) – which (ironically, given the populist rhetoric) has lost contact with 'the specific relationships through which works are made and move' (1989: 173). Ironic, also, has been the continuity with literary humanism in what Williams describes as the new formalism's effacing of a specific, situated history.

> Blocks of ideology could be moved around in general historical or cultural analysis, but in practice . . . they lacked almost any useful form of specifiable . . . agency. . . . [W]hat was now being said, by nearly everyone, was that specification depended on the excision of such naiveties as 'external' content and agency, and the name for this specification was *text*. Ironically this was the same vocabulary as the academic 'canon'. A text: an isolated object to be construed and discoursed upon: once from pulpits, now from seminar desks. (1989: 172)

In this developing 'cultural studies' context, Williams, like Meaghan Morris, became suspicious of the alibis of 'resistance' and 'appropriation'.

> Nor could it make any useful difference when this isolated [textualist] object began to be opened up to its internal uncertainties and multiplicities, or to the further stage of its entire and helpless openness to any form of interpretation or analysis whatever: that cutting loose of readers and critics from any obligation to social connection and historical fact. For what was being excluded, from this work reduced to the status of text or of text as critical device, was the socially and historically specifiable agency of its making: an agency that has to include both content and intention. (Williams, 1989: 172)

Like Hughes-Freeland et al., Williams emphasizes agency and intentionality, creativity within constraint, the participatory nature of (historically placed, socially situated) spectatorship, and the specified relationship of different (time/space) cultural framings of performing 'reality' and 'illusion'. In this regard, Williams's influence on analysis of the relationships through which 'works are made and move', and on a concern for '*people's* questions' – especially in the area of high culture – has been more profound in recent versions of literary theory than in cultural studies. He has also, because of the popular democratic orientation of his work, had a significant influence on writers for television and theatre who shared his early interest in adult education and New Left politics, like Trevor Griffiths. In the next chapter I will look at the performative 'transforming' of some of Frow's key high-cultural 'regimes of value' (the universities, theatre and television) to examine 'border crossings' between them, and ways in which liberal humanism's liturgical narratives of 'the modern' may be challenged, transformed and performed again as 'voices of the everyday'.

4
(HIGH-) CULTURAL RE-FRAMING

The isolated, estranged images of alienation and loss, the narrative discontinuities, have become the easy iconography of the commercials, and the lonely, bitter, sardonic and sceptical hero takes his ready-made place as star of the thriller. These heartless formulae sharply remind us that the innovations of what is called Modernism have become the new but fixed forms of our present moment. If we are to break out of the non-historical fixity of *post*-modernism, then we must search out and counterpose an alternative tradition taken from the neglected works left in the wide margin of the century. (Raymond Williams, 1989: 35)

It is worth elaborating some of the key concepts *vis-à-vis* 'performance' that were emphasized in the Introduction and opening chapters, because as we move in this and the next chapter more fully into the situated analysis of 'formal performance' and spectatorship in theatre and television we will see that all are as relevant here as earlier. These key concepts were:

- that performativity is endemic to the process of constructing human reality;
- that the power of performativity 'turns crucially on its *inter*active edge, and hence on the nature of the relationship between "performers" and others in the situation to whom the performance is directed' (Schieffelin, 1998: 200);
- that therefore the analysis of performativity should focus on actions more than on 'text', on the social construction of reality rather than representations of reality (Hughes-Freeland, 1998: 21);
- that a focus on performance as social action, and on the dialogical agency of situations, allows us to understand these situations in terms of participatory and rhetorical models rather than (linear) communication ones;
- that 'actors' are 'double agents' embedded in the skills, strategies and tactics of both the 'liturgical' (canonical) and the 'ironic' (transformative);
- that there is a need to resist residual tendencies to exoticize ritual and performance, but rather to analyse them as locally situated practices;
- that performances are narratives of personalized exchange with the potential to subvert routine;
- that separated ('aesthetic') performative events like theatre, film and television are, like everyday 'ordinary' routines, 'systematised and collated within particular performative local contexts' (Hughes-Freeland, 1998: 22);

- that it is important to emphasize 'margins and border crossings' between different kinds of performative event as social action (whether Baumann's 'formal performance' as displays of expressive competence or Goffman's performance of 'everyday social life');
- that if 'the degrees of technological intervention differ between media events and live ones, this is not an intervention which negates the agency of the viewers or audiences' (Hughes-Freeland, 1998: 10);
- that nevertheless we do need to articulate the different 'liminoid' discourses, practices and embodiments of formal performance;
- that a 'key dynamic in performance theory . . . is the audience's conceptualization of the relationship between performer, performance and the context of which it is a part' (Brown, 1998: 162);
- that the various sets of distinctions – liminal/liminoid; strategy/tactic; script/bricolage; language/utterance; theatre/performance; performance/ performativity – demonstrate 'the essentially contested essence of the term "performance", with some theorists viewing it as reinforcing cultural givens, others seeing it as at least potentially subversive' (Carlson, 1996: 24);
- that agency and structure, creativity and constraint, performance and 'spectatorship' are co-present and co-dependent in performative practice.

These key features of both the framing context and the interactivity of performance as both high and popular cultural event will be evident in this and the next chapter. In Chapter 3 I focused on liberal-humanist and 'modernist' framing contexts within high culture. In this chapter I will consider significant performances of 'lay voices' *within* 'expert' high-cultural discourses which seek to transform liberal-humanist frames. In this and the next chapter I will also examine 'margins and border crossings' between different kinds of performative event as social action; as the 'theatrical event' is itself understood as everyday work or leisure-time performance.

We have seen in Chapter 3 that as in everyday life, so too within high-cultural framing, performativity 'is not unfettered agency but creativity contingent . . . on a liturgical script' (Hughes-Freeland, 1998: 7). But on the other hand, as we will see in this chapter, in the play of global relations 'one never actually leaves the local' (Hirsch, 1998: 223) – whether the local is the high-cultural classroom, theatre space or television production. It is in this relationship of local and global that we can understand Hughes-Freeland's point that (for all the talk about a world of simulacra) theatre and media can be alternate frames which militate against (as much as commoditize) fixity, reification and essentialization.

Academic sites: Shakespeare, Chekhov and new historicism

Shakespeare and Chekhov have been, quintessentially, *the* representatives of 'high culture' in many western countries. In Britain, for example, they come first and second in popularity as 'canonical' theatre. Similarly, in leading postgraduate theatre training schools, such as at Florida State University in the USA, Shakespeare and Chekhov are the two key models.

> Chekhov is the Shakespeare of contemporary drama. It is where we really say . . . this will stress our abilities because the text itself is not going to do it for you. The whole idea of a subtext . . . is a skill that the actors cannot possibly master without an understanding of . . . what Chekhov is dramatizing. (Brant Pope, 1994, personal interview with Tom Barvill)

Yet Shakespeare and Chekhov are currently embedded in very different representational orders within the 'regimes of value' of academia.

The attempt to theorize high culture in Raymond Williams's terms has gone furthest in canonicity's heartland: Shakespeare studies. Yet cultural theory came to Shakespeare studies not, as Williams might wish, via adult or 'work experience' education, but through top-down changes in the university sector. As a recent Australian Vice-Chancellors' report on academic standards in English put it (and broadly the same account could be given of Britain and the USA):

> It was in the late 1970s that something loosely called 'theory' began to transform English in Australian universities, though the change was confined at first to a few fairly new institutions and arrived much later in some quarters. . . .'Theory' in this context . . . is . . . a commitment to scrutinise thoroughly the underlying notions that constitute the field of study itself – notions such as 'English', 'literature', 'reading' and 'writing'. By the beginning of the 1990s almost every English Department or similar teaching area in the country had ceased to take these at face value. . . . The purpose of reading anything is no longer seen as to extract meanings that an author supposedly implanted within it. Rather it is to trace the processes of framing by which textual practices attempt to control interpretations. (Australian Vice-Chancellors' Committee, 1994: 16–17)

As we will see, this emphasis on re-framing English studies by analysing the way in which *textual practices* control 'reading' has led to a continued effacing of situated analysis. However, the transformative process in English has been far ahead of that in Russian studies, where 'literature' has hardly been exposed to the 'critical theory' debate at all, and continues to be taught by and large in the more traditional universities and departments.

Virtually none of the leading Chekhov scholars we have interviewed in the USA, Britain and Australia deny this major distinction between current Shakespeare and Chekhov studies; and the very few younger academics in the USA who do teach critical theory all emphasize the entrenched conservatism of Russian literary studies, related in part to the formalist influence of Russian émigrés in American university departments, in part to the power of age and generation differences, in part to control of professional associations, journals and publishers. The following comments were replicated by all the other younger Slavist scholars in the USA that we interviewed.

> I would attribute it to the conservative tendency . . . within Slavic studies, and a hesitancy to accept the sorts of theoretical approaches that seem more widely

accepted outside the field – for example among colleagues . . . who teach in the English department, teach in French, and what you might call comp. lit. type programs. Feminism, postmodernism, cultural materialism, those theoretical approaches are more widespread in the criticism which *they* read, and it's then incorporated into the courses that they teach. . . . It's much slower finding its way into our field. . . . I don't know if it's a reverence for the tradition of formalism, structuralism in Slavic studies . . . but certainly . . . the new Left appropriation of Bakhtin is not a Slavic one. If you look at work that's been written by Slavists about Bakhtin . . . [it] has very little to say about carnival . . . yet that's a very central one everywhere else, like in popular culture. The notion of prosaics seems to have some currency in the Slavic field but doesn't outside it. So I don't think Bakhtin is really an exception to an almost innate conservatism that . . . permeates the teaching of American Slavists at the undergraduate and graduate levels. (Le Blanc, 1993, personal interview)

The academics' 'expert' interaction with Bakhtin is thus 'multi-accented', according to institutional 'regimes of value'. Raymond Williams has written about this development also in Britain, where Russian Formalism,

as it came through into an influential tendency in literary theory, was a disastrous narrowing of the very facts to which it pointed. It became tied to rejections of what were called 'content' . . . and even more damagingly 'intention', which actually missed the point of active literary uses of the very quality that Voloshinov called 'multiaccentual', an inherent semantic openness, corresponding to a still active social process, from which new meanings . . . can be generated. (Williams, 1989: 75)

Rather than the 'distinct historical practice, by real agents in complex relations with other . . . varying agents and practices' which Bakhtin, Medvedev and Voloshinov described, the new formalism, Williams argues, invented a rationalism no less acute than in Wynne's 'objectivist' science.

Thus the a priori rejection of history as relevant or even possible, which has distinguished this tendency from Formalism through structuralism to what has called itself post-structuralism, was actually a move away from some key forms of specificity . . . which Medvedev and Bakhtin defined. . . . Excluding the real and serious pressures on the actual making of art, the formalists and their successors necessarily reduced the language of culture to a rationalism. As Medvedev and Bakhtin put it: 'They reduce both creative and contemplative perception to juxtaposition, comparison, difference and contrast, i.e., to purely logical acts. These acts are treated as equally adequate to both the perception of the reader and the creative intention of the artist'. (Williams, 1989: 167–8)

In contrast, what the recent critical Shakespeare studies have achieved (partly influenced by Williams himself) – in its 'rival' traditions of new historicism and cultural materialism – is a new performance of text, culture and (especially) history. Crucially here, the text has been lifted away from its 'expert' – the author – and its language has been embedded dialogically in intertextual contexts, which are by no means themselves always 'high-cultural'. Both new historicism and cultural materialism have thus refused to elevate the literary text (in the way that Middleton Murry elevates Chekhov) 'above' history.

In this and the next section I want to look at new historicism within academia and cultural materialism within theatre and television to consider what kind of 'performativity' these new high-cultural traditions embrace. As I have said, cultural studies has been remiss in by and large ignoring these movements within high-cultural analysis, and part of my intention here is to restore them to cultural studies' own canon (of texts, monographs, courses, and so on).

As a symptomatic example of the re-framing of high culture within new historicism I will consider Stephen Greenblatt's juxtaposition of Harriot's *A Brief and True Report of the New Land of Virginia* with Shakespeare's *Henry IV/Henry V*. Greenblatt uses this conjuncture of a 'true report' with the Shakespeare trilogy to establish:

> a poetics that is inseparably bound up with the figure of Queen Elizabeth, a ruler without a standing army, without a highly developed bureaucracy, without an extensive police force, a ruler whose power is constituted in theatrical celebra-tions of royal glory and theatrical violence visited upon the enemies of that glory. Power that relies upon a massive police apparatus, a strong, middle-class nuclear family, an elaborate school system, power that dreams of a panopticon in which the most intimate secrets are open to the view of an invisible authority, such power will have as its appropriate aesthetic form the realist novel; Elizabethan power, by contrast, depends upon its privileged visibility. (Greenblatt, 1992: 107–8)

Greenblatt's is transparently a Foucauldian history, embracing the shift from the early modern (a regime of power where the performed public spectacle of the few made visible to the many – the theatrical event, the public execution, the destruction of the rebellious subject – reaffirmed the glory of monarchy) to the 'disciplinary society' (of 'panoptican' surveillance of the many by the few: in prison, hospital, school and army). Greenblatt here contrasts different forms of modernity, exposing one early modern historical moment in particular when the public 'theatrical event' was at its centre.

By way of *first* analysing Harriot's *Brief and True Report*, Greenblatt establishes the discursive utterances foundational to this Elizabethan poetics of 'privileged visibility'. These are:

- **testing**: in Harriot's case, of 'the Machiavellian anthropology that posited the origin of religion in a cunning imposition of socially coercive doctrines by an educated and sophisticated lawgiver upon a simple people' (Greenblatt, 1992: 87);
- **recording**: in Harriot's text of the native American voices which subvert the English view (that the locals are dying because of moral inferiority; that God is protecting his chosen people) with more 'realistic' accounts of 'the lethal biological warfare that was destroying them' (Greenblatt, 1992: 91);
- **explaining**: in Harriot's response to the natives that they cannot appeal to the English God to similarly kill off their own local enemies, and yet

also in Harriot's acceptance of the 'marvellous accident' when the measles, smallpox and common cold do indeed spread to these other American tribes: the 'explanatory moment manifests the self-validating, totalising character of Renaissance political theology – its ability to account for almost every occurrence, even (or above all) apparently perverse or contrary occurrences' (Greenblatt, 1992: 93).

Greenblatt then moves to his Shakespearian texts to find the same discursive tactics at work. *2 Henry IV*, for example, **tests** *Henry V*'s proposition that rulers earn their exalted position through sleeplessness and suffering via Falstaff's parody of it '*before* it makes its appearance as official truth'. Here rhetoric, 'marked out as something with which to impress whores and innkeepers to whom one owes money one does not intend to pay', precedes its appearance in 'the innermost thoughts of the king'.

> At such moments *2 Henry IV* seems to be testing and confirming an extremely dark and disturbing hypothesis about the nature of monarchical power in England: that its moral authority rests upon a hypocrisy so deep that the hypocrites themselves believe it. (Greenblatt, 1992: 105)

This process of testing is achieved via the further tactic of the **recording** of

> voices that seem to dwell in realms apart from that ruled by the potentates of the land. These voices exist and have their apotheosis in Falstaff [and his] company, marching off to Shrewsbury: 'discarded unjust servingmen, younger sons to younger brothers, revolted tapsters, and ostlers trade-fall'n, the cankers of a calm world and a long peace'. (*2 Henry IV*: 27–30, cited in Greenblatt, 1992: 95)

But if this recording of 'the speech of an "under-skinker" and his mates' (Greenblatt, 1992: 97) is the equivalent of Harriot's accessing of native American voices, it is equivalent also in its **explanatory** strategy. Diversity of voices, in *Henry V*, is, in the end, the yoking of subversive voices on behalf of power.

> By yoking together diverse peoples – represented in the play by the Welshman Fluellen, the Irishman Macmorris, and the Scotsman Jamy, who fight at Agincourt alongside the loyal Englishmen – Hal symbolically tames the last wild areas in the British Isles, areas that in the sixteenth century represented, far more powerfully than any New World people, the doomed outposts of a vanishing tribalism. He does so, obviously, by launching a war of conquest against the French, but his military campaign is depicted as carefully founded upon acts of what I have called 'explaining'. The play opens with a notoriously elaborate account of the king's genealogical claim to the French throne, and, as we found in the comparable instances in Harriot, this ideological justification of English policy is an unsettling mixture of 'impeccable' reasoning . . . and gross self-interest'. (Greenblatt, 1992: 106)

Three aspects of Greenblatt's account are relevant to my own project in this book. First, by his typically new historicist refusal to privilege high-cultural texts 'above' non-literary texts – by his discovery, in fact, of a modern Elizabethan poetic *first* in the co-text of Harriot rather than in Shakespeare – Greenblatt is giving a particular 'English studies' twist to our earlier account of 'expert' and 'lay' knowledgeabilities. In the context of literary studies, in other words, new historicists are rejecting the 'creative expertise' (and elevation, as in Middleton Murry) of the canonical author.

Secondly, Greenblatt's Elizabethan poetic gives a temporal twist also to Brian Wynne's 'Risk Society' thinking, by pushing back the issue of 'expert' and 'lay' voices into the pre- or early modern. Wynne's 'Andean Farmers' now reappear as akin, in their way, to Harriot's native tribes – in both cases, they are traditional voices which 'know' more than the voices of modernity that control them. Literary theory, in other words, is now reaching *for* 'ordinary utterances' in its account of high-cultural aesthetics – as these are positioned dialogically in history.

> Drama, and artistic expression in general, is never perfectly self-contained and abstract, nor can it be derived satisfactorily from the subjective consciousness of an isolated creator. Collective actions, ritual gestures, paradigms of relationships, and shared images of authority penetrate the work of art, while conversely the socially overdetermined work of art, along with a multitude of other institutions and utterances, contributes to the formation, realignment, and transmission of social practices. Works of art are, to be sure, marked off in our culture from ordinary utterances, but this demarcation is itself a communal event and signals not the effacement of the social but rather its successful absorption into the work by implication or articulation. This absorption – the presence within the work of its social being – makes it possible, as Bakhtin has argued, for art to survive the disappearance of its enabling social conditions, where ordinary utterance, more dependent upon the extraverbal pragmatic situations, drifts rapidly towards insignificance or incomprehensibility. (Greenblatt, 1992: 97)

So here the mark of the difference between 'everyday' and 'formal' performance is an historical mark: canonical works preserve, in their own way, the voices of past oppressed cultures. Like Sylvia Lawson in the case of Australian silent cinema, Greenblatt is seeking his 'ordinary utterances' as dialogical traces in the historical texts he analyses; but as in Butler's and Patton's notion of 'performativity', these 'alien voices' are opposed yet never finally quite controlled by the texts in which they are implicated. As with Patton's epidemiological discourse (which calls into being 'risk groups' and thus helps gay voices to become performative), so with Greenblatt's 'alien voices'. Renaissance discourse (especially in its high-cultural forms) resonates and makes public these 'ordinary voices' down the centuries.

Like Brian Wynne, new historicists are also challenging the normative claims to universality of 'expert knowledgeability'. The *differences* between Greenblatt and Wynne – for example the historic*ist* rather than historical focus of Greenblatt et al. (that is, their interest in history as recorded in written documents, in history-as-text) – are not simply that new historicists are dealing with 'aesthetic' compared with 'scientific' expert systems. It is also that new historicists are examining the risks to native peoples and 'ordinary utterances' in the past. As in the case of Sylvia Lawson, there is no direct access to our builders' labourers or Wynne's Cumbrian farmers, and therefore no empirical methodology on behalf of Wynne's 'necessary and legitimate involvement of lay publics' (Wynne, 1996: 78). Greenblatt finds his 'lay knowledgeability' instead in the *textually inscribed* 'subversive voices' of Harriot's native Americans and Shakespeare's ' "under-skinker" and his mates'. And in this case, unlike Cindy Patton, Greenblatt does indeed find 'performativity' inscribed in the dialogical relationship between 'expert' colonizing discourses and 'the already-discounted-native'.

Thirdly, as indicated by Greenblatt's reference to 'a panopticon in which the most intimate secrets are open to the view of an invisible authority' (Greenblatt, 1992: 108), new historicist theory is strongly embedded in the Foucauldian debate of 'power versus subversion'. The common criticism (by cultural materialists) of new historicism – that there is a tendency to political pessimism via their concentration on 'containing' ideological and social structures – is supported by Greenblatt's own analysis.

> The mood at the close [of *2 Henry IV*] remains, to be sure, an unpleasant one – the rejection of Falstaff has been one of the nagging 'problems' of Shakespearian criticism – but the discomfort only serves to verify Hal's claim that he has turned away from his former self. If there is frustration at the harshness of the play's end, the frustration is confirmation of a carefully plotted official strategy whereby subversive perceptions are at once produced and contained. . . . Within this theatrical setting, there is a remarkable insistence upon the paradoxes, ambiguities, and tensions of authority, but this apparent production of subversion is . . . the very condition of power. I should add that this condition is not a theoretical necessity of theatrical power in general but an historical phenomenon, the particular mode of this particular culture. (Greenblatt, 1992: 105, 108)

Despite Greenblatt's final disclaimer that his 'pessimism' is a matter of empirical rather than theoretical necessity, his comparison of Elizabethan theatre with the nineteenth-century realist novel (which also successfully contains subversion) and the work of new historicists quite generally on Shakespeare and other theatre, does tend to support the view of cultural materialists that North American new historicists 'find power containing resistance' while British cultural materialists 'stress the potential for dissidence' (Dollimore and Sinfield, 1994: 260). Even a recent theorist like Scott Wilson who contests this 'crude opposition' between the two 'debating' theories, still says: 'Now, Greenblatt certainly [like Foucault] also highlights the productivity of power (or the law); power produces desire, but ultimately only to repress it: or to turn desire back on to itself and make repression a form of enjoyment, and exercise of domination. . . . Falstaff and the Eastcheap gang are banished as Hal identifies his rule with the law' (Wilson, 1995: 64).

Part of the problem here is, as I say, practical and methodological: there is no way today for those lost 'alien voices' either to perform outside the (western) texts that constrain them, or for us to access them in any other manner. But part of the problem is also theoretical. As Wilson says, Greenblatt would agree with Dollimore that 'the "subversion-containment" paradox "disappears when we speak not of a monolithic power structure producing its effects but of one made up of different, often competing elements, and these not merely producing culture but producing it through appropriations" ' (cited in Wilson, 1995: 62–3). To reject the notion of a monolithic power structure and to discover 'other voices' is as important to Brian Wynne as to Dollimore and Greenblatt. For all of them the notion of 'competing elements' is important. Yet the tendency also to forget about alternative agency is striking. Wynne's account of current government/ corporate 'environmentalist' discourse tends to subsume the 'scientific/ expert' voice within the 'official' state discourse, against which he contrasts 'lay knowledgeability'; while this lay knowledgeability is itself subsumed in Greenblatt within the self-reproducing power of the state.

Raymond Williams can help us here. For him, it is a condition of modernity that an important part of the 'competing elements' within the modern state has been the antagonism *between* scientific professionals and official state ideology – or at least, a significant ambivalence in that relationship. If we return, via Williams to Chekhov and to Foucault's 'disciplinary society', I want to argue that Foucault's narrative (and with it much of new historicism's) has too simplistic an emphasis on surveillance as the defining moment of modernity (see here also Thompson, 1995: 134). At the same time, I want to argue that new historical approaches can still be a valuable contribution to the kind of high-cultural analysis of the local, the situated and the agentive that Raymond Williams worked towards.

There were, I have argued, a number of 'experts' in social change at the end of the nineteenth century in Russia, and Chekhov responded very carefully to the utterances of each of them. One important example in Chekhov's works was the revolutionary, and via a new historicist-style juxtaposition of 'co-texts' it is quite possible to explore the way in which Chekhov described, in Greenblatt's terms, a 'power structure producing its effects but . . . made up of different, often competing elements'.

In *The Cherry Orchard* Act 2, Trofimov denies the reality of modernity in Russia.

> But it is clear to anybody that our workers are fed abominably and are forced to sleep without proper beds, thirty to forty to a room, with bed bugs, filthy smells, and a penetrating damp and immorality. It's perfectly plain that all our high-sounding talk has the simple function of misleading ourselves and other people. You just tell me: where are these creches everyone talks about, and where are the reading rooms? We write about them in novels, but in fact they simply don't exist. There's only filth, bestiality, Asiatic habits.

In fact, Chekhov answered Trofimov's question by way of his own daily practices. His medical group was setting up children's crèches, and libraries were being provided by the *zemstvas* – like the one at Taganrog which Chekhov supplied with his own books. Moreover, when we juxtapose Trofimov's speech with a co-text by Chekhov's close friend and *zemstvo* doctor P.I. Kurkin, the revolutionary's speech is resisted. Kurkin co-authored a book (which Chekhov had in his library) about the functioning of sanitary surveillance in the local factories. Prior to 1889, Kurkin said, medical surveillance of the factories was unsystematic; but all this changed after 1890 when plans for factory construction had to be submitted to the local *zemstvo*, to various medical councils, and after which factories had to be open to medical inspection. Kurkin then continues with a description strikingly close to Trofimov's:

> Erisman's research of 1880–1 showed that workers were living in very bad conditions – sleeping quarters that were ill-lit by day, badly constructed, over-crowded; these shanties were covered with bad straw, wet matting, earth floors, and in general such places resembled in no way human habitations.

However, as a result of Erisman's research and the new *zemstvo* regulations, Kurkin continues:

> Now everywhere have been constructed vast, clean and dry barracks with proper floors and camp beds covered with straw mattresses. According to the research of 1880–1 factory owners, with few exceptions, paid no attention to the ventilation of their workshops. Now one can no longer find workshops without practical ventilators on the windows, and in some important factories mechanical ventilators have been employed to refresh the air. (Osipov et al., 1900: 247)

Chekhov had read Kurkin's book. He had been a student of Erisman (whom he much admired) at Moscow University when the latter's research was being conducted. And, as a factory sanitary inspector himself, Chekhov had been active in giving effect to the improvements by the *zemstva* that Kurkin was describing. It is inconceivable that, knowing these 'utterances', acting professionally on them, and as a writer who was always punctilious about accuracy in medical details, Chekhov should have intended Trofimov's speech to be taken at face value. Critics (from at least Middleton Murry on) are right to point to the rhetorical emptiness in Trofimov's vision of change; but wrong to assume that Chekhov therefore sided with the 'immutable', the 'unanswerable' and the 'infliction of pain as processes . . . inevitable, natural and beautiful'!

In this section I have focused on academic institutions and their regimes of high-cultural value. In particular I have looked at relatively new theoret-ical work in literary criticism that challenges high-cultural 'expert know-ledgeability' and its liberal-humanist normative frames. This I see as a parallel to the discussion of Wynne's critique of scientific knowledgeability in Chapter 2. Consequently, I have discussed new historicism as an approach which reaches for Wynne's 'alien voices', here underlying the official discourse of historical texts. Like the new historicists, my own account of Chekhov is based on a parallel reading of theatrical texts and non-literary co-texts of the same historical period. So, for example, elsewhere (Tulloch, 1981) I have used as co-texts the evolutionist psychiatrist Merzheyevskii's 1887 lecture to the Medico-Psychological Association in Moscow on 'degeneration' within the Russian intelligentsia and Chekhov's text *Ivanov*; and also as co-texts the scientist Il'ya Metchnikov's lecture at the Moscow

International Medical Congress in 1897 and Chekhov's own description of 'sterile and fragile flowers' in *The Cherry Orchard*.

However, there are also two important difference between the 'new historical' analysis I am suggesting here and the new historicists' own approach which bear directly on my analysis of 'performativity' in this book. First, my account of Chekhov is more situated in his daily work activities, and the rhetorical relationship between his 'voices' as doctor and writer on the one hand, and the various and different 'utterances' of modernity on the other. Chekhov was educated at Moscow University within a new, symbiotic version of Social Darwinism, was active as a *zemstvo* doctor, went to the lectures of Merzheyevskii and Metchnikov, read Kurkin's book, and engaged in regular 'border crossings' between these everyday 'ordinary' routines and more formal 'aesthetic' performance events. Indeed, his struggle with 'modernist' forms was precisely to shift what he saw as the 'expressive competence' of one discourse (medical) into another (literary/theatrical) – thus his well-known letter agonising over the fact that he 'knew' the condition of his main character in *Ivanov*, but was unable to convey it satisfactorily to his audience and critics.

New historicists do *not* claim a situated and contextual relationship between text and co-text of this kind. Indeed, many new historicists adopt a poststructuralist radical scepticism about the possibility of establishing 'sure' knowledge. Instead, drawing on a post-Foucauldian position, new historicists have addressed the multiplicity of discourses operating at societal level – as found embedded in colonial, penal, medical and other co-texts – which positioned Renaissance culture at the beginning of modernity. As Wilson and Dutton describe this approach:

> Read within this archival continuum, what [Renaissance texts] represented was not harmony but the violence of the Puritan attack on carnival, the imposition of slavery, the rise of patriarchy, the hounding of deviance, and the crashing of the prison gates during what Foucault called 'the Age of Confinement, at the dawn of the carceral society.' 'My subject', Foucault told the Californian professors, 'is our subjection: how we turned ourselves into the objects of our own social science, our prisons, asylums and hospitals, and of our own conscience'. (Wilson and Dutton, 1992: 8)

Chekhov was a positivist by training, who looked at all of these things – people as the objects of social science, prisons, asylums, hospitals – and was undoubtedly part of Foucault's surveillant modernity. And one of the major weaknesses of my own account is the need for analysis that looks at his own multiple identities in relation to these differently situated narratives, as well as to his own terminally ill body (see Popkin, forthcoming).

Nevertheless, it is also important that we get beyond new historicism's *Foucauldian* sense of performativity; since this is the performativity of 'subject-effect' which (with Threadgold) I criticized in Judith Butler in the Introduction. Chekhov's grand narrative of science was very specifically situated in the vernacular. Like his medical colleagues, he believed in an holistic psychiatry that did not surveillantly incarcerate, but looked to an out-of-asylum positioning and understanding of 'neurasthenics' as agents (like Ivanov) not as 'others'. It was this aspect of a *zemstvo* psychiatry which a surprised British medical profession described in *The Lancet* (after the Moscow International Medical Congress of 1897) as leading the world. Nor was Chekhov's environmentalism contained by what Lash, Szerszynski and Wynne describe as the 'environment-as-technology coalition' (1996: 6), but based on the more humanity-focused, culturally-differentiated and locally-agentive response to environmental risk that Wynne and his colleagues call for. And like the Renaissance texts described by new historicists, Chekhov's texts did speak with the 'other voices' – of peasants as much as of the gentry.

The second difference between this kind of account and new historicism is evident in the *processual* agency that Williams points to, for example in his discussion of the relationship between new theatre forms (Chekhov), new theatre institutions (Stanislavski), and new theatre audiences (progressive sections of the Russian upper-middle class (Williams, 1991: 124). One of the constraining frames which even the more innovative (historically and materially based) literary theories have themselves placed around their field is lack of the institutional/processual analysis needed to examine high culture as 'expert system' *in its actual practice of the everyday* – whether of artists or audiences. This failure to take up Ien Ang's 'ethnography as storytelling' has not been the result only of new historicists' focus on the Renaissance past. As the Director of the Shakespeare Institute at Stratford-upon-Avon, Peter Holland, has said:

> The [new] theoretical work is not actually concerned with Jacobean theatrical performance, and it is certainly not concerned with modern theatrical perform-ance. Most of the theory people that I know do not go to the theatre. . . . The text exists as a reading text and not as a performance text. (Holland, 1994, personal interview)

By and large this is as true of cultural materialism (despite its valuable discussion of institutions of high culture like the RSC) as of new historicism. However, not all cultural materialists work on the academic page. In the next section I will turn to two other semiotic institutions of high culture – the theatre and BBC television – where a *practitioner* cultural materialist found those 'alien voices' in Chekhov. As John B. Thompson has said in his own critique of Foucault, 'it would be quite misleading to focus our attention exclusively on activities of surveillance while neglecting the new forms of publicness created by the media' (1995: 134). Thompson notes that this crucially '*mediated*' aspect of modernity depends not on a Panoptican rendering of many people visible to the few, but of a few appearing before many. It was precisely this historically contingent, mediated aspect of modernity which led dramatist Trevor Griffiths from theatre to television, and thus to my final case study of this chapter.

Theatre and television sites: high-cultural re-framing from academic page to public stage

One of the customarily noted values of cultural materialist analysis of Shakespeare is its contemporary political engagement. Like new historicism, cultural materialism refuses to privilege the literary text above non-literary co-texts. But whereas new historicism finds these co-texts in the past, cultural materialism finds them in the present: in speeches in Parliament that use Shakespeare to justify the Falklands War; in newspaper attacks on a primary teacher who takes a feminist line on *Romeo and Juliet*; in RSC programmes and advertising; in the design of the English syllabus (in Australia as much as England) to privilege Shakespeare for 'brighter' students; in contemporary film and television versions of *Henry V*, *Richard II*, *Romeo and Juliet*, and so on.

In that sense cultural materialism engages with these current co-texts, and often appears more agentive – and optimistic – than new historicism. In a foundational cultural materialist text, *Political Shakespeare*, Dollimore and Sinfield quote Marx that 'men and women make their own history but not in conditions of their own choosing' (1994: 3), going on to say that whereas new historicists tend to focus on the 'not of their own choosing' ideological structures, cultural materialists concentrate more on the agency of people in engaging with history. Sinfield, for example, argues that 'Shakespeare does not have to work in a conservative manner. . . . It is partly a matter of reading [the plays] differently – drawing attention to their historical insertion, their political implications, and the activity of criticism in reproducing them' (Dollimore and Sinfield, 1994: 161).

In this section I will look at a cultural materialist performance which did 'read differently'. I will look at Trevor Griffiths' 1977 Nottingham Playhouse stage version of *The Cherry Orchard* and his 1981 BBC television intervention *as* a cultural materialist, focusing on the dialogic process of 'border crossings' (from academic co-texts through theatre to television production).

Griffiths' co-texts: relating academic and theatrical utterances

It was Raymond Williams, as one of its foundational theorists, who coined the name 'cultural materialism'. And Raymond Williams's late-1960s academic writings on Chekhov were important co-texts in relation to Griffiths' own 1978 version of *The Cherry Orchard*.

In an important sense, Williams's concept of 'structure of feeling' (which he developed between his editions of *Drama from Ibsen to Eliot* and *Drama from Ibsen to Brecht*) did some of the same important 'power/resistance' work as Foucault's concept of 'discourse' that is so central in new historicism. For Williams, structures of feeling are 'lived and felt' values, and frequently evident in 'semantic figures which, in art and literature, are often among the very first indications that such a new structure is forming'

(Williams, 1977: 133). 'Structure of feeling' does work at the level of mundane daily experience as 'a set of local wisdoms and folklore about a local place' (Taylor et al., 1996: 32); hence Taylor, Evans and Fraser make Williams's concept the foundation of their analysis of the many different 'mental maps' people (according to age, class gender, sexual preference and ethnicity) have of the cities of Manchester and Sheffield in the postindustrial 1990s. But Williams's emphasis on semantic figures and form in structures of feeling also mark this as an *aesthetic* kind of 'resistance', which he distinguishes from what he calls the 'more formal concepts of "world view" or "ideology"' (Williams, 1977: 132) with which it is in tension. Consequently, it is a concept which leaves space for high-cultural authorship as a practical (rather than articulated or 'official') consciousness (Williams, 1977: 130–1). This is the sense that Williams emphasizes when he talks about the socially and historically specifiable agency of a text's making as 'an unease, a stress, a displacement, a latency: the moment of conscious comparison not yet come' (Williams, 1977: 130).

In Williams's account, for example, Chekhov's plays were a worked-at but fragmented (and far from 'organic') relationship between existing naturalistic conventions and a new Russian structure of feeling. Unlike Ibsen's isolated and compromised (heroic) individual in deadlock with 'society', Chekhov's 'crucial emotion is that of the group'. His developing polyphonic form was 'attempting to dramatize a stagnant group, in which a modern consciousness has turned inward and become, if not wholly inarticulate, at least unconnecting' (Williams, 1993: 108). Not finding in naturalistic action a form for this drama of interiority and inaction, Chekhov's modernist Naturalism 'attempted to develop a new kind of dialogue which, paradoxically, would express disintegration without weakening the sense of common condition' (Williams, 1993: 109). Williams believes that Chekhov was only intermittently successful, failing sometimes because of an 'imprecise' symbolism, at others through an idiosyncratic caricaturing. But in Act 2 of *The Cherry Orchard* – 'which as a theme for voices, a condition, and an atmosphere created by hesitation, implication, unconnected confession, is more complete and powerful than anything else Chekhov wrote' (Williams, 1993: 109) – a new form of modernist theatre was invented. Thus here, and to some extent in *The Three Sisters*, Chekhov, in Williams's view, began that connection between the inner emotional state and the wider social history which traditional naturalist conventions could not reveal.

Trevor Griffiths has emphasized that he worked with Williams's 'notion of the inaccessible, the hidden, the unknown, the unexplained – *the need for somebody to fill in the silences and ellipses of the text*' (my italics). Griffiths followed Williams in especially emphasizing Act 2 of *The Cherry Orchard* (hence Williams's, Griffiths' and my own 'new historical' accounts of this Act 2 make an interesting comparison as narratives of modernity).

The opening of the second Act is the least naturalistic of anything in Chekhov. . . . It's like expressionism, the interior being turned outside, the subtext bursting through the text and becoming the text and the text getting washed away. . . . You frame the play as a naturalist play with Act 1, but Act 2 bursts out of that for 2 or 3 pages, and then when it seems to recover its naturalist impulse, I would keep elements of that first three pages going through it – the vagrant [for instance] is an incredible disjuncture. (Griffiths, personal interview)

Griffiths' text: The Cherry Orchard

In his own 'Chekhov' text (a new translation with Helen Rappaport), Griffiths constructed in the first few pages of Act 2 a Chekhov in the image of Williams's account, a Chekhov whose modernist Naturalism was continuous with – and precursor to – later versions of modernism (like Expressionism). But Griffiths then turned Williams's Chekhovian 'silences' into *historical* utterances in three ways. First, Griffiths transformed Williams via a series of what he sees as alienating strategies and devices, such as the taped Russian voice of Charlotta at the beginning of Act 2 – which he describes as his 'modest Brechtian input to the piece'. Charlotta became, for Griffiths, 'a character edging towards Kafka, edging towards statelessness, edging towards . . . "Who am I? How can I define an identity, a self identity, without a state, without values, without history?" ' Together with the other class-disconnected characters at the beginning of Act 2, Griffiths' Charlotta acts as 'a kind of objective lampooning of the class they serve'.

Secondly, the Rappaport/Griffiths translation of *The Cherry Orchard* restored lines to the revolutionary student Trofimov which Chekhov self-censored. Trofimov has consistently been constructed in the West as the 'eternal student', and this has been a significant part of conventional humanist-melancholic, non-agentive readings of Chekhov – as, for example, in Middleton Murry's 'inevitability' reading. However, as Griffiths empha-sized when working with his actors at rehearsals, Trofimov was an eternal student because his exam results were withheld for political reasons. In his English version, Griffiths *uttered* Chekhov's silence, with 'I'm still a student. If the authorities have their way, I suspect I'll always be one.'

Mick Ford, who played Trofimov in the Eyre/Griffiths production of *The Cherry Orchard* at the Nottingham Playhouse (1977), emphasized that these re-articulated lines were central to the success of his own performance.

The most important thing to me of the production . . . was that Trofimov . . . was an eternal student . . . because he was not *allowed* to go on . . . which to me made a big difference, just in terms of how you come on and do it. . . . [W]hat I find so often when I watch Chekhov is that actors . . . make the characters slightly ridiculous, or try and get the audience to like them in some way. And what happens usually . . . is that by the time you get to the end you can't get the audience back to treat you seriously. And the moments that hurt or that give the real insight get lost. So in Trofimov's case, that idea that he was being *held* back, and then being left behind slightly as the world was changing, was important. He was someone who I felt would be, by the time of the Revolution, . . . sunk and no longer needed, like all of them in that place, outside of Lopakhin. . . . Those are the moments that allow you as an actor to have a bit of weight. That's what I remember of the production. . . . People knew what they were doing. (Ford, 1993, personal interview by Tom Burvill)

Thirdly, in Act 2, Trofimov's lines to Anya about her family's exploitation of the serfs (written in Griffiths' version as 'From every tree in your orchard there are people hanging') are inscribed as part of a subtext, linking together Charlotta and the other servants at the beginning of the Act, Firs's comments about giving up his freedom (after the Emancipation of the Serfs) and the 'explosion on to the stage' of the vagrant. For Griffiths,

> that word 'freedom' has now been unleashed in this text, and it resonates throughout the play. . . . The heart of the scene for me is the arrival of the stranger. . . . Nobody from that underclass has ever appeared . . . in Chekhov's kind of drama. . . . Released by the French Revolution a hundred years previously and still wandering, still looking for social justice, equality, fraternity. And, clearly, failing to find it here. But, in an odd way, by putting this person into the set and presenting that person with such extraordinary menace . . . [Chekhov] menaces and metamorphoses at one and the same time the property loss that is facing them as a problem . . . and destabilizes any notion the audience might have had of a settled world, *their* settled world. Even if you see it satirically and critically and comically, as Chekhov invites us to do, I think this moment really says there is a great unavoidable black hole underneath our world, and very soon we will disappear into it and become a pellet of energy for a new world. (Griffiths, 1993, personal interview)

In addition to Trofimov, Lopakhin is read in Griffiths' version as a second – and alternative – agent of change. Performed by Bill Patterson in the 1981 BBC TV version as one of Thatcher's new Tories sweeping away the old and effete Tory landed gentry elite in an intra-class struggle, Lopakhin also needed to be performed, in Griffiths' view, as a more fragmented and ambivalent future-oriented character.

> In Act 4 Lopakhin begins to talk about the poppy fields in bloom. Now, there's two things going on here. He talks about the poppy field and he talks about how much it's worth. And in *my* version of that play both things have got to be very strong; both the natural, organic dimension of a poppy field, and the accountancy. At Nottingham, Dave Hill got that on the stage, though he leaned towards the natural dimension of the poppy field. Bill never got anywhere near that. He always had a calculator in his pocket. He was clicking up what it was worth. (Griffths, 1993, personal interview)

For Trevor Griffiths, Lopakhin and Trofimov, as agents of change, *energize* the subtextual narrative and contextualize in different ways Act 2's 'breaking string'. This famous 'symbolic' moment in Chekhov's play is thus, in Griffiths's performance of the text, far from being Williams's 'inert symbol', but rather a signifier of discontinuity with the past: of rupture, dislocation, a 'cable groaning under stress'. In Act 2, Chekhov, in Griffiths' version, is working 'below the text, rather than arching above it in monumental, statuesque symbolism. There's so much that is alive and pulsing below the line that it's almost unplayable' (Griffiths, 1995, personal interview).

Trevor Griffiths is very aware in this version both of his debt and his *performativity* in relation to Raymond Williams's 'Chekhov'. It is in this Act 2 subtext that Griffiths (like Williams) finds Chekhov's new modernist form.

But while the two narrative agents providing the energy of change are Lopakhin and Trofimov, it is in his peasants and the underclass that Griffiths finds Chekhov's 'alien voices'. The narrative conjuncture of the stranger (wearing in Griffiths' text a First World War greatcoat) and Trofimov's speech about 'people hanging from the trees' allows Chekhov's peasants – who (as Griffiths emphasizes) populate his stories but, for reasons of stage conventions and theatre audience ideologies, are absent from his plays – to explode on to the stage.

> I saw a production . . . in New York . . . in which, as [the vagrant] begins his speech, these peasants come on to the stage and peer at you through the foliage, the back stage. And so you've got these post-realist peasant presences. I think they're there in the [Chekhov] text, within the realist mode. They're there, and I think that they have been put there, very concretely and specifically by the traveller, by . . . that image of an underclass. (Griffiths, 1995, personal interview)

Griffiths' cultural materialist 'rediscovery' of Chekhov is actually *in the different readerships and interpretative communities for Chekhov's plays and short stories in his own historical time*, then re-released – performed, juxtaposed, put into conjuncture – on contemporary television, in Thatcher's Britain with its own increasing army of street-people.

> Chekhov's peasant stories are amazing, but they don't reach the stage in the 1880s, 1890s and 1900s . . . or are there only coded. . . . He knew so much that never got anywhere near the stage. . . . So with the peasants [in *The Cherry Orchard*] . . . I think I was rediscovering Chekhov. (Griffiths, 1995, personal interview)

For Griffiths it was Chekhov's coded release of details from his peasant stories which defined his new form. It was *this* subtext of the inaccessible and the unexplained 'alien voices', the hidden peasants, and their silence on the Russian stage which for Griffiths articulated the profoundly alienating action of Act 2.

Cultural materialist academics were later to adopt a similar underclass function in their readings of Shakespeare: Jonathan Dollimore's discussion of the prostitutes in *Measure For Measure*, for instance, and Terry Eagleton's analysis of the witches in *Macbeth*. But Griffiths was, at the time, relating back to Raymond Williams, reconnecting the latter's dialogue of disintegration with socially, historically and generically contextualized stage performance – with human *action* which in Williams's reading of Chekhov had disappeared into group silence and gesture.

Trevor Griffiths' intervention as a playwright 'rediscovering' Chekhov was cultural materialist in at least three ways. First, his emphasis was on the agency of men and women in making their own history. Trofimov was rescued from being the psychologically hopeless 'eternal student', and placed in an historically situated state structure which he actively resisted. Likewise, Lopakhin was rescued from being the familiar western real estate agent, and became an historically positioned maker of environmental change. Further, in addition to the sense of Lopakhin as active worker and transformer of the land 'then' (1903/4), Griffiths was also emphasizing the contemporaneity of Lopakhin 'now' (1981).

Secondly, Griffiths (like cultural materialist theorists in their criticism of new historicists' poststructuralist scepticism about the 'real') is not a relativist. In his collaboration with Ken Loach on the film *Fatherland*, Griffiths, for example, had substantially changed the ironic and reflexive 'polyphony of variations' of Milan Kundera's novel *The Book of Laughter and Forgetting* which was the text Loach had originally brought to him as a starting point for the film. Griffiths had found Kundera's Bakhtin-style 'laughter of variation' too 'terminal', and had constructed instead a screenplay with a 'hard affirmation of the future' (see Tulloch, 1990: 153–5). Similarly, with both his 'canonical' transformations for television – D.H. Lawrence's *Sons and Lovers*, and Chekhov's *The Cherry Orchard* – Griffiths performed (in a Raymond Williams/Lukàcian sense) the 'underlying real' via what he called a 'materialism of forces', rather than the more descriptive naturalism of a 'materialism of detail'. His 'alien voices' subtext was central to this in his 'rediscovery' of Chekhov.

Thirdly, Griffiths' 'co-texts' are always, in part, in the present (as with the 'Thatcherite' reading of Lopakhin). For his television series about Robert Falcon Scott in the Antarctic, a co-text was a Tory Minister's speech in Parliament linking 'Scott of the Antarctic' to the recent British military intervention in the Falkland Islands. But another co-text was documentary footage of soldiers dying in Flanders during the First World War. This was the ultimate example, in Griffiths' view, of the disintegrating, masculinist, British imperial quest for death and glory emblematized just a few years before by Scott; just as the same First World War greatcoat on his vagrant in *The Cherry Orchard* represented that key vehicle of exploitation and revolt – the Russian soldier – which made the underclass agentive as revolutionaries.

In his historical pieces, Griffiths generally juxtaposes co-texts of both 'then' and 'now' (as in the case of Lopakhin) as part of his performance as dramatist: history is seen as a relevant part of the Enlightenment project, the stirring of freedom from 'the French Revolution to the days of Thatcher'. Moreover, Griffiths' versions and forms of Chekhov change according to historical change – from the 'dog days of the Callaghan Labour government' at the time of the Nottingham Playhouse *Cherry Orchard* to the television version in the early days of Thatcher. By early 1990s Griffiths was saying that were he to do Chekhov again, his form would change again given the devaluing of 'mass' television in the days of satellite and cable.

Griffiths and the commodification of high culture

Most of what I have looked at so far is Griffiths' cultural materialism on the written page, and his translation of this into the rehearsal process. To explore the process and performance of high culture on BBC television or as theatre event we would need to take more space than I have here to examine what

Thompson calls the 'mediated visibility' so symptomatic of modernity. However, central to this account would be John Frow's point about the absorption of high culture within commodity production.

As this Chekhov play by writer Trevor Griffiths and producer Richard Eyre 'border crossed' from theatre to television, familiar 'globalized' features of television as a mass commodity medium intervened. First, the **television-naturalism** emphasis of the BBC set designer gave Act 2 'a lot of depth' (despite the producer telling her that 'he certainly didn't want anything naturalistic at all'). Naturalistic depth was exactly what Griffiths did not want either. As he explained, his preference (in terms of an Act 2 'alienation' effect) was to have the kind of 'flat' staging achieved at the Nottingham production.

> In the theatre it didn't pretend that it had more space than it had, except in a very cardboard way . . . a very strange, almost painted tree for example, rather than what we have here [in the television production], which was dried plants brought into the studio and potted and rooted and covered with shale and elephant grass and things like that. (Griffiths, 1995, personal interview)

Griffiths' whole point in Chekhov's 'crucial' Act 2 was for the *mise-en-scène* to challenge the naturalism of the 'country-house nostalgia' of Acts 1 and 4; and he felt that this was lost in the television production.

Secondly, Griffiths worried about the '**star charisma**' that the famous Judi Dench imported to the television version, replacing the much less well-known actors of the theatre performance.

> Richard imported a whole set of actors into the production who are substars or stars. And some of the old English [class] sense of Chekhov I think is reimported when you get a Judi Dench . . . playing Ranevskaya. Because she has such weight as an actress she necessarily pulls my play, or the structure of that play, out of kilter. The weight of Ranevskaya as against the relative weight of Trofimov and Lopakhin, that's really what I'm talking about. (Griffiths, 1995, personal interview)

Thirdly, there was the television **scheduling** of the production. Griffiths had wanted his generic 'country-house' pairing of *The Cherry Orchard* and his own play *Country* to be scheduled in direct opposition to the huge ratings success of *Brideshead Revisited*. These two Griffiths plays were thus to be an ironic parody of the high-rating, canonical country-house genre. But ratings-conscious television channels do not normally schedule in terms of this kind of 'ludic excess' (Coleman and Eisner, 1998), and Griffiths complains that his political/generic challenge – scheduled separately from *Brideshead* – was totally lost in the wash of adulation accompanying that popular television series.

However, as Hughes-Freeland emphasizes, it would be a mistake to assume that mass media *only* globalize, fix and reify performativity in a world of simulacra. To speak of the 'commodifying' of Griffiths' version of *The Cherry Orchard* according to the standardizing tendencies of television is to ignore, as Hirsch would argue, the local and the contextually situated aspect of television practices. Two brief examples must suffice to make my point; and both involve the intertextual performance of another high-cultural form – paintings – in this production. They offer, also, examples of Frow's point about the mediation of 'class' modernist forms by a broadly-defined 'intelligentsia'.

The first example relates to the lighting of *The Cherry Orchard*. Both then (in 1981) and now this production was regarded as important for its camera and lighting. It was one of the earliest BBC productions to use new portable cameras and to light each shot separately, as for film. To achieve his 'very subtle . . . light, yet . . . no light' effect in Act 1 (just prior to the opening of the shutters when the family look out of their house to the cherry orchard), lighting director Howard King was looking for a visual concept. It is quite common in 'art' television to draw on classical paintings for concepts – Griffiths, for example, complained that his earlier television version of *Sons and Lovers* had been reduced from a political intervention to 'art house' television by beginning each week's episode with a painting. In this case, also, King looked to a painting.

> I was impressed by a painting by Josef Israel in Amsterdam. . . . There was a subtlety about it. . . . I looked at this painting and I thought it somehow or other gives you a sense of . . . being in a cube of light. In other words, light all around you. There's no particular direction. It's just a sensation. It's very difficult to describe in words, but I thought that's what I would like to do – because I'd read *The Cherry Orchard* by then. I was thinking about this room and I thought it must be possible to do. . . . The painting was two people, a person down stage and a four-poster bed, looking at someone who had just died, and a window up stage. But I think what actually impressed me . . . was the fact that the floor . . . was right. So often . . . when you look at television lighting . . . people . . . are all obsessed with vertical surfaces – in other words, faces and things like that; but not with the horizontal surfaces, like tops of tables, tops of settees . . . and floor. . . . Yet we have light coming down . . . and it all accumulates on the floor eventually, with multiplicity of shadows.

This was Howard King at work, drawing on his daily routines, competences and practices to perform the lighting for *The Cherry Orchard* via a high-cultural intertext. However, his 'cube of light' effect, as our audience research indicated, could help establish the opposite meaning from the one that Griffiths and Eyre intended. One audience group read the lighting in Act 1 as follows.

> They had such realistic lighting when they were all inside the house and looking out the windows, and there was that bright sunlight. And it seemed so kind of inviting. You could see why they were valuing the orchard. And then they go out [in Act 2] . . . and it seemed so unnatural . . . to have this whole gentry setting in the middle of the desert. . . . It just didn't fit. I was expecting much more of a lush setting to go with the people and see what they're giving up. (Columbia University audience group)

Consequently, this audience group read Act 2 not as a politically alienating effect, as Griffiths wanted, but as a 'jarring transition' which they rejected. King's lighting thus helped them to reinforce the canonical, liberal-humanist 'empathy and compassion' with the landowners.

The second example of the intertextual use of a painting was planned to have quite the opposite effect. This was producer Richard Eyre's use of John Berger's television analysis of the Gainsborough painting 'Mr and Mrs Andrews' for his staging of the gentry sitting on *their* bench in *their* landscape in Act 2. 'It wasn't long before that that John [Berger] did his "Ways of Seeing" and I remember him talking about that painting. So I think his whole idea of [painting] landscape as property was very much in my mind'. This use of a painting for selection of props, set design and actors' blocking in Act 2 – unlike the King example – worked *with* Griffiths' 'old way of owning, experiencing and possessing land' (1995, personal interview) reading of the play, since Berger emphasized Gainsborough's celebration of class, and of the gentry *ownership* of all they survey. Here Griffiths and Eyre were seeking to deny not only Chekhov's play, but theatre itself, their status as ' "extension" of cultural property' (Kruger, 1993: 56). The degree to which these local intertextual 'utterances' were negotiated by actual audiences will be looked at later.

Conclusion

In this and the previous chapters I have moved from the analysis of performance in daily routine to formal performance within the semiotic institutions of high culture. In particular I have argued for a new emphasis within cultural studies on high-cultural framing and performance, especially as high culture's definition of modernism and modernity has ongoing rhetorical effects in a wide range of important semiotic institutions. I have examined here a few of these, focusing on the kinds of transformative performing of the 'canonical' and 'liturgical' that have recently been occurring within the academic, theatrical and televisual frames of high culture. In each I have asked questions about the *kinds* of performativity that are in place in these different semiotic institutions, in relation to the definitions and discussions of performance at the beginning of the book. Above all I am arguing – polemically, as Raymond Williams did – for a new performativity of cultural studies itself in relation to the sites of high culture. That way, 'neglected works' (in the sense of their own history and our own history) may, as Williams said, be 'imagined again'.

5

CULTURAL READING

> The third generation [of reception studies] resumes an interest in the programmes and programming, but not as texts studied in isolation from their usage as an element of everyday life. Furthermore, it adds a neglected layer of reflexivity to the research on the 'reception' of media messages by addressing the audiences' notions of themselves as the 'audience'. (Alasuutari, 1999)

The notion of performing culture implies an audience that receives the performance. As Judith Butler says, the 'effects of performatives, understood as discursive production, do not conclude at the terminus of a given statement or utterance. . . . They continue to signify in spite of their authors, and sometimes against their authors' most precious intentions' (Butler, 1993: 240–1). In a different, anthropological approach, Brown argues that a 'key dynamic in performance theory . . . is the audience's conceptualization of the relationship between performer, performance and the context of which it is a part' (Brown, 1998: 162). And Hughes-Freeland emphasizes the similarity of spectatorship whether in everyday interactions or in globalized and other formal performances: 'If the degrees of technological intervention differ between media events and live ones, this is not an intervention which negates the agency of the viewers or audiences' (Hughes-Freeland, 1996: 10).

'Audience' has been a constant preoccupation of most of the 'expert' archives I have investigated in this book: the 'lost audience' of our Australian film/cultural studies readings (Chapter 1), the 'at risk' public that AIDS policy makers are trying to reach (Chapter 2), the RSC marketers' 57,000 potential subscribers (Chapter 3), the 'alien' and 'hidden' voices of new historicism and cultural materialism (Chapter 4). Theories of audience and reading are therefore one focus through which we can begin to tie together the various themes of the book: of the 'positioned truths' of cultural theory; of cultural policy and its 'lost' (or 'everyday') voices; of the commoditizing of high culture; of cultural framing and 'ordinary utterances'.

What, then, is my own 'mandated' interpretative schema in the area of 'cultural reading'? Ang, as we have seen, describes a range of audience 'theories' – uses and gratifications, resistance, interpretative community etc – as a series of representational orders via which the academic as 'expert' confers upon the reader provisional closures of order and coherence in an 'otherwise chaotic' world. Here I am positioning the book in relation to what is currently being described as cultural studies' 'third generation' audience theory (Alasuutari, 1999). This theoretical trend in media studies is an attempt to restitch 1970s notions of encoded texts and their inscribed readers with 1980s ethnographically-oriented 'active audience' theory. Often the 'second generation' work of 'going to the audience' examined popular cultural fandom (for example, Hobson, 1982; Ang, 1985; Radway, 1984; Penley, 1991; Bacon-Smith, 1992; Jenkins, 1992), and this same 'fan' orientation has been carried over to 'third generation' studies that deal with texts in the context of production ethnographies as well as 'active audiences' (Tulloch and Jenkins, 1995).

Current 'third generation' theory starts from a focus on **'audiencing'**, that is the point of Grossberg and others that an audience, far from being a facticity 'out there', is in fact a discursive construct located within multiple interpretative frames. On the one hand, coming from 'active audience' theory and the ethnography of daily life, 'audiencing' theory asks about the frames via which we *constitute* ourselves as audiences among our other daily practices. An example of research from this perspective in relation to formal performance was based on my spending a day with four people from country New South Wales, whom I was interested in because they were prepared to drive as much as seven hours to and seven hours back from the Belvoir Street Theatre in Sydney as regular Saturday evening subscribers.

- Why did they constitute themselves as regular subscribers at such a distance from home?
- Given that they did make that decision, why did they choose this particular theatre rather than the more fashionable harbour-side sites of the Opera House or Wharf Theatre?
- Given that they chose this theatre and not those ones, how did their horizon of expectations associated with this theatre give them specific expectations as to how Chekhov's *The Seagull* would be designed, set and played in this particular theatrical space?
- What would the relationship be between the Artistic Director's familiar idiolect (described by one reviewer as Neil Armfield's 'sustained experiment with old chairs and an empty Belvoir space') and this expectation?
- How would this audience group read the city-Australian reflexivity of Belvoir Street theatre via their own country-Australian position, especially given that *The Seagull* is set in the country, and that this is in part reflected in Nina's 'squatter's daughter' costumes in Act 1 of the production?
- Given the profiled stage/audience intimacy of this theatre, how would they relate that woman on stage, Nina, with the 'strong women' they could see in the same eyeline sitting in the audience, and with whom they identified as subscribers?

By spending the day with this audience group, interviewing them pre-, during and after the performance, the relationship between their constituting themselves as an audience for this particular theatre and their 'reading' of *The Seagull* could be examined. The emphasis here was very much Hirsch's performance emphasis on analysing globalized commodities (in this case internationally popular canonical theatre) as *locally* situated practice.

On the other hand, returning to the notion of the encoded production and text, third-generation 'audiencing' research examines the 'frames or discourses about . . . audiences inscribed in the programmes [or performances] themselves' (Alasuutari, 1999: 12). This is often a matter of cultural framing and policy – as we saw, for example, in Trevor Griffiths' attempt to release 'hidden voices' from their suppression on Chekhov's contemporary stage on to our television screens.

In my choice of theoretical narrative, I am supporting here also W.B. Worthen's holistic approach to performance theory, where he situates 'readings' as one among a number of formations which give us access as spectators to the text. Criticizing conventional high-cultural theatre-performance theory, Worthen argues that to 'displace the enervating polarisation of "criticism against performance" (the subtext, so to speak, of the "text against performance" controversy)', the first move is in recognizing 'that our access to the text is always through its performance, a performance continually taking place offstage – as reading, education, advertising, criticism, and so on – before any stage performance is conceived' (Worthen, 1989: 455) In other words, Worthen is encouraging a performance theory which embraces the reading formations, frames of discourse and everyday working practice within and through which a text is 'accessed' to a public; and this includes advertising, publicity, academic criticism and reviewing as much as it does directorial interpretation and actors' embodiment. The important emphasis here is Worthen's point about performance *continually* taking place – both offstage and onstage; and in this chapter I want to look at examples of the process of 'reading' formal performance in both these areas.

Offstage performance 1: marketing high culture

We start here from John Frow's observation that high culture 'is now fully absorbed within commodity production' (1993: 208); but also from the point that I was beginning to develop in Chapter 4 that this absorption always occurs in situated and local ways, so that it is important to take account of specific institutional values of practice. I also want to develop this point about commodity production past where I left it in the Trevor Griffiths example in Chapter 4. There Griffiths' talk about the 'success' of the theatre version of his *Cherry Orchard* and his significant 'worries' about the television version risks slippage into the high/popular-cultural distinction that Frow warns us about – where it is the high-cultural theatre that 'gets it right', and popular culture which degrades the author's text. In fact, as Frow would predict, high culture is commoditized even in the theatre, even at the Royal Shakespeare Company; and I want in this section to discuss how high culture and commoditization are *performed together* offstage in Britain's most prestigious high-cultural institution, the Royal Shakespeare Company.

In designing the advance brochures for the RSC Stratford's 1995–96 season, the marketing officer, Sian Sterling, 'came up with a summing-up paragraph' for Adrian Noble's *The Cherry Orchard* (which I touched on in Chapter 3). This was 'about the historical reference . . . that this was the point just before Russia went into Revolution. . . . So it was very much to do with the family being in turmoil, but it was also to do with the country being in turmoil' (Sterling, 1996, personal interview).

In fact, the circulation of meanings around modernity and history in the 1995–96 RSC *The Cherry Orchard* began with discussions between director Adrian Noble and the RSC marketing office which led to the first, pre-performance images and utterances in leaflets sent world-wide to the 57,000 RSC mailing-list members. Here a marketing officer in Stratford, a director who at that stage had few ideas as to which direction his production would take, and an artist working in New York combined to create pre-rehearsal publicity which juxtaposed the marketing officer's copy about 'masses of white blossom' faced by 'axes . . . ready to swing through the cherry orchards of Russia' on one page, with a painter's image of 'these trees which you weren't sure whether they were dying or dead' (Sterling, 1996, personal interview) on the adjoining page of the brochure.

A particular reading of history and place was being performed for the RSC's future audiences through the marketing office here: of beauty and nostalgia that must inevitably die in the face of the brute facticity of a history that had 'already happened'. But this was a sense of history and context which arguably was already consonant with an expected audience's horizon of expectations. Alan Sinfield has written extensively about the RSC and its location of 'culturalism' within the shifting politics of welfare capitalism and then Thatcherism between the 1960s and 1990s. In particular Sinfield focuses on the 'confusion about its audiences and roles' of the RSC as 'a liberal, consensual institution in a society which was polarising' from at least the 1970s (Dollimore and Sinfield, 1994: 196). But for Sinfield three things have been constant throughout these uncertainties at the RSC: (1) 'the assumption that human nature is always the same' so that 'the plays can be presented as direct sources of wisdom'; (2) the continuing nihilism of successive artistic directors of the RSC where 'in effect [Peter] Brook's anguished Modernist disdain for history, politics and material reality approximated to [Peter] Hall's despondent argument that nothing can be done because we are animals and unable to live up to the Elizabethan World Picture'; and (3) a 'feeling its way' by the RSC towards the greatly expanded postwar youthful, left-liberal, 'culturalist' intelligentsia without losing its more conservative 'over 45' audience. As Sinfield says, this attempt to appeal to different audiences 'no doubt accounts for much of the vagueness of stance of the RSC' (Dollimore and Sinfield, 1994: 182–203) and its tendency, under these pressures, to succumb to the formula: 'The implacable roller of history crushes everybody and everything' (Dollimore and Sinfield, 1994: 185). The similarity with Adrian Noble's 'sinking Titanic' *Cherry Orchard* at the RSC could hardly be closer.

So, long-term RSC audience dispositions were re-written for *The Cherry Orchard* as advertising discourse, which itself drew in half-remembered ways on other 'offstage' co-texts. Sian Sterling told us, there 'was a bit of baggage left over from O-Level education', and she was also conscious that *The Cherry Orchard* was likely to have 'a huge audience among schools . . . because it's an A-Level text and GCSE text' (Sterling, 1996, personal interview). At the same time, perceived audience dispositions were positioned historically, post-Soviet Union, *post-closure* of that 'axes . . . ready to swing' (Revolutionary) event supposedly predicted by *The Cherry Orchard*. Already, as the first brochures were being circulated, the programme cover was being designed, with its toppling red sickle 'C' for 'Cherry Orchard'.

Later – by the time that the first brochure's initial words and images had been translated into 'phenomenal uptake . . . an absolutely amazing hit' (Sterling, 1996, personal interview) in terms of box office pre-booking sales to RSC mailing-list members – rehearsals had taken place and production ideas had developed. Consequently, RSC images and utterances around Noble's *The Cherry Orchard* had 'significantly changed, so that the original image produced so early on may no longer be as relevant' (Sterling, 1996, personal interview). For the next (and first public) brochure, new star images (of 'two magnificent actors recruited for this production, Penelope Wilton and Alec McCowen') were used, while the director's idea of 'doing a photograph outside a stately home that looked slightly Russian with everybody dressed in the relevant clothing' was discarded because 'it wasn't economical to do it . . . just because the production was selling so well' (Sterling, 1996, personal interview).

Like other subsidized companies, the RSC post-Thatcher is forced to think commercially, adding to its 'company idea' what Sir Peter Hall has called 'short-termism and . . . one-off, TV-dominated casting' (*Guardian Weekly*, 11 August 1996: 27). Thus a photograph of Jennifer Ehle, star of the international TV hit, *Pride and Prejudice*, heads *The Painter of Dishonour* pages in the same RSC brochure; thus a photograph of television sitcom star Josie Lawrence in her *Taming of the Shrew* lead role (Lawrence played Dunyasha in Noble's *The Cherry Orchard*) dominates the cover of the RSC's London brochure; and thus the 'star' images of Wilton and McCowen now anchored this stage of the advertising of *The Cherry Orchard*.

But in this first public brochure, the star imagery does not float free of the earlier 'doomed class' critical history of the pre-sales brochure. The marketing officer's copy still has 'generations of Russian people living on the brink of tremendous social upheaval'. Wilton is shown full-page, in close-up, unsmiling, eyes ringed with care, the beauty and elegance threatened. McCowen is shown sitting on one end of his bench, not (as in the John Berger 'Mr and Mrs Andrews' intertext) as *owner* of this land, but alone, marginalized and – like Wilton – against an empty black backcloth that seems to emphasize their lack of lifeworld context.

Later still, as the 1996–97 RSC London season was being prepared, a third brochure for *The Cherry Orchard* was sent out by the marketing office.

For this London brochure, the play was signified by a production photograph of the 'company from the original Stratford production'. The production image chosen was of the 'breaking cable' moment of performance in Act 2. Thus, again, a conventional embodied 'history' of Chekhov was imaged. For the production's movement designer Sue Lefton, her work with the actors at this particular 'breaking cable' moment was her major contribution to the Act.

> Very close to my heart was the . . . incredibly important . . . moment when the string breaks in the mine. . . . It somehow says something deep down, about premonition of the Revolution. I did some work with the actors so that they would be hit in the middle of their *breath*, so that when they heard the noise they wouldn't just hear it with their ears, but they'd hear it like a creature, like an animal full of fear. It is a straightening, it's a kind of [gasp of the breath] moment, rather than what the actors might have chosen to do, which was to beat it a little less and just look around which would make it more of an intellectual thing. I thought it should go right through the body, a real animal fear. . . . That can be found through the *body* unintellectually. Very often you can have that transformer moment, just finding the breath of fear. (Lefton, 1996, personal interview)

The London RSC brochure, announcing the play's 'Transferring to the West End in Autumn 1996', chose this 'transformer moment . . . breath of fear' premonition of the Russian Revolution as its image to attract an audience. Box office transferring (from Stratford to London) and historical transforming (from aristocratic to revolutionary Russia) were thus merged and blended in a familiar mix of high-cultural and commoditized activity. The 'financial ruin [that] looms' for the Ranevsky family was juxtaposed with the 'sell out' financial success of the production at Stratford. So the 'sell-out success when it played in the Swan Theatre last year' was used to encourage further box office success in London – clearly a tighter hold on enterprise reality than Madame Ranevskaya's!

It is clear that invoking *both* cultural *and* material capital is central to the RSC theatre marketing project: the London brochure quoted the *Financial Times* that this was the 'finest RSC production for several seasons' (clearly a major high-cultural claim in the RSC's own brochure) and 'a sell-out success'. It was within this particular and conjoint marketing context that, six months into the Stratford performance of *The Cherry Orchard*, the RSC marketing office promoted further images and ideas of Chekhov via an onstage 'In Conversation' interview at the Swan Theatre (just prior to the penultimate evening performance of the play at Stratford) between director Adrian Noble and Cambridge University theatre academic Peter Holland.

As a materialist theatre academic himself, a strong advocate of Griffiths' *The Cherry Orchard* (and indeed of my own reading of Lopakhin), this was a key moment (for one particular audience) when critical theory entered the performance for an audience, as I will describe in the next section. But mainly this interview was part of a new marketing exercise by the RSC.

> It always surprised me that as a text-based company we actually never talked publicly in any sort of forum or workshop of the work that we do on classic

texts. . . . Our new 'In Conversation' events . . . were . . . therefore trying to find
ways in which the audience can take part in the way we work with texts. . . . I
thought there was probably a market for people, adults, who have a good
knowledge of Shakespeare or a new play or whatever . . . to engage in some sort
of communication with the creator of that production. . . . I don't believe the
marketing department is just about selling tickets. Sure that's one of our
functions. But I do believe that we're also there to communicate and relate better
. . . with our audience at different levels. It's a relationship as opposed to just
somebody coming in and buying a ticket. (Sterling, 1996, personal interview)

So the RSC marketing office was interpellating its own 'active audience'
('the audience can take part in the way we work with texts'). But, of course,
Sterling and the RSC were in the comfortable position that the ticket sales
had been 'phenomenal from the start' of pre-bookings with RSC mailing-list
members, so that it was virtually impossible to just 'come in and buy a
ticket' anyway. Once this material exchange had taken place, it was the
audience's cultural capital that RSC marketing was especially interested
in.

The marketing orientation of the RSC is symptomatically high cultural:
Sterling's references are to classic texts, to audiences that 'have a good
knowledge of Shakespeare or a new play', to school students who can be
encouraged 'to return as adults' to the RSC via 'different levels' of educational event, to 'communicating with creators', and to other high-cultural
institutions like 'the National, the Royal Court and lots of other Arts
organizations in England' who are also establishing 'a relationship as
opposed to just somebody coming in and buying a ticket' (Sterling, 1996,
personal interview).

The implication is that this kind of 'just buying a ticket' commodity
audience can be left to 'popular culture'; and even the RSC's major
commercial sponsor, Allied Domecq, is profiled in the theatre programmes
as enabling the RSC to undertake 'an enhanced education programme'.
The relationship between Allied Domecq (distributors of Teachers and
Ballantine's Scotch Whisky, Beefeater's Gin, Courvoisier Cognac, Kahlua
Coffee Liqueur and Tia Maria) and the RSC is signified as a symbiotic one:
of 'international reputation', 'quality' and expanding 'client' service. Notices
hanging over the entrance to the auditorium of the Royal Shakespeare
Theatre announce: 'This innovative partnership links Allied Domecq's
world class portfolio of brandy with world class classical theatre whilst
taking the RSC to a wider international audience.'

So the 'relationship' that Sian Sterling is referring to is with sets of
'quality' competencies and the propensities of a world-wide high-cultural
leisure habitus (we should remember here those priority pre-sale brochures
sent nationally and internationally to 55,000 mailing-list members as potential audience). Within the field of cultural production, the marketing and
education departments of the RSC are characteristic agents in Bourdieu's
sense, maintaining the aesthetic disposition (emphasizing the creative form
rather than the substance of the theatre), and exchanging symbolic capital as

an entry fee to a high-cultural habitus in return for young people's future box office fee.

In this conjoint cultural/economic marketing context, where an aesthetic disposition is the stake, it may well be a useful professional performance to fetishize the substance of the play in terms of a liturgical ('inevitable') history: 'The axes are ready to swing through the cherry orchards of Russia . . .'. The 'active' high-cultural audience thus 'knows' the content (the inevitable march of history: from 1903 to 1917 to 1996), and is then invited to the RSC 'In Conversation' events to revisit its form. That is one of the contexts in which we can understand Adrian Noble's interview comment to Peter Holland that:

> It seemed to me that there's a way to the heart of Chekhov that isn't the realistic or naturalistic way in. . . . It's very abstract actually, what we eventually came up with and indeed the way it's played. (Adrian Noble, 1996, public interview by Peter Holland)

Further, in the context of this high-cultural promotional exercise, the choice of Peter Holland to interview Adrian Noble was a precise one on the part of the marketing office. He was both a governor of the RSC and at that time a senior academic at Cambridge University 'who was very well thought of on that whole period' (Sterling, 1996, personal interview), so he had cultural prestige (soon after, indeed, Holland was to become Director of the Shakespeare Institute at Stratford).

Offstage performance 2: the academic institution

Worthen points to marketing, education and criticism as key areas of offstage performance 'before any onstage performance is conceived'. One important area of this is the relationship of 'expert' academic criticism to embodied stage performance, which normally takes place in isolation from the theatre – in the classroom, newspaper reviews, journal articles etc. However, in the case of Adrian Noble's *The Cherry Orchard*, one such typically 'offstage performance' took place *onstage* as a result of RSC marketing strategies. This 'In Conversation' discussion between academic Peter Holland and director Adrian Noble became not only a part of the RSC constituting its audience (it was put on immediately before a performance of the play, and was watched by a paying audience, as well as by some of the actors), but also a public dialogic exchange *between* 'offstage' and 'onstage' performers.

To repeat Ien Ang's caution, a poststructuralist 'ethnography of storytelling' needs to be reflexively aware of its own closures, its own 'representational order'. The 'positioned truths' that we establish in our stories will depend significantly on the questions we ask – whether we ask them of our 'texts' (like Shakespeare and Chekhov in Chapters 3 and 4) or of our 'respondents' (in qualitative research like that with the building workers in Chapter 2). One of the significant absences, for example, in my analysis in Chapter 3 was the same kind of reflexivity about the *academics'/ interviewers'* questions that I displayed in the analysis of the Heterosexual Men's Campaign in Chapter 2. What, in other words, was the particular conjuncture of two kinds of 'expert knowledgeability' as the Cambridge academic Peter Holland interviewed the RSC Artistic Director Adrian Noble in front of a paying audience on the stage of the Swan Theatre? The interview was, after all, not only embedded as part of the new high-cultural marketing strategy of the RSC; it was also *my research access* to Noble's stories about the production, in a public negotiation in which Chekhov's 'history' was made overtly dialogic – a dialogue that depended on the 'reading formations' of the two participants involved.

Bill Worthen has argued that:

> Theatrical production writes the drama into stage practice. Performance criticism should reveal the affiliations between this writing and the very different acts of inscription that make the theatre readable. To understand the drama, we need to understand all the ways that we make it perform. (Worthen, 1989: 455)

One fundamental way that we, as researchers, 'make it perform' is through our methodologies and theories of criticism. In the case of Sylvia Lawson (Chapter 1), 'going to the audience' meant trying to retrieve its 'lost voices' through traces revealed in the silent films that remain. But the 'In Conversation' interview between Holland and Noble allowed us not only to go to the 'actual audience' for Chekhov (sitting in the theatre waiting for the evening's performance), but also to embody *onstage* that affiliation that Worthen seeks between the 'writing' of theatrical production and the 'writing' of theatre criticism. I want to refer briefly to this interview here to illustrate the relationship of my theory (as 'positioned truth') to 'offstage performance' and audiences.

Holland, like his former Cambridge colleague Raymond Williams, was broadly working within a cultural materialist framework, distinguishing as he asked his interview questions the naturalism which Chekhov disliked in Stanislavski's frogs, trains and corncrakes, from a real history of social movements, theatre conventions and intertexts in the play. Like the dramatist Trevor Griffiths, whose work on Chekhov he admires, Holland (again like Raymond Williams) was adopting the Lukàcian distinction between 'materialism of detail' (empiricist naturalism) and 'materialism of forces' ('deep structural' realism). Holland's choice of 'Chekhov' quotations in preparation for his interview with Noble was closely related to this cultural materialist agenda, especially in:

- his comparing of the English audience's 'National Trust' reading of the play with the centrality of Lopakhin as an 'environmentally' positive character, close in his 'summer cottages' scheme to Chekhov himself;
- his querying of Noble's articulation of 'history' and 'class' for audiences (through the programme) but not for actors (in rehearsal);
- his questioning Noble's choice of the Stanislavskian Method, thus

probing the director's hesitation between personal and socio-historical determination of agency; and,

- his questioning of stage naturalism, which led Noble to negotiate (via a different reading formation) the staging of Chekhov's 'poetry' and his history-as-modernity.

There is little space here to develop this argument (see Tulloch and Burvill, 1999). But a small sample will I hope illustrate the way in which this kind of reflexivity (since Holland was in an important sense *standing in* – both bodily and epistemologically – for me as interviewer in this public performance) can respond to Ang's call for revealing the politics of 'what kind of representational order we . . . establish'.

> *P.H.:* You say that Chekhov is writing the play for a particular company . . . but it is also a company with which he had a terrible time and a great deal of tension. All the arguments whether *The Cherry Orchard* is a comedy or a tragedy begin with Chekhov saying it's a comedy and Stanislavski saying you're wrong. . . . And indeed the same thing was going on with performance style. Famously, Stanislavski loved littering any production with sound, and Chekhov writes this letter to Stanislavski . . . 'Haymaking usually takes place between 20 and 25th of June at which time I think the corncrake no longer cries. And frogs also are silent at this time of year. If you can show a train without any noise, without a single sound, then carry on. I haven't anything against a single set for Acts 3 and 4 as long as the entrances and exits are convenient.' And I think it's very striking that Chekhov's concern is about convenience, not about 'realism'.
>
> *A.N.:* That's right, yes. I mean, we were very keen not to create a set of rooms, not just because of the nature of this theatre but also because it seemed to me that there is a way to the heart of Chekhov that isn't the realistic or naturalistic way in. . . . It's very abstract, actually, what we eventually came up with and indeed the way it's played. In terms of what you just read out I would be of Chekhov's camp. He had this great skill to offer to an audience just a *few* objects or a *few* effects or images that, like a drip in water . . . will reverberate through the play. So the trains were, to me, terribly important, the thing of arriving, travelling – 'oh, the old master used to go by coach, now they travel by train' – they arrive back on the train, and they leave on the train. Most of the great and usually tragic moments in twentieth-century European history involve trains. I've always found that a rather frightening matter.

Holland's continuing critique here (via Chekhov's letter to Stanislavski) was against stage naturalism. However, because of his use of the phrase 'about convenience, not about "realism"', and especially because this was introduced via Chekhov's comment about combining sets for Acts 3 and 4, Noble was able to say that he too cut down on the sets in *The Cherry Orchard* in order to get to the 'heart of Chekhov', which is an 'abstract' rather than 'realistic or naturalistic way in'. For Holland, an uncluttered Chekhov set meant stripping away the sensory sights and sounds with which Stanislavski 'littered' it in order to see 'that resistance of the real' (see Holland, 1982: 241). An uncluttered Chekhov set for Noble was 'to really

allow the poetic qualities of the language and the play to blossom un-
hindered'.

Despite the slippage between Holland's and Noble's utterances of the
'real', the 'trains' reference makes their differences especially clear. For
Holland, 'train noises' represented to Chekhov the 'clutter' of surface naturalism, and so he didn't want them. For Noble, his use of the train sound, on an
'uncluttered' stage at the Swan, represented a central way of tying his
performance in to what he called the 'mighty tides' of history 'running
underneath the play that you can't show very often, you have to know
they're there'. What *could* be shown, in Noble's view, are the 'secret grief or
joy' – those conventionally 'Chekhovian' inner states of being – to which
the particular stage of the Swan Theatre is supposedly 'sympathetic'.

In this particular piece of analysis, I am examining interview talk
(including academic talk) as contextually situated narrative, that is as 'text'
mobilized within interpretative communities – and so I need to make it clear
from my *privileging* of the intertexts of Holland, Griffiths and Worthen in
the analysis that my own interpretative 'bid' is from within a specific
materialist/poststructuralist reading formation. In that sense, the choice of
the Holland/Noble interview as the dialogic site for this research was at one
and the same time agentive (privileging our own reading formation),
reflexive (foregrounding the critic/theatre relationship), and pragmatic (as
my only opportunity of 'going to' Adrian Noble). My political strategy was
thus no different from the general tendency within cultural studies in engaging
critically with high-cultural discourse. The difference was in trying to reveal
high-cultural discourse as text/performance/audience *event*, since my view
was that much postmodernist writing about 'slippage' and 'bricolage'
(between high and popular cultural forms) either effaces these processes or,
worse, contents itself with celebration of the forms it describes.

Rather than reading these interview narratives and stories as the prior,
unitary and originating 'truths' of self-consciousness, I am examining them
as local, context-bound utterances through which different voices, subjectivities and modalities of utterance were performed and negotiated. Thus
in an extended analysis I would also emphasize Noble's own multiple
subjectivity:

- as **Artistic Director** of the RSC (highly aware of the commercial
  implications of playing Chekhov in the Swan Theatre);
- as **director** of *The Cherry Orchard* 'authentically' deferring (as he said
  in interview) to a Stanislavskian improvisatory method 'quite contrary to
  my own style';
- as director of Chekhov **in the Swan Theatre**, with the implications of an
  'honest sharing' of 'a secret grief or joy' in an 'intimate' theatre space
  that contrasted in definition of both 'character' and 'history/modernity'
  with Griffiths' more Brechtian imaging of the underclass;
- as dialogic **negotiator of pre-performance marketing promotion**;
- and as **programme negotiator** (with the programme compiler), so that

the audience who read it were exposed to the 'serious research' about the results of the Emancipation of the Serfs that the actors never received in rehearsal.

At the same time, I have not accepted that Noble's production simply represented a fragmented set of identities. His 'performances' – via the rhetorics of marketing, writing, staging, lighting, acting, directing and so on – reconstructed a liberal-humanist problematic within the shared mental representations of dominant theatrical cultures. And there was an homologous relationship between this dominant culture and that of theatre reviewers who (within their own high-cultural forms) reproduce 'expert' discourse. I was not surprised, in other words, that this was the most *critically* acclaimed 'Chekhov' on the British stage in years.

Onstage performance 1: acting Lopakhin

How can 'ethnography of storytelling' and 'third-generation' cultural studies attempts to synthesize production, textual and reading theory engage with recent critiques of the objectivism and lack of reflexivity in traditional ethnographic theory, as well as the rejection of the 'metaphysics of presence' in postmodernist theory. In particular, research which is based on interviews (where producers, writers, actors, or audience members construct narratives about meaning) is subject to the dual critique that talk (including interview talk) is contextually situated and as such 'text'; and that interview narratives (where taken as 'evidence') are subject to the postmodern critique of a prior, unitary and originating self-consciousness which is dependent for its 'truth' on 'lived experience'.

In fact my own position, while accepting the notion of a decentred subject, is not radically postmodern. My view is that speaking subjects are indeed composed of movements of difference, resistances and negotiations between multiple identities (so that the subject rather than being originating is 'territorialized by discourse'). But it is also important to examine the *shared* mental and cultural frames of speaking and performing subjects as members of professional groups, subcultures, theatrical organizations, university reading formations (as in Holland's case and my own), fandoms and other interpretative communities. In particular, I will suggest in this and the next chapter that humanist notions of subjectivity, embedded in the commercial as well as intellectual practices of state-funded theatre, still underpin the 'multiple subjectivities' and 'territories of discourse' which flow through the various stages of high-cultural theatre performance – as far as the audience.

'Going to the theatre' (or to the advertising agency that designs an HIV/ AIDS campaign, or to the Sydney builders' labourers, or to the Chekhov audience) becomes a way of engaging critically and dialogically with these mental and cultural representations, rather than reading them simply from within our own reading formation. We learn here more about the 'mandated schemas' surrounding the research – for example those of the researchers, the advertising company, and the State government that I drew attention to in discussing the 'Heterosexual Men's Campaign' in Chapter 2. This parallels Alasuutari's emphasis that 'the task of the emerging third generation cultural audience studies is to study different phenomena related to contemporary media cultures empirically, and in such a way that the researchers are not blinded by their own fears and concerns' (Alasuutari, 1999). The point of this approach, says Michael Pickering (in a book I agree with substantially), is 'not to use an ethnography of experience as "the authenticating test of cultural analysis", but instead to explore the methodological possibility of "being surprised" by the ethnographic evidence, and so moving to "knowledge not prefigured in one's starting paradigm" (Hall, 1989: 62; Willis, 1980: 90)' (Pickering, 1997: 200).

More specifically, 'going to the theatre' to observe and interview actors, directors, marketers and others is to undertake the kind of *questioning* of performance discourse that Worthen encourages. This is to examine performance

> as both an interpretative and a signifying practice, articulating a dialogic relationship between the text and the *mise-en-scène*, and between the *mise-en-scène* and the audience. How does acting reproduce a text? How does the actors' training enable them to conceive the text as *telling* them to *do* anything in particular? . . . A similar line of questioning might, of course, be trained on directors, designers, and so on. (Worthen, 1989: 447)

As Worthen says, all of these different kinds of stage 'performance' – acting, directing, designing (and importantly he extends 'performance' to marketing and criticism) – require

> a highly formalised body of activities: techniques for training and preparation; conventions of acting and staging style; habits of audience disposition, behaviour, and interpretation. Richly diverse and historically localised, these practices articulate the text as 'acting' within the wider range of signifying behaviour specific to a given theatre and culture. (1989: 447)

It is to get access to these framing practices of articulation *as* 'high culture' – to the formalized techniques, conventions and dispositions (in the moment when they become enabling devices for 'performers' to 'conceive the text as *telling* them to *do* anything in particular') – that we 'go to the theatre'. It is here that we can begin to probe the 'difference' of formal performance.

Where in the range of signifying behaviour, where in the 'map' of our theatrical event, we choose to *locate* our theoretical focus is both an analytical and pragmatic question. Access to working performers, whether in theatre or television or advertising, can be a chancy business, and we may have to take what we can get (see, for example, Moeran's discussion of his failure to get access to advertising sales campaign and marketing talk, resulting in a more limited textualist account: Moeran, 1996: 78). An advantage of re-focusing on high culture is that here issues of 'culture' are so centrally articulated, framed and negotiated across Moeran's full gamut of campaign, marketing, process and text.

But the moment of the process that we choose to study also has theoretical implications. In the RSC's theatrical event around Chekhov, we might wish to examine:

- the marketing of high-cultural competence and framing (drawing on Bourdieu);
- methodological reflexivity within the ethnography of 'offstage' and 'onstage' performance (Bakhtin's 'dialogic');
- rehearsals (via a critical ethnography);
- the reading formations and interpretative communities of academic and newspaper reviewers (drawing on Carlson, Bennett, Frow, Fish; but also using content analysis and quantitative methods);
- 'active audiences' (Morley, Ang, Radway etc).

The specific methodologies we use will be determined by our choice of theoretical focus; but my suggestion is that to take on 'third generation' audience analysis we need to be open-minded without being simply eclectic.

The problem here is that even the more innovative approaches to high-cultural reading of performance texts (within theatre studies, Marvin Carlson, for example) have tended to provide *simply* a map of discrete 'moments' of reading (programmes, newspaper reviews, etc) and a simple description of method. There has been little attempt to analyse the framing and reading moments *as* process, and thus provide the kind of 'third generation' synthesis of 'formal' and 'everyday life' performance/audience theory that we have been looking for in this book. Given the space restrictions of this chapter, I will focus on just one 'onstage performance' moment of production to begin to sketch out how this analysis of the 'audiencing' process might occur: an actors' reading of a character in rehearsal. The character is *The Cherry Orchard*'s Lopakhin, and the performance moment is David Troughton's physical response to other characters' dismissal of his 'land fit for giants' lines in Act 2.

Lopakhin 'in the text'

As Peter Holland emphasized in his questions to Adrian Noble, Chekhov described Lopakhin as the central character in the play which, if Lopakhin was not played well, would be 'a flop'. Holland also knew and supported my own analysis, emphasizing the centrality of Lopakhin in *The Cherry Orchard*, saying to me after the interview with Noble 'I did my best for you with those Lopakhin questions' – so in a very direct sense there was an engagement here between Holland's, my own and Noble's reading of the play. My focus in this section is the *actor's* construction of the part of Lopakhin *within* the sequence of theatrical performances that I have been describing.

I have chosen to focus on Lopakhin in particular because in my view this character represents one of high-cultural performance's more successful

elisions of issues of class history, modernity and sociocultural change. At the same time, this radical elision of 'ideological' interpretation has conventionally led to a fetishization of the aesthetic (the beauty of the cherry orchard) as 'pleasure'.

Because of the timing of Chekhov's play (1903/4, just before the first revolutionary outbreak in Russia in 1905), and because of the representation of the revolutionary student Trofimov in the play, 'history' in the interpretation of *The Cherry Orchard* has been overdetermined (via publicity, programmes, directors etc) *by* the revolution and its aftermath (thus: Noble's Stratford programme cover in 1995, soon after the break-up of the Soviet Union, with its falling red sickle). Little account has been taken of the fact that Lopakhin's 'environmental' vision of new classes working the land more productively than the defunct cherry orchard (and its gentry owners) was close to Chekhov's own evolutionist values, stemming from his education as a doctor at Moscow University.

Chekhov's 'being' as a doctor (in the sense of Rostas's contrast of the 'being' and 'becoming' of performativity: see Introduction) is often recognized by interpreters on page and stage. It was, for example, drawn on a number of times during Noble's rehearsals to explain 'why does Ranevskaya not take her pills?', even 'why does Chekhov start Act 1 in the early morning?' But this 'doctor' is customarily removed from his particular situated history of Russian *zemstvo* medicine, and hence universalized and fetishized as 'objective', 'scientific', etc. In this objectivist (*and* humanist) reading, the man of clinical precision replaces the man dedicated to social agency and environmental change.

The Lopakhin most visible in public performances of *The Cherry Orchard* in the West has been brutalized by his serf father as a child. The text tells us that his wounds were often tended by Liubov Ranevskaya, the owner of the estate, and that he loves his mistress beyond all else. Yet, he has become a rich businessman who (when Ranevskaya ignores his advice to save her family from debt by subdividing and selling the cherry orchard to the new 'summer villa' class) buys the estate himself.

Lopakhin's actor must perform one of the only two characters in the play whose discourse is about action and social change: the other is the revolutionary Trofimov (the tutor to Ranevskaya's now dead son, who, like Lopakhin, is emotionally dependent on her). Because of this tension between the backward-looking personal attachment to the attractive female representative of the old order and their future-oriented (but alternative) discourses relating to social change, Trofimov and Lopakhin have conventionally been represented as 'sociologically' determined in their resolution of this personal/ social dilemma. Consequently, Ang's noted separation between 'ideological' instrumentalism and aesthetic 'pleasure' in cultural studies' audience theory has – in theatre productions in the West – been conventionally framed as between characters in the play, between Lopakhin/Trofimov on the one hand, and the gentry group who want to save the beautiful cherry orchard, on the other.

While Trofimov has conventionally been depoliticized as the 'eternal student', Lopakhin has been represented as either the brash capitalist who sweeps away the old order by converting its fragile beauty (the cherry orchard) into real estate, or as the businessman despite himself, who is forced by the class ineptitude of those he loves (and by his own serf anger) to betray them. In the case of actors performing both Trofimov and Lopakhin, then, the characters' discourse about social change (Trofimov's revolution, and Lopakhin's love of the environment, based on Chekhov's own evolutionist grand narrative) tends to be effaced or reified within a simple, personal socialization. Trofimov as a 'typical' student talks a lot about the future but is idle. Lopakhin may love the cherry orchard people, but when the chips are down (especially when he is drunk after buying the cherry orchard in Act 3) his serf/business ruthlessness shows.

Issues of modernity's agency trapped into an emotional dependence on structure (that is the old order represented by the cherry orchard) seem foundational in these readings. Within cultural studies, of course, notions of structure and agency have been under severe poststructuralist review – especially in relation to grand narratives of modernity. Some theorists, however, have usefully revisited this issue of agency and structure within a poststructuralist framework (or even post-poststructuralist framework: see Barbara Adam and Stuart Allan, *Theorizing Culture*, 1995). For example, Bronwyn Davies argues that a feminist, poststructuralist agency would not be part of the masculinist, elitist and humanist definition of a unitary identity based on 'the choices of the rational self'. As she points out, the humanist notion of rational agency controlling the irrational is closely allied with the boundaries it has constructed between the conscious and the unconscious, and between mind and body. But once 'the boundaries between conscious and unconscious thought are recognised as boundaries both constructed around and constitutive of a particular humanist vision of the person . . . then women's disregard for these boundaries becomes a strength to be tapped in the deconstruction of the dualisms that are constitutive features of modern discourse' (Davies, 1991: 45).

Agency is never, as Davies says, 'autonomy in the sense of being an individual standing outside social structure and process'. Rather, a post-structuralist agency would always be located dialogically in relation to dominant discourses 'in so far as it persuaded them to change themselves, to become more multiple, flexible and inclusive of different points of view'. Especially, this would mean liberating them from 'the burden of a rationality which controls, dominates and negates feeling, the concrete and the real in favour of the abstract' (Davies, 1991: 51). This latter would include also, of course, Ang's posing of 'pleasure' against the over-rationalized and instru-mentalized 'ideological' emphasis in reading the fictional text.

In an important sense, the canonical Lopakhin has been framed and performed across this binary of reason/feeling that Davies critiques. But in the end the ex-serf/male is generally read (by directors, reviewers, audiences etc) as prevailing; his emotional attachment to Ranevskaya is outflanked by deterministic 'sociological' events, and the aestheticism of the old order is destroyed. 'Pleasure' and instrumentalism are separated, and thus the aesthetic is celebrated in the face of a one-dimensional modernity.

Fundamental to this framing of 'Chekhov' are the foundational humanist notions of: (1) a distinction between rational thought and irrational aspects of the self (the distance between Lopakhin's summer cottage scheme and Ranevskaya/Gayev's 'irrationality' and emotionalism; or between Lopakhin's own environmental fantasies and his instrumental action); and (2) a continuity of individual identity arising from early socialization (Davies, 1991: 43): thus not only Ranevskaya but Lopakhin too are understood as continuous identities trapped in their early upbringing. The notion that Lopakhin's multiple subjectivities could lie in *alternative futures* that embody both pleasure and instrumental dedication to social change (as represented in his emotional relationship with Trofimov, who tells him he has 'an artist's hands') is generally not countenanced. Humanist critics would do well to take note here of Chekhov's own multiple subjectivities; as, struggling with his literary form even as he 'knows' (scientifically) how to represent his 'superfluous man', Ivanov, he rails against his own 'serf mentality'. But Chekhov (unlike the humanist's Lopakhin) worked *between* modernity (as both writer and doctor) and his brutalized socialization.

The failure to 'perform' Lopakhin as a 'decentred' identity occurs for various reasons in various high-cultural sites. For example, among newspaper reviewers (who, as content analysis of reviews of Noble's *Cherry Orchard* revealed, tended to focus on Lopakhin's 'drunken, stamping dance' Act-3 image rather than on his more 'aesthetic/environmentalist' lines) a humanist reading formation is strongly in place. Among actors in rehearsal – and *especially* actors playing Chekhov – a training in Stanislavskian naturalism is nearly always significant. All the actors we interviewed emphasized the importance of Stanislavskian exercises to Noble's structuring of rehearsals, and the director himself emphasized that he had drawn on Stanislavski in contrast to his usual directing style.

As Worthen says, actors tend not to occupy the familiar 'decentred' postmodern position of subjective fragmentation as they confront the duality of the 'past' traced in the text and the 'present' of their performance. The Stanislavskian sense of a 'single whole, coherent "character"' whose behaviour flows from a concrete past into a determined present' generally constructs a Lopakhin who, as Peter Holland said of the Noble production, is 'locked into the notion of the child; and Lopakhin is, for me, prevented [in this production] from adulthood. . . . You cannot conceive of Lopakhin as a positive, progressive character' (Holland, 1996, personal interview).

Despite all of the familiar 'ambivalent Lopakhin' performances and readings – between the brutalized son of a serf and the man who acquires sensitivity in the intimate milieu of the gentry class – fundamentally this is still the 'socialized' Lopakhin relating him to the past of the gentry (their aestheticism) or to the past of a serf class (their brutalism). The 'infantilizing process' which Holland critiques in Noble's production is fundamentally a humanist framing, in the sense that the adult 'character' has an identity understood as arising out of (and given coherence by) early socialization. There is little sense of a continuing fragmentation and contradictory subjectivity, based on the one hand on *future* investment in the agentive and material force of discourse, and on the other hand in a pleasure that expands beyond the gentry class so that all of Russia fulfils its resource potential in modernity as a 'land fit for giants'.

Lopakhin in Troughton's performance

In canonical theatre there are many 'quotable' lines which create audience pleasure. Newspaper reviewers told me, for example, that Masha's 'I'm in mourning for my life' line at the beginning of *The Seagull* is a pleasurable indicator for them of how the production will be played. Such lines are looked for in advance, and the play between the expected line and a new interpretation seems central to that pleasure.

Caliban's line in *The Tempest*, 'This isle is full of noises, sweet sounds . . .' is one such line. But Lopakhin's 'Russia has *vast* fields, *vast* forests, we should be giants living in a land like this' is **not** another 'looked for' line, even though there is a parallel tension in these *Tempest* and *Cherry Orchard* passages of the unexpected recognition and verbalization of beauty by a 'brute'.

Lopakhin's actor in the Noble production, David Troughton, had also played Caliban recently for the RSC at Stratford. But whereas his sense of the 'plausibility' of Caliban's 'sweet sounds' lines could draw on a post-colonial framing of *The Tempest* which has been widespread not only in academia but in the theatre too in recent years (Vaughan and Vaughan, 1991), Troughton's other 'brutalized' character, Lopakhin, could work off no similar recent 'critical' reading.

Yet, Troughton *felt* equal pleasure in delivering the Caliban and Lopakhin lines. Despite Noble's emphasis in rehearsals as director, Troughton *worked for* both the aesthetic pleasure and the ideological instrumentalism in performing Lopakhin.

> That's his dichotomy, his inner struggle, his inner [being]. I *feel* beauty, I can actually *feel* it. . . . I say 'at the moment they just like to sit on their verandahs, drinking tea, but I can see a time when they'll start cultivating their lives, and your cherry orchard will have made way for rich, prosperous, active lives'. . . . Now . . . that's not unlike . . . what Trofimov is talking about, helping each other. . . . But what I'm saying is that you give them the opportunity . . . by setting up these holiday villas. (Troughton, 1996, personal interview)

The 'sociological' Lopakhin is a still a significant part of his performance, however, and Troughton weaves into this framing his professional knowledge of the English stage.

> All Lopakhins have trouble, until. . . . the actor playing them realizes that he's not the same as anyone else on stage. You tend in rehearsals, because it's English,

and it's about aristocrats, to get into their rhythms, their manners . . . their 'Chekhovian' way of delivering, and it leads you up the wrong path, because Lopakhin, above all, is common, he's a peasant, he's a beaten child, and he loves one person only, and that's Liuba. . . . He's still a serf, and that's what drives through to the big speech in Act 3 when he's drunk. . . . Caliban drinks and then speaks the most beautiful language that possibly Shakespeare has ever written, the island speech. . . . But the two comics, when *they're* drunk, get greedy and stupid and power mad; and Shakespeare's saying something about drink, what it does to lower classes, and what it does to a so-called animal. So drink varies us, and that's why I decided to be as strong as that, as aggressive with Liuba, because again, the people you love you always go for in the end, and all the peasant upbringing comes out in that anger. . . . He doesn't want to but he just can't help it.

This performance of Lopakhin embodies his 'pleasure' (in Liuba) *in* his anger and 'socialization'. This is the Lopakhin whom the newspaper critics most noticed (as my content analysis revealed), clinging in Act 3 to the hem of Liuba Ranevskaya's skirt. Here the 'sociology' of Lopakhin ('his peasant upbringing') is one crucial component of his identity. 'He should be like an animal who's been suppressed on a lead and suddenly let loose. The drink does it' (Troughton, 1996, personal interview).

But, as we saw, there is Troughton's *other* 'pleasure' in Lopakhin – with his 'artist's hands' and his 'I *feel* beauty' in his poppy field and 'land fit for giants' lines. Troughton had to construct his part across this decentred subjectivity of the 'cultivating . . . active lives' Lopakhin (of Acts 2 and 4) on the one hand and the drunken Lopakhin of Act 3 on the other. Both were crucial to his reading of the part.

On stage, David Troughton (DT) as Lopakhin and Sean Murray (SM) as Trofimov wanted to emphasize a shared sense of emotional bonding around a future positivity that was against the grain of Noble's production. Consequently, they *inserted a visual exchange* to emphasize Lopakhin's 'land fit for giants' speech, and to carry this mutuality forward to the poppy field scene.

SM: When we were at that point in the outside scene when Lopakhin has said 'We ought to be giants living in a place like this' and then Ranevskaya says 'Giants. Who needs giants? They're always in fairytales' and they all laugh, David does this sort of hurt look, because they're laughing at him again. Something that was *heartfelt* has been turned into a joke. So he sort of looks down, and as he looks up again he just catches my eye and we're looking at each other for a moment. Then we both look away because there's an embarrassment of the recognition that . . . I have seen . . . a sensitivity . . . in Lopakhin. . . . So it's *recognized* at that point, and then later on there's a resonance of that same moment when we've embraced and again can't look at each other. . . . *What he feels and what he thinks*: when they don't go together it creates a big conflict in him and a confusion in him. (Murray, 1996, personal interview)

DT: I try and enter into the conversation they're having about death and life, and the irony of Trofimov going on about people talking too much when he has a four-page speech. Then I say 'but people in Russia, we've got all these resources, we've got the most fantastic country and yet we're lazy, we don't use it'. . . . Liuba takes the totally wrong end of it . . . 'giants, we don't want giants . . .', and that's the moment where Lopakhin's frustration comes through. . . . Well, Sean and I try and make a moment of it, and then later [in Act 4] I hug him and say 'goodbye, dear friend', and . . . that was the crossing point, 'poppy fields . . . do you want some money?' is the only way Lopakhin can reply . . . 'thank you'. But it completely backfires and from that point they diverge. (Troughton, 1996, personal interview)

By reading Troughton's Lopakhin via Worthen's notion of the 'decentred' postmodern acting position (Troughton's 1996 'I *feel* beauty'), and by emphasizing (to use Holland's words) Lopakhin as 'a positive, progressive character . . . [who] does . . . have a sense of a future' as well as an embedded socialization in the past, we can then take a number of useful directions in relation to Troughton's *process* of framing his part.

● We can examine the rehearsal moment when directors, writers and actors negotiate a formal performance within broader ideological and high-cultural frames (comparing, for instance, Hill's, Patterson's and Troughton's preparation of the part of Lopakhin in 1977, 1981 and 1995). For example, as a result of his close contact with Trevor Griffiths during his Nottingham Playhouse rehearsal, as well as his own recent experience of Eastern Europe, Dave Hill avoided Troughton's rehearsal difficulties. Hill's 'poppy field' words (relating to Lopakhin's earlier 'we should be giants living in a land like this' lines) were delivered as a combination of aesthetics and work, of pleasure and instrumentalism. '[They] were a wonderful combination of beauty, almost like it was a painting but also the feeling of getting your hands dirty at the same time, which I think is some sort of key to unlocking the man – that he has the ability to actually get down and dig . . . and plant the field himself. . . . The beauty of what you gain from life is enhanced by the fact that that's what *you've* done. (Hill, 1993, personal interview by Tom Burvill)
● We can conduct 'actual audience' research. So, for example, I interviewed and surveyed Stratford audience members to see how many noticed the Troughton/Murray (Lopakhin/Trofimov) eyeline in Act 2 of Noble's production, and to what degree it influenced their reading of Lopakhin. In this quantitative survey of RSC members only 20 per cent of respondents noticed this Lopakhin/Trofimov look; and, asked how they interpreted it, most of these read it fairly similarly to David Troughton. 'They had something in common. Each knew change had to come.' 'A brief understanding between the two of them. This was further developed in Act 4.' I also asked questions in the survey to compare audience responses to this moment of actor framing with responses to a major signifier of change framed by the director, the train noise with which Noble began the production. I should say that the train noise was not the conventional, naturalistic 'whistle and puffing steam' sound that would have been familiar to the audience from heritage television, but rather was a somewhat ominous sound that neither of the researchers watching the production initially identified *as*

a train sound. Yet 64 per cent of the audience said they noticed the train noise. Asked 'If you did notice it, what did it imply to you?', responses broke down between those who read it denotatively ('That Ranevskaya etc would be arriving shortly': 36 per cent) and those who read it symbolically ('The modern changing world was about to intrude and shatter their world'; 'Inevitability'; 'Arrival – Imminent happenings/changes': 52 per cent). Not surprisingly, perhaps, Adrian Noble's 'inevitable history' signification seems to have had a stronger impact on the RSC audience than David Troughton's 'two sensitive people of change' inflection; and this would have been further influenced by the newspaper reviews.

• I analysed newspaper reviews of the production and compared their reporting (following Marvin Carlson) of specific performance 'images': particularly the more 'aesthetic Lopakhin' images and the more *discursively* favoured 'frightening, stamping dance' drunken-serf Lopakhin at the end of Act 3. A content analysis of national and local newspaper reviews of Noble's *The Cherry Orchard* revealed that 18 per cent of *all* 'images' mentioned related to Lopakhin's 'drunken stamping dance'; 18 per cent related to the 'tilting/toppling' Titanic ball scene; 6 per cent to the 'entrapping' gauze box which came down on stage at the beginning of Act 1, accompanied by the train noise; and 6 per cent mentioned Lopakhin kissing Ranevskaya's hem. *None* mentioned any of the 'land fit for giants', 'poppy field' or other Lopakhin/Trofimov moments of 'pleasure' and 'feeling'.

My following analysis of Troughton's 'giants' performance framing of his eyeline moment with Murray situates itself in relation to these 'reading contexts' and also the audience analysis which concludes the chapter.

My methodology for this particular section is based on observing the performance itself four times (three at a six-month interval in Stratford, and once at the Albery Theatre in London), interviewing David Troughton, and also analysing images published of the performance (available to the audience as postcards and posters). In particular, a published postcard shows the 'eyeline match' moment. The following account is based primarily on the last of those watched performances (in London), the interview, and the Stratford postcard.

Developing the notion of the doubly 'habituated' agency of the theatre actor (Hastrup, 1998), it seemed to me that this moment of performance embodied a number of idiolects and 'expert' knowledges which Troughton brought to the role as a professional actor who was reaching (as he put it) 'towards lead status'.

• The sense of being recognized as a quality actor of comedy (Troughton once found a list of first-choice comic actors in the RSC Artistic Director's desk draw) linked to his received history of Stanislavskian 'misreadings': 'I like comedy and a lot of things I do make people laugh. . . . Obviously

Adrian saw in me something that he thought could be Lopakhinish, so it is a funny play, it's a comedy, Chekhov said it was a comedy, it's only Stanislavski who perpetuated this rumour of all this tragedy'. (Troughton, 1996, personal interview)

• Knowledge of other actors' difficulty with the part and their resolution of the problem: 'I've been speaking to other Lopakhins. . . . I had a terrible time rehearsing this. . . . I think I'm the only person [in this production] who did really have quite a difficult time. All Lopakhins have trouble, until . . . the actor playing them realizes that he's not the same as anyone else on stage. All Lopakhins I know had the same difficulty and came to it that late as well. Norman Rodway played it Irish, another actor played it Mancunian, and I played it Cornish. . . . So two days before the technical [rehearsal] I put the accent on, and immediately . . . it worked . . . suddenly I *found* Lopakhin. It came that late!' (Troughton, 1996, personal interview)

• Advice from Russian language experts: 'We had a Russian lady come in to tell us how to speak, how to say the Russian names, you know . . . "Lopaacheen", and you think "well I'm not going to say that, don't be silly", but . . . she also said that the Russian aristocrats speak in very old-worldly Russian and the only two modern Russian speakers in that play are Lopakhin and Trofimov which then sort of opens it out; you say "well, why not, I've got to be different, in England we understand that accents mean a different upbringing".' (Troughton, 1996, personal interview)

• Textual cues and an idiolectal convention to *embody* them: 'In Richard III, Shakespeare says he has a halt, he's got a hump, and he's got a withered arm, you can't get away from that; and similarly Lopakhin does something with his hands, for Trofimov to say "stop flapping your arms about". So technically you have to find something, and . . . why he does it. I decided that it's awkwardness within, not fitting into a situation. He is *able* to [fit in] because he's rich enough but it's his upbringing, he's still a serf. . . . I'm a physical being [as an actor]. I believe in the expression of the whole body in acting. I mean, my Richard [III] is the ultimate of that, but I must feel right . . . internally. I don't work on physical extremities first, I try and get it from here inside, but *then* unless I feel right physically, for me I'm not in the part.' (Troughton, 1996, personal interview)

• The intertextuality of performance of a 'repertory' actor playing Richard III in the main Stratford theatre at the same time: 'I'm not a [Stanislavskian] bacon-and-egg actor . . . thinking what [as a character] I had for breakfast. Especially with Shakespeare . . . what you say is what you think at the time you're saying it . . . you don't *have* to do a Russian pause. . . . It's wrong I think, it breaks rhythm, it slows it down and it makes the language dead. The enjoyment of Shakespeare is hearing someone think and speak at the same time . . . I don't like a lot of subtext.' (Troughton, 1996, personal interview)

• The narrative construction of Lopakhin as a doubly ambivalent character (based on his future vision and his past socialization).

A number of these knowledges and framings seem evident at the 'eyeline' moment of Lopakhin's shared intimacy with Trofimov in Act 2. The actor with a status for comedy who expresses it 'in a physical way that at the same time expresses his inner state of mind' plays this moment sitting immobile, bulging out of his (actor-chosen) over-tight suit like a sack of potatoes, his legs and arms fixed immobile to the ground. Only his head moves, to the left to look briefly at Trofimov, his expression uncertain and comically hangdog. The Shakespearean actor who prefers to 'think and speak at the same time' can totally forget his (Stanislavskian/serf) socialization at this moment. But the actor who rejects 'Chekhovian' pauses makes this a very brief eyeline exchange indeed, before he launches himself physically into his next (and completely changed) 'think and speak' lines. The actor who knows that a successfully performed Lopakhin must be unlike anyone else on stage will soon be making a macho (and solo) defence of Ranevskaya's group (*unlike* Trofimov) against the vagrant when the latter launches almost a physical assault on Varya.

Thus Lopakhin's 'embarrassment of recognition' exchange of looks with Trofimov in Act 2 is performed without lingering – as a momentarily humorous head and shoulders move that expresses his own inner social uncertainty. The exchange of looks is very easy to miss altogether as a communication with Trofimov, since the latter could be read as simply happening to be in the path of Lopakhin's bodily exaggerated, comic and frustrated head move.

By 'mapping' a particular Chekhov production, and then focusing on the acting of Lopakhin within it, bringing together these various theatrical performance 'moments' as a sequence of sequential frames, we can restore 'process' to our theories of communication and audience without either the empiricism of American 'effects' theory (which is where we last heard of 'process' theory in communication) or the 'unitary identity' humanism of high-cultural analysis.

By focusing on this process of framings as *readings* (from the first marketing brochures through to specific audience interpretations; from actors' construction of character identities to reviewers' and audiences') we can then begin to address Alasuutari's 'third generation' intention: where the 'ethnographic turn' of audience theory is reinvested in institutional and textual readings, but where texts are not 'studied in isolation from their usage as an element in everyday life.'

In this case, though, the everyday life that we 'go to' as researchers is not simply that of audiences (as dominated cultural studies in the 1980s) but includes the daily rhetorics of practice-as-performance of marketers, directors, actors, reviewers, academics, 'fan' audiences, and school audiences (in their own 'A-level' frames).

I turn, finally in this chapter, to 'active audience' case studies. These have been chosen as 'research object' deliberately, in so far as both are also the object of the commoditized high culture that John Frow reminds us of:

school A-level students, for example, were a particular 'target' of the RSC marketing and education offices.

Onstage performance 2: constituted audiences

Following Hughes-Freeland, I have been arguing that separated ('aesthetic') performative events like theatre, film and television are, like everyday 'ordinary' routines, 'systematised and collated within particular performative local contexts' (Hughes-Freeland, 1998: 22); and further, that a 'key dynamic in performance theory . . . is the audience's conceptualization of the relationship between performer, performance and the context of which it is a part' (Brown, 1998: 162). Nevertheless, if it is like 'ordinary' routines in being local and situated, I have also been agreeing with Carlson and others that formal performance is also different in having particularly institutionalized semiotic and embodied relationships 'on' and 'off' stage.

   In the local, situated and contextual sense, the live audience is an important part of onstage performance, and in this final section of the chapter I will discuss examples of the relationship between performer, performance and an audience's local context in two very different theatre 'geographies'. The first is the RSC, Stratford, which aimed its *The Cherry Orchard* strategically at the 'A-Level' school audience. This strategy was successful in terms of numbers, though Troughton hated playing to students taking notes in the front row. The second is the small Q-Theatre in Penrith, a town 60 kilometres west of Sydney, New South Wales, where again there was a determined and successful marketing of their canonical play (*A Midsummer Night's Dream*) to school students.

   My two analyses will have different emphases. In looking at the audience group of English 'A-Level' students' responses to Lopakhin and Trofimov, I will look at the cultural framing as 'audience' of a group of young people already commoditized by RSC marketing. As in the case of the building workers analysis of Chapter 2, in a longer account this would need to be both (a) a situated analysis (what was the students' reading formation? And how did this relate to their pleasures and interpretations of the Noble production?) and (b) reflexive (what were the roles of their teacher and the researcher in this interview 'text'?). In the case of the Q-Theatre's *A Midsummer Night's Dream*, as well as capturing 'bums on seats', Artistic Director Mary-Anne Gifford was aiming at 'performing gender differently'. In this case, I will look briefly at how both female director and female audience members were constituting themselves *as* audience. The relationship I describe is between the Shakespearean text as performed and significant readings of it by teenage schoolgirls in the audience. As we will see, while these two approaches (one based on commoditizing high-cultural rhetorical strategies, the other on the situated analysis of audience self-construction) are both necessary and compatible in a fuller analysis, they lead to different conceptual frames for 'further work'. I elaborate on these

audience case studies at greater length elsewhere; here there is only space
for a few summary findings, and no space at all for the kind of 'dialogic'
analysis I applied to the building workers earlier (see Tulloch, forthcoming).

The RSC's The Cherry Orchard, 1995/96

This first school audience study is part of my wider analysis of the
'audiencing' strategies of the Chekhov production by the RSC marketing
department. Certain key conceptual markers framed this study; in particular
the emphasis on the interweaving of different high-cultural (semiotic)
institutions in this particular theatrical (text/performance/audience) event.
Crucially these included:

- the commoditizing process of school 'audiencing' by the RSC marketing
  department;
- the liberal-humanist (anti-naturalist, but also technologically determinist)
  construction of Chekhov's 'history' in this particular theatrical event
  according to the multiple and overlapping (but not always consistent)
  identities of Adrian Noble: as director of the production, as Artistic
  Director of the RSC, as compiler of the theatre programme notes, as
  Stanislavskian rehearser of the actors, and so on; and
- the constitution of the student audience as 'A-Level' viewers of this
  production.

In other words, a variety of Frow's semiotic institutions and regimes of
high-cultural value were interacting here to produce student 'readings' of the
RSC *Cherry Orchard*. I will point briefly to key findings and methodological
implications that I expand on more fully elsewhere.

- The school students interviewed were from Cumbria (like Brian
  Wynne's farmers) – carrying their strong northern accents into a heartland of high culture, Stratford-upon-Avon. However, unlike Wynne's
  'situated' farmers, they were in Stratford not to reflect their 'local'
  adaptive culture; but rather to partake of elite culture – via their
  A-Levels in Russian or English studies.
- Like many student groups, this was a targeted audience for a 'package'
  of Stratford plays relevant to their studies – primarily Shakespeare, but
  also Chekhov. With them was their Chekhov teacher, and he was present
  during the focus-group interview. So the context of the interview – the
  'A-Level' texts, the teacher occasionally offering his comments, and the
  interview conducted by an Associate Professor of English and Drama –
  was inevitably associated with the 'formal curriculum', however hard we
  tried to make it informal.
- Just occasionally a more informal 'risk and daily life' discourse broke
  through, as when a (male) student said 'We've had the sex [Trofimov/
  Anya], and the drugs [Lopakhin's poppy seeds/'opium'], now what
  about the rock 'n roll' [the Jewish orchestra]. But overall, the formal

school curriculum dominated their 'northern voice', in their pleasure as well as in instrumental terms.

The following comments were symptomatic of the focus-group discussion.

Female: 'In our version, did Lopakhin do that massive speech? . . . That huge speech in the ballroom?' . . .
F: 'You know where Lopakhin's in the ballroom, saying "This is mine . . ." '
F: 'Like he's trying to be a peasant.'
Male: 'Oh yeah.'
F: 'That was the social standard. That's what the play's on – peasants rising up to their sort of aristocracy, 'cause he was never accepted totally into them.'
M: 'Are you an English student?'
F: 'Yeah.' [laughter]
M: 'Who's our aristocracy?' [laughter]
F: 'I'll shut up now.'
F: [Laughs] 'Good!'
F: 'Eh . . . I forgot what I was going to say now'. [laughter]
F: 'Yeah, that he was never truly accepted, because they used to ignore him, and didn't feel he was an equal to them.' . . .
F: 'I thought it was really effective when, like, he was saying to them . . . "your estate's going to have to be sold. Your cherry orchard's going to have to be, like, pulled down", and, like, they just turned away, and he's standing there and they're turned away like, eating biscuits and drinking tea, as if, like, he wasn't even there! And you just thought, well! . . .'
F: 'He brought more of Lopakhin's lines to life. . . . When you read it, it was flat. But last night . . . it really showed, like, their ignorance.' . . .
F: 'I think a lot more of the humour was brought out last night.'
F: 'Yeah.'
F: 'Ours was more flat.'
M: 'Visually it was brought out.'
F: 'When we read it I totally missed it. Well, I know it's funny – you [to the teacher] kept pointing it out – the relationship between Gayev and Firs, I just missed that, but it really brought out last night how funny' . . .

The importance of comedy in the play (which the teacher confirms also during the interview) has been conventionally emphasized both in schools and on the stage since, at least, Michael Frayn's translation of *The Cherry Orchard* in the early 1980s. We also know that Noble cast key characters (such as David Troughton as Lopakhin) because of their reputation for comedy. At the end of the Noble production these A-Level students could *see* ('Visually brought it out') what earlier they had been told: the comic authority of their 'Chekhov' A-Level text.

But if the comic Chekhov has prevailed in recent years, the 'class' aspect of *The Cherry Orchard* has been much less popular in conventional academic writing (Donald Rayfield, for instance, has described this 'sociological' reading of the play as 'a betrayal': 1995, personal interview). The western 'expert' rejection of a class reading is undoubtedly partly because of the negative model of the Soviet Chekhov. Yet the class mobility reading – as we see from this part of the interview, focusing especially round Lopakhin – is still resilient with the school students. A major reason for this is the character/theme focus of school studies of canonical texts. However much the teacher might be trained in 'close reading', the type of questions asked at A-level (part of the conditions of production in schools where, as Sinfield says, 'the complexities of knowledge and method in professional academic work' become 'the simplicities imposed by the set book and the examination question', Dollimore and Sinfield, 1994: 285) make it impossible to avoid Lopakhin's class relationship with a family that is itself on the edge of class change.

Thus it is that in an earlier part of the discussion, about Firs, a student spoke of her personal emotions of 'I felt really bad for him' as he was left to die at the end. Another student replied, 'We weren't really thinking about that because we understood' the class symbolism that Firs's death connoted. This latter was a surrogate voice for the teacher: 'I understood the meaning of it, and I understood what was happening, so . . . [I didn't emote like you did]'. On the other hand, this girl (who consistently talks about symbolism) is soon after sent up by her peers: 'Are you an English student? . . . Who's our aristocracy?'

There is a rather overt ironic play here on the differences between 'lay' feelings and the 'expert' knowledge of the A-Level course and the teacher. As Henry Jenkins has argued, drawing on de Certeau, 'School children are taught to read for authorial meaning, to consume the narrative without leaving their own marks upon it. . . . The teacher's red pen rewards those who "correctly" decipher the text and penalizes those who "get it wrong", while the student's personal feelings are rated "irrelevant" to the task of literary analysis' (Jenkins, 1992: 24–5). In this interview, the students who respond with 'personal feelings' are getting a little of their own back – just momentarily – against the teacher's surrogate 'red pen'.

Still, overall, the students rarely come away from the formal performance of the play separate, as it were, from their 'A-Level' reading of it. Mainly it was as a matter of actors 'bringing to life' the 'flat' and 'stilted' page, clarifying it, confirming the comedy they had been told was there, and successfully blending the 'reality' and the 'social symbolism' of the text. It is as though the actors *restored* the stilted 'A-Level' text of 'expert knowledge' to the students' mundane daily life.

It was a feature of this entire focus-group discussion how little the Russian Revolution, which so often hangs like a dead weight over interpretations of *The Cherry Orchard* – as we saw in the earliest marketing brochures for the RSC production – affected readings among the 'A-Level' students. Nevertheless, the formally performed text *has* altered 'A-Level' (official) textual readings for some of its audience – at least two students (in my focus group of seven) debated the ambivalent Lopakhin that Troughton was working for, the man who *both* realizes that the orchard has lost its beauty in relation to 'the people' *and* 'likes money'. Further, if David Troughton's multi-faceted character proved too difficult to achieve for other students, Adrian Murray's

Trofimov did launch himself beyond the canonical 'eternal student' for most of them.

> *F:*   '*Everyone's* an eternal student if you think of it like that. Everyone learns, don't they? Every day of your life you learn something new.'
> *M:*   'He's open to, like, the new things but some people just close their minds and shut themselves away . . .'

A fuller analysis would look more dialogically and reflexively at the interventions during the focus group of the teacher (who draws for example on the 'expert' history of the programme notes to establish his 'A-Level' authority) and the researcher/interviewer (who has his own political agenda – evident in questions about Lopakhin at the end of the interview – in comparing this liberal-humanist production of Chekhov with other, more radicalized performances being researched; see Tulloch, Burvill and Hood, 1997). However, I want to turn at this point – with my second case study – in the opposite direction, away from a reflexive focus on 'expert' discourse in audience analysis, to an emphasis on the situated, self-constituting quality of 'audiencing'.

The Q-Theatre A Midsummer Night's Dream *1998*

In contrast to my *Cherry Orchard* school audience case study, certain points are worth noting here. My first point is that here I am telling the story of a Shakespeare production from the point of view of 'everyday' encounters with the Shakespeare text, rather than from the perspective of an 'expert system' (like a marketing company that is in the business of 'audiencing' high culture). Both producers and audiences of this A *Midsummer Night's Dream* drew reflexively on a range of biographical and social histories as they encountered others, whether as on-stage performers or offstage audiences. Thus director Mary-Anne Gifford wove this Shakespeare text through memories of her own daily childhood encounters with her left-wing parents' favourite music (and indeed, through her own later musical experience as lead singer in a rock band). Thus, also, young women in the audience referred to their own dating memories as on stage Helena offered herself, bodily and without words, to Demetrius in the woods. As an 18-year-old school student said, she found this moment deeply disturbing as a woman. Yet, she also felt in it a moment of positive identification. Her own biography negotiated with the performance; 'because . . . for me it *was* a decision and it was a strength that she has thought the process through and she has intelligence and therefore she has a certain amount of power and strength.' She and the other women in the focus group went on to argue that at the end of the narrative 'the men get what they want – *all* of them'. Yet, they still felt that Hermia and Helena in the woods were *driving* the narrative actions in the play. Here the interaction between their own experientially-based narratives and those of the women on stage created a dynamic that challenged the (male) happy ending. My point here is that for 'third generation' audience/performance analysis we need to go further with a critical ethnographic (and/or qualitative) approach to the situated and reflexive negotiation of meanings by both individual performers and individual audience members.

Secondly, while recognizing the importance of emphasizing 'margins and border crossings' between different kinds of performative event as social action (whether separated performative events like theatre, film and television, or everyday 'ordinary' routines, Hughes-Freeland, 1998: 22) we do need also to focus on the differences *between* everyday and formal performance narratives. This is particularly the case at the level of the economic and institutional embedding of these performative micro-narratives. We can contrast here, for example, the 'everyday' and 'formal' performances of two personally strong and determined feminists before their own particular audiences: Julie's 'street performance' (Introduction) and Q-Theatre director Mary-Anne Gifford's *A Midsummer Night's Dream*. At a general level, both Julie, the Australian lesbian woman who feared the threat of zero-tolerance policing more than she feared crime, and Mary-Anne who had recently joined a theatre company that had lost its government subsidy, were operating within and against economic rationalism. But their micro-narratives were different. The performers and audiences of formal performances at the Q-Theatre were placed within a number of very specific time/space frames that were unlike Julie's street performance/audience event. Running the only remaining regionally-based touring professional theatre in New South Wales without a federal government subsidy, Mary-Anne Gifford's audiences are not Julie's street 'strangers', but rather are commoditized 'bums on seats'. Among these economically necessary audiences, there are the targeted school student audiences studying the text for Higher School Certificate, whose readings are often embedded in specific (generally liberal–humanist and/or Stanislavskian) reading formations. There are also other distinct processes of audiencing in formal performance. There were the different audiences the *A Midsummer Night's Dream* actors noticed during the stage performance itself, as for example between city 'theatre-ati' (with lots of what the actors call 'judgmental' knowledge from other Shakespeare productions) and those country audiences in places like Gunnedah or Taree who were encountering Shakespeare (or even the theatre itself) for the very first time. Further, there was the audience as an implied construction of Mary-Anne Gifford's gendered and leftist politics. All her productions since she arrived at the Q-Theatre in January 1998 had played with gender, class, ethnicity, sexual preference and so on. In the *A Midsummer Night's Dream* production, her implied audience was constructed in part by economic constraints (the need for very small casts and thus a tripling of parts for many actors), which then required some cuts in the final Court/Pyramus and Thisbe scene. But it was an implied audience too in Gifford's reflexive sense of the relationship of the text to Shakespeare's audience and her own. Gifford was quite comfortable with the cuts she necessarily made in the final scene to the aristocratic wordplay that puts down the working class mechanicals. Her view was that the dialogic energy of this scene would have been viewed very differently in Shakespeare's time. In her production this linguistic energy was replaced by what Gifford called a working-class 'joy of popular culture' (both music and film). This included the play between various popular cultural styles ('silent film' melodrama, 1920s/1930s cabaret, Busby Berkley, Gifford's parents' love of Mario Lanza) and the potential naturalism of the canonical high-cultural text. My point with these examples is that, while focusing on the situated daily experiences, memories and negotiations of individual audience members and producers, it is also important to see how these *interact* with the very particular 'audiences' constructed via the daily economic, political, and aesthetic practices of 'formal' performance.

My third point is that there is also a difference between 'everyday' and 'formal' performance narratives at the level of the semiotically dense theatre performance space. Our teenage female audience respondents consistently emphasized the emotional closeness that the cramped Q-Theatre space gave them with both young and older performers, for example, as Hippolyta, with big silent-screen facial gestures, suffered her sisterhood in oppression to Hermia's father's shocking lines 'As she is mine, I may dispose of her'. Here we are talking of Carlson's 'liminoid' relationship between live audiences and live actors in this or that particular theatrical space. In the case of the Q-Theatre's *A Midsummer Night's Dream*, as compared, say, with the also sexually embodied production of the play at Stratford-upon-Avon in 1999, that relationship was especially felt because the young women on the apron stage were often within touching distance of the audience.

This was, in Loren Kruger's words, a moment of live, *local* theatre: 'a *liminoid* space in which alternative or *virtual* public spheres can be performed, tested, *entertained*' (1993: 68). The teenage audience watched (felt, laughed) closely through the male/female chases in the woods; or as the only two women on stage in Act 1, Scene 1, moved breast to breast (Hippolyta ignoring Theseus's 'Come, *my* Hippolyta', as she transferred her 'silent screen' silver lamé shawl slowly to Hermia). All the school focus groups we interviewed noted the long silence as the shawl briefly hid both women's heads from the raging males. This was a moment worked for in rehearsal by two female actors enjoying performing for a woman director, and in turn helping recreate personalized narratives for the girls who watched.

Yet, it was not always interpreted according to the preferred reading of the director or actors. Nearly all of my survey and focus-group audience of 200 school students missed Gifford's 'defeated Amazon Queen'/defeated German militarism analogy which cued her 'ten-year party' choice of music and the 'cinema melodrama' form. Instead, the students read this embodied moment as a mother-to-daughter 'passing of the burden from one to the other'; or else as somehow woman-to-woman 'symbolic. . . . It wasn't clear what of'. Our interviews revealed how the physical (audience/actor) proximity, and the emotional (audience/character) closeness to the male/female, love/hate lives on stage impacted on the young audience, establishing what one teenager called an everyday 'feeling and doing . . . more like real life' emotion. At the same time, though, no-one was ever in doubt that this was formal performance. The students particularly liked the actors changing their parts by changing clothes visibly on stage; and many said that the production brought out for the first time the formalized pleasure of the Shakespearean language and poetry.

Conclusion

This has been a complex chapter, covering a lot of 'onstage/offstage' performance ground. In my analysis of the RSC's *The Cherry Orchard* I have wanted to bring together a variety of these around Lopakhin: marketing, academic, rehearsing, staging, acting and audience readings. We saw how a profoundly humanist and 'sociologically' determinist positioning of the play across a variety of formal performance sites could intersect transparently with an 'A-Level'-constituted audience and its 'class' reading. Minor 'resistances' were seen: among actors for brief moments; among school students for brief moments; with the most sustained resistance developing out of the particular 'political' acting of Sean Murry as Trofimov and the school students' *positive*, agentive reading of the sign 'eternal student'.

In my much too brief reference to the Q-Theatre's *A Midsummer Night's Dream*, I have wanted to suggest that the same commoditizing strategy towards the school audience can lead to a more sustained 'resistance' depending on the director's frames for inscribing her female audience in the performance, and on the particular theatre site. Here all of our audience respondents noted positively the interactions of women with women, as well as the young female lovers so close to them onstage as they offered themselves to/resisted their men. While these girls were unable to read the director's broader ideological frame (as Athens/the capitalist 1920s 'west' parties after military conquest), they did read personalized gender issues via their own experiences. For them, this local production not only created enormous enjoyment (particularly in the positive 'carnival' performance of the mechanicals), but also helped them think about the ambivalences involved in 'performing gender differently'.

As Kruger argues, there is a case for examining local and decentralized theatre practice like this one in the face of the centralized and rationalized power of the media. These girls at the Q-Theatre emphasized their feeling of physical proximity to the women on stage, in an experience they said they found much more pleasurable than television. Thus, as Kruger says, 'the intermediate technology of small-scale actions may provide an effective stage' for alternative daily practices (Kruger 1993: 66). As Kruger adds, in diverse performance contexts the 'object itself' is neither the 'immutable touchstone of eternal value' ('Shakespeare') nor 'a simple sign of class domination' ('high culture theatre'). Rather, 'its *critical* significance, its *identification* as "art" or "entertainment", changes with the occasion and the place and the *kind* of audience of its performance' (1993: 63). The significant question on each occasion is: what is the particular, situated *relationship* between the 'formal' performance space and practice and the 'ordinary, everyday' performance of the audience as each one 'places' the other's occasion?

6

CULTURAL METHODS

[I]n a bureaucratic-technological society, numbers talk . . . [W]e cannot afford to live like hermits, blinded by global, theoretical critiques to the possible analytical and practical uses of quantification. (Silverman, 1993: 163)

We are at the moment, in cultural theory, between a rock and a hard place. The rock is what Silverman describes as a bureaucratic-technological society's demand that 'numbers talk'. The hard place is postmodernism's insistence that there is no 'innocent' knowledge, no 'reality' external to our own situated theorizing, no neutral 'detection' available via 'impartial' methods of analysis – and hence no point whatsoever in cultural studies engaging with 'scientific' methodologies of quantification. The result of this latter position is, of course, a much greater emphasis on analysing all our talking (to use Sparks's phrase) 'in determinate settings' – whether as 'subjects' or 'objects' of research. To borrow Adam and Allan's comment in their useful review/critique of cultural theory 'after postmodernism', the 'situated, constitutive self can no longer hide behind the imperialism of unifying conceptual schemes embodied in "master" narratives; rather, each one of us has to engage with the fluid ambiguities and uncertainties of tentative, "local" stories or accounts' (Adam and Allan, 1995: xv).

In my view, this 'rock and a hard place' positioning makes the asking of questions about cultural *method* more not less important. Or, more specific to the methodological project of this book, 'we become concerned with *meta-methodology*: primarily . . . we become interested both in the procedures and devices we use in "socially constructing" the subject matter of our investigations in concert with our fellow investigators' (Shotter, 1993: 21). These 'fellow investigators' may be other 'expert stakeholders' (as for example with various theatre and television professionals in the 'ethnographies of production' covered in this book), or they may be the Sydney building workers with whom we collaborated in designing a health campaign. In either case, we have had to move away, as Shotter says, from 'the stance of individual, third-person, contemplative observers, away from collecting *fragmented* data from a position socially "outside" of the activity observed' (1993: 21) towards a *more* hermeneutic, reflexive and often practical interest. I emphasize 'more' because it is, of course, neither possible nor in the end desirable to move away from one's 'expert' position altogether. It is at that point that Ien Ang's insistence on 'ethnographies of storytelling', which draw attention to the provisional closures that both 'lay' and 'expert' narratives are mobilizing, become a major focus of our method.

As Adam and Allan argue, postmodern cultural theory's 'controverting of the validity of the "metaphysics of presence", that is, the assumption that something real exists "in the world out there" independent of the observer, constitutes an attack on narrative knowledge. In its place, this theoretical project looks to affirm the contextual and constitutive nature of culture' (1995: xiv). Adam and Allan also argue, however, against postmodernism's resulting (often 'startling') implication, embedded in its 'all too frequent conceptual dis-articulation of questions concerning how cultural power is woven into the very texture of everyday life' (1995: xiii).

In contrast, in this book I have emphasized the importance of narrative knowledge in relation to power embedded in the dialogic negotiations of daily life (whether of Julie in the streets of Seattle, Trevor Griffiths in BBC television, or the teenage girls watching Shakespeare at Penrith). Here the constitutive and agentive aspects of culture have been mapped as a series of performative events: whether these be theoretical writing, attempts at making cultural policy, framing, marketing, acting and spectating high culture, or establishing a reflexive and dialogic method for doing any of these things. Consequently I have emphasized also the importance of a critical 'ethnography of storytelling' as a cultural methodology that engages with the 'margins and border crossings' that have conventionally separated (not least in cultural studies) the 'aesthetic' performative events like theatre, film and television from everyday 'ordinary' performances.

Part of this theoretical move has been the refusal to exoticize 'ritual' or 'performance' as anthropological 'other' (Hughes-Freeland, 1998: 1); part of it has been a focus on the 'transformativity' of different forms of performance within ritual, 'liturgy' and constraint; part of it engaging with what we mean by saying that performance is somehow 'more' than the everyday, even though (as with Julie in Seattle) it is also as much *part* of the everyday as it is part of the formal expressivity of theatre or television. An active *spectatorship* has been crucial to this understanding of performance as a particular kind of social action. 'What validates the performance is that it is made real by the audience. . . . The agency of situations is one which is constituted by a range of participants' (Hughes-Freeland, 1998: 15). This has been equally true of our methodology; for example, in the performance of Sue and Jeff in interviewing our building workers, and in their active spectatorship of the different stories these interviewers told.

It is then this model of performativity as living bodily expressivity, conversation and social interaction (rather than textual representation) that underpins Rapport's theory of social reproduction and the subversion of routine. 'It is through narrational performance that we maintain conscious selves; through the performance of narratives we continue to write and rewrite the stories of our selves' (Hughes-Freeland, 1998: 20). Thus, in working through this model of performance as social action, I have found no problem with *both* affirming the importance of the contextual and constitutive nature of culture *and* affirming narrative knowledge.

Yet even as, in the wake of postmodernism, we survey the 'micropolitics' of fragmented, multiple, situational logics of performance – from Sydney building workers designing an HIV/AIDS campaign to Stratford theatre-goers re-reading in public their 'A-level' text – so too it is important (as Adam and Allan also say) 'to reflexively examine how we are temporally and spatially situated within the institutional dynamics of theoretical produc-tion so that we may then, in turn, proceed to challenge their attendant "micropolitics" ' (Adams and Allan, 1995: xvi). That reflexivity about the institutional dynamics of our theoretical performance has been a feature of this book, as has the process of challenging their attendant 'micropolitics' – whether this has been in the dialogic critique of Australian neocolonialism within film theory, the researching and formulation of 'below-up' HIV/AIDS campaigns, the alternative constructions of the modern as between literary humanism and new historicism, or the relationship between 'research', 'A-level' and 'professional theatrical' performances of Chekhov. It is *that* relationship between 'ritual' and 'performativity', 'constraint' and 'creativity', the 'global' and the 'local', 'structure' and 'agency', and so on that I have been emphasizing, each within their own 'micropolitics' of personalized, situated exchange. And it is for that reason that so much of this book has relied on qualitative (and where possible) ethnographic methods to help access situated narratives.

Angela McRobbie has written particularly clearly about this in relation to cultural policy in post-Thatcher Britain. She notes that

> the overwhelming impact of psychoanalysis and post-structuralism [has] posed fairly damning critiques of what I have recently labelled 'the three Es: empiricism, ethnography and the category of experience. The efforts given over to exposing these sites of "truth" and "knowledge" as artificially coherent narrative fictions (!) made it difficult for media and cultural studies to participate in facts and figures-oriented policy debates. (McRobbie, 1996: 337)

Consequently, she notes that it 'has instead been left to sociologists like James Ditton in Glasgow to do the dirtier work of developing policies on youth cultures like rave, which necessitates having access to reliable facts, figures and even "ethnographic accounts" to be able to argue with angry councillors, police and assorted moral guardians' (1996: 337–8). McRobbie herself has done work on 'the debates and discussions that go on behind the scenes in magazines like *More!* or *Just Seventeen*', arguing that it is important not to dismissively consign all popular cultural production in Britain post-Thatcher to 'enterprise culture'. She argues for the need to do ethnographies of, and collect facts and figures about, 'a sprawling sector of micro-economies of culture which now traverses the boundaries of social class, ethnicity and gender' (1996: 339); and where cultural workers very often tend towards the political left, many trained in media and cultural studies, and fighting 'to balance the input of feminist ideas with the need to keep sales high and circulation figures healthy' (1996: 340). For these cultural workers cultural and media studies are performative discourses, but not so much 'as counter-discourses (which implies a starkly oppositional relation) but rather one set of competing discourses within a professional field of others' (1996: 340).

So, says McRobbie,

> Despite all the problems of dealing with 'personal accounts' as evidence, testimony or simply data, it still seems worthwhile to me to ask how these cultural workers experience this form of activity. . . . I am not suggesting that those 'raves from the grave', the three-'Es' are simply exhumed, but rather that they are reconceptualised . . . so that one strand of cultural and media studies is at least better able to position itself in the field of policy. This would mean doing more empirical research, it would also mean re-instating ethnography despite and in response to Clifford's testimony to its poetic character. . . . We need to be able to do more than analyse texts, we need data, graphs, ethnographies, facts and figures. (1996: 339, 338, 341)

So we *are* still left with the 'rock' of Silverman's account. All of us who do cultural research face the issue Silverman and McRobbie refer to, especially if we are doing policy-oriented research or consultancies. For example, in a recent consultancy for the Australian Federation of AIDS Organizations (AFAO) on 'Best Practice in Social Marketing as Applied to HIV/AIDS Prevention', even though the ostensible focus of the review was practitioner performance in social marketing via a range of different interactive health campaigns, and even though the majority of these health workers (like McRobbie's cultural workers) are probably left-leaning, Deborah Lupton and I were faced immediately in the consultancy brief with these definitions of 'best practice'.

- Efficacy: the measurable influence of a particular intervention of the health behaviours, attitudes, practices, morbidity or mortality of individuals and groups.
- Community acceptability: the extent to which the individual or group subject to the health goal are prepared to support . . . the direction, qualities and delivery of the health promotion policy.
- Effectiveness: the extent to which measurable change can be extended to other individuals and groups in various social and cultural settings, in a way that produces the best health outcome for the community at large.
- Efficiency: concerns the comparative cost of the particular intervention in relation to its impact on a particular health goal. (Lupton and Tulloch, 1997: 1–2)

Most of the emphasis here is on the 'measurable influence', the 'extent of reach', the 'comparative cost', and while governments (and their advertising agencies) are increasingly talking about 'various social and cultural settings', the 'community at large' must remain the rhetorical goal of state policy. It is even arguable that the reason why social marketing has become the current fashionable health communication model is less to do with 'cultural imperialism' (in so far as this approach derives from a fusion of marketing with health communication models from the USA), and more to do with the fact that social marketing ostensibly deals with 'cultural differences', while remaining firmly committed to the *measurable* 'four Ps':

price, product ('packaging', 'brand name' etc), promotion (advertising, public relations), place. In other words, it is to do with the rhetorical manoeuvres within the multi-identitied mix of health bureaucracies and their advertising agencies. Symptomatically, the 'place' of social marketing is less the situated, dialogic 'stories' of daily performance that I have talked about in this book, and more a matter of 'top-down' distribution outlets, inventories and channels for delivering services to 'target adopters'.

Increasingly in a neo-conservative, economic-fundamentalist state, government emphasis is on a 'contracts and outcomes approach' that focuses on 'products'. Governments are concerned about cost-effectiveness. Consequently, 'larger reach' rather than labour-intensive small group performative strategies are encouraged because maximum reach is assumed to equate with cost-effectiveness (the 'efficiency' goal of 'best practice'). Contracts and consultancies thus tend to be specifically about broad campaigns; and (Lupton and Tulloch, 1997) for many working daily in the field there is a concern that mass campaigns may become 'core work' at the expense of related community development and educational issues such as negotiated safety in different subcultures. This is particularly ironic since many leading members of government health agencies have long experience of situated community collaboration around sexual practice and risk in the gay community; and there is a concern among these that a return to 'scary' campaigns with hard-line outcomes like reduction in serioconversion rates will replace the policy of actively creating ownership of issues among people at risk.

Operating within the state, Australian health agency personnel who are close to gay, womens', ethnic and other communities, do try to shift 'social marketing' from its emphasis on 'product' and 'consumer' to tactical community participation – an example of the 'performative' contextualization of epidemiology that Cindy Patton speaks about. One senior project officer told us that he had 'concerns about social marketing identifying people as consumers because it is divisionist. It doesn't identify people as active participants in their health'. Another said that the 'content of social marketing campaigns needs to be sophisticated. It is not just a matter of putting a product out there for people to buy. It can be used as a way for the community to think through an epidemic on a community scale, to support the community in some kind of objective without necessarily selling a product.'

However, this kind of definition of 'product' is increasingly hard to sustain in the current political-economic climate. In our report we said we believed that this tension accounted for the adjacent mix of 'techniques' in the AFAO brief, where an under-defined 'social marketing' model was said to need combining with community development and peer group education. As workers in the field told us, for them social marketing is 'a strategy rather than the total answer to the problem'.

I will quote our report's conclusions, because it offers a recent example of the dialogic in policy writing itself. Here cultural researchers attempted to negotiate (via the 'voices' of health workers in the field) the *realpolitik* of government's 'expert' models in health campaigns, thus trying to achieve some transformative shift in perspective. Our five conclusions were:

- 'Health practitioners will increasingly need to emphasise an "outcomes", product-focussed approach in their submissions for funding, because health bureaucracies are increasingly emphasising accountability measures in the HIV/ AIDS field. In this context the map provided by social marketeers is a useful and rewarding one since it offers a framework and a set of procedures for planning and implementing a campaign. At its best, social marketing can be used in campaigns to establish norms about "best practice" (trust in a relationship, equality in sexual negotiation, etc) which can then lead to dialogue and curiosity for more information within individual partnerships. At the same time, social marketing offers a necessary costing "discipline". As [one of our health campaign respondents] says, "marketing has to be cost effective because it is driven by dollars and social marketing will help health to be cost effective because it is also driven by dollars".'
- 'The current division between "community development" ("where affected communities mobilise and engage in health promotion activity") and "social marketing" is an arbitrary and unclear one, which very few practitioners operate with in the actual work place. Furthermore, governments' emphasis on "product" can often work against social marketing's core focus on "consumers", with the result that campaigns (as "products") can draw attention away from more fine-grained and complex community work. The view among health practitioners that "social marketing HIV" means that the communities the campaigns are designed for are the ones that are doing the campaigns often underpins this more complex approach. But it must still take on board current theories of community empower-ment, embodiment and pleasure, and structural change within the risk society. This emphasis on embodied social and structural change in a postmodern context needs to become at least as much a part of government agendas as the current focus on maximising individual behaviour change.'
- 'The confusions and ambiguities that we have traced as between "voluntary" and "manipulative", "consumer" and "product", "individual" and "community" emphases will continue because they are inherent both in social marketing literature, and in marketing rhetoric generally (including that of governments). At the same time, however, current theories of "the risk society" (Ulrich Beck) can help clarify this problem to the degree that these focus *on* the issue of "expert-led" as against "community-led" risk evaluation, and there are signs that this particular paradigm is gaining broader political and bureaucratic acceptance. Health bureau-crats can help in this development by advising funding bodies (as has occurred in the UK in the case of the Economic and Social Research Council) of the need to target funding to "risk" conceptualisations and research (for example, it could become an Australian Research Council "priority" area).'
- 'The ambiguity that we have noted between "community" and "larger reach" campaigns will also continue, but can probably best be negotiated via the emerging current policy of broad national campaigns (eg for urban gay communities) which are then modified, inflected and re-imaged at a local level. At the same time, though, these national campaigns themselves need to be based on the kinds of active community participation that the "new public health" movement advocates, and on the "consumer"-focussed methodologies and segmentation advocated by both social marketing and "active audience" communication theory.'
- 'The issue of evaluation will continue to be problematic. As [one health officer respondent] argues, a useful first step is to "identify what we can evaluate

and what we can't evaluate". Then, on the one hand, health workers may be able to agree with [a campaign leader] that engaging people in critical self-evaluation "is a quantum leap, the actual notion that you can change your behaviour is huge and empowering"; while on the other hand looking for performance and output measures that will satisfy governments and health bureaucracies. In the current health "market", the trick . . . is to define one's audience as *both* "an action force" *and* "a target audience".' (Lupton and Tulloch, 1997: 31–3)

In our report we were trying to explain what was in fact happening in the field – active local and community-based performances within the *liturgy* of social marketing – without losing contact with its 'market-based' comparabilities (the 'four Ps'). It was another example (along with Davies's discussion of the Eisteddfod, and Coleman and Eisner's analysis of the pilgrimage as social action referred to earlier) where without the preconditions of 'canonical forms' to 'act against or play with, creativity would not emerge' (Hughes-Freeland, 1998: 7).

On their part, this particular consultancy was a classic case of state bureaucrats wanting top-down 'expert knowledge' (social marketing) fused with 'lay knowledge' (as health workers in the field drew on local voices). In turn, Deborah Lupton and I were employed to use our 'cultural studies' expertise to overview current 'social marketing'-based health campaigns in the field. This gave us a certain surveillant power (at least as far as the report stage).

On the other hand, in the case of the Heterosexual Men's Campaign, the boot was on the other foot. The low-tech health campaign that we had designed collectively with the builders' labourers was later evaluated quantitatively by a separate (and very senior) marketing company. This 'independent evaluation consultancy' now had the surveillant power, proclaiming our campaign 'mildly successful in getting recognition to its sexual health warning messages, in being of personal relevance, making men consider their own sexual behaviour and improving knowledge about safe sex, STDs and HIV/AIDS' (AGB McNair, 1993: 47).

It would be too easy to point to the way in which this independent report – its two pages of 'facts' placed at the end of the 47-page 'Your Little Head Thinking Instead of Your Big Head' qualitative report – closed *our* narrative with its top-down, mild commendation. Of course it did that; but then so too did our 'Best Practice in Social Marketing Report'. The 'creativity and constraint' of performing cultural policy is always embedded in political and economic materiality, and can work in different directions.

But my point here is (as it is in David Silverman's header quotation to this chapter) that quantitative research is not simply a political fact of life that we have to endure (and moderate where we can). Rather, it can be important to us *as* cultural researchers. Silverman says,

The real issue is how our research can be *both* intellectually challenging and rigorous and critical. . . . This means overcoming the temptation to jump to easy conclusions just because there is some evidence that seems to lead in an interesting direction. Instead, we must subject this evidence to every possible test. (Silverman, 1993: 144)

Ien Ang, in our header quotation to the Introduction, also emphasized the importance of continuing methodological rigour ('accurate data gathering and careful inference') – even as she emphasized telling our 'ethnographic stories'. Her difference from Silverman is in drawing closer attention reflexively to the fact that our 'tests' are (to use Stuart Hall's term) ' "arbitrary closures" in our storytelling practice' (Ang, 1996: 78). They are 'provisional closures', overlaying 'the ultimate intransigence of audience chaos' (Ang, 1996: 77) with a certain kind of 'representational order'. But Ang and Silverman would both agree that one's 'provisional closure' needs to be systematically related to one's *theoretical* propositions rather than to *populations* or universes' (Silverman, citing Bryman, 1993: 160); and this is because, as I have tried to indicate since Chapter 1 of this book, our theoretical propositions are situated voices, performing dialogically in the context of other voices, other 'citations'.

Given the clearly situated propositions underpinning our beer coasters and toilet door stickers in the Heterosexual Men's Campaign, it was thus a valuable follow-up that McNair conducted 401 interviews 'at pubs and clubs featuring campaign materials' and 'at households in the vicinity of pubs/clubs featuring the campaign' (AGB McNair, 1993: 46). Here the quantitative survey was based on the *time/space co-ordinates of the campaign's own 'expert' and 'lay' propositions*. It 'tested':

- at the men's chosen venues the degree of unprompted notice of our two campaign signs ('beer coasters were recalled most often: 3:1 over stickers in toilets');
- prompted recall of campaign elements among all men interviewed ('beer coasters at venues were seen most (at 19%), followed by billboard or bus ads (13%), stickers in pub/club toilets (11%), and magazine ads (7%)');
- beer coasters as conversation starters ('Among the one in four who recognised beer coasters or stickers at venues, three quarters had read them. Among these, for 19% it had helped as a conversation starter on safe sex with their partner while for 27% it helped start conversation with their mates, representing 4 to 5% effectively of the total sample. It also had other effects such as "made them laugh", "made them think" or "increased their knowledge" ');
- knowledge of the link between STDs and HIV ('for those familiar with at least one element of the campaign . . . 45% stated their knowledge about safe sex, STDs and HIV/AIDS had improved due to the campaign information. This was particularly so for NESB [non-English-speaking background] men at . . . 63%');
- sense of effectiveness ('The campaign was seen as being . . . effective for 84% in giving people information to help protect themselves against STDs and HIV/AIDS');

- age of greatest 'reach' ('the campaign and sexual health messages were best recalled by 18–24 year olds, single (sexually active men). . . . Further the campaign had greatest influence and was of the most personal relevance for single sexually active men, condom users and 18–24 year olds'. (AGB McNair, 1993: 46–7)

We can see from the figures 'representing around 4 to 5% effectively of the total sample' why McNair called this a 'mildly successful campaign' (remembering what is at stake in *any single change* of safer-sex behaviour). At the same time, the fact that the beer coasters 'helped act as a conversation starter on the subject of safe sex for around one in five men' (AGB McNair, 1993: 47) can be counted a significant success for our jointly chosen vehicle, place and time of intervention (considering the very short period the campaign had been running before the McNair survey, and that some of the men will not have had 'pick ups' in that time). Other aspects of the McNair research would have been useful knowledge if *more precisely* focused on the campaign intentions. For example, the statistics of 45 per cent who stated that their information 'about safe sex, STDs and HIV/AIDS' had improved due to the campaign information; and the 84 per cent who said it would help protect them against STDs and HIV/AIDS seem encouraging, but it is unclear that they derive from questions focusing on the *link* between STDs and HIV, which was one of the foundational propositions of the campaign.

Overall, though, our jointly designed, low-tech, 'below-up' and situated HIV campaign gained the imprimatur from a company that is used by the major political parties for national opinion polls. As a sampling company that is used to the most 'hard-edged' wing of data quantification, perhaps it was an achievement that McNair said, 'As the campaign was low-level media based (with no television exposure) it had achieved a reasonable level of awareness, recognition of its elements and impact amongst men of Sydney' (AGB McNair, 1993: 47). Strategically, at least, this was a win, and methodologically, in my view reasonably useful and appropriate; though one has to note the continued assumption here of the greater 'impact' of 'high-level media-based (*with* television exposure)' campaigns.

From qualitative to quantitative methods in popular cultural and policy research

Clearly, given these continuing assumptions among policy decision-makers about 'top-down' media-based research, it would be myopic for cultural researchers to focus *only* on small groups like builders' labourers! How can the kinds of theoretical parameter emphasized in this book be applied as a methodology for *mass* media policy?

One method I have adopted extensively is to use 'ethnographies of story-telling' (in relation to the production and 'audiencing' of popular culture) as a basis for quantitative work. For example, I observed all stages of pro-duction (from forward planning, through story conferences, rehearsals, studio, editing and publicity) for the Australian peak-time soap opera, *A Country Practice* (*ACP*) when, in different episodes in different years, it tackled (a) unemployment as 'a health hazard', and (b) a 'third wave' (needle-sharing → sexual transmission → heterosexual epidemic) HIV/AIDS story.

In this research I was aiming at what Alasuutari calls a 'third generation' audience agenda, that is re-tying audiences and programming. But here the 'everyday life' I concentrated on was initially that of *formal performance* rhetorics and technologies, as producers of the programmes implied their 'audiences' in performing their texts. Because a soap opera works especially strongly *at* the 'quantitative' (popular ratings) edge of television, these globally dominant frames and discourses of commercial television were very strong. But I also discovered other, less expected formal performance and 'audiencing' frames – of quality writing and 'Shakespeare' in the context of mixing 'downer' and comedy narratives for a popular audience; of a 'bonus' emphasis on current one-parent and step-parent family audiences conceived to be looking for something 'less sentimentalising than *The Brady Bunch*'; of a perceived public interest in current 'downer' social issues like unemployment, AIDS, and drug cultures. Thus the canonical 'Shakespeare' (tragedy/comedy) and the 'liturgies' of medical discourse ('the three-waves of AIDS') were both performed and transformed in popular television, indicating that aspects of 'high culture' (both as 'information' and as 'entertainment') can be important performance frames in soap opera, as they are in more expected venues of high-cultural ritual.

These are some of the attempts in one particular independent production company making soap operas to 'rearticulate' the enterprise culture that McRobbie refers to. In her own research field of teenage girls' magazines, she indicates how media studies-trained editors and journalists may, through a 'self-consciously superficial style of writing, signal the existence of a space of knowing that it is not to be taken seriously and that girls are no longer passive female subjects, the victims of romance' (McRobbie, 1996: 340). This 'space of knowing' is quite different from the one I observed being constructed for teenage girls at *A Country Practice*. But in both cases, there were distinctly 'left' discourses at work in the 'micro-economies' of the production, constructing their own audiences among the 'set of competing discourses within a professional field'. The point is that we need to do ethnographies, we need to collect McRobbie's 'facts and figures', and we need, as she says, to get beyond the 'debates on these kinds of questions [that] have been so bifurcated along the lines of those on the side of political economy against those on the side of meaning and consumption' (1996: 341).

It is *as important* to trace the very rich contexts, processes and dialogic interactions of these frames and discourses of performance in the 'everyday' of television, media and cultural production as it is among television audiences. It is important to situate the various moments of writing, designing, acting, recording, editing and marketing an 'AIDS story' or a *Just Seventeen* article in their own professional everyday time and space co-ordinates, to understand *them* in processes of dialogic negotiation between professional and other rhetorics (just as elsewhere I have examined the dialogic negotiation between theatre researchers and theatre directors/writers, or between HIV researchers and building workers). It is important to understand the formal performance frames within which these different professional identities and rhetorics are set if we are to shed light on the particular historical and institutional globalizing of 'the cultural concerns that surround media use and media messages' (Alasuutari, 1999: introduction).

At the same time, we can draw on these commercial industry-based performance frames of 'audiencing' (which as McRobbie says are seldom 'just' enterprise-commercial) to examine actual audience readings among different (by age, gender, class, ethnicity, etc) audience groups. Here we can *bring together the different formulations of 'truth' of different, plurally situated narratives*: for example McRobbie's actual readers of *Just Seventeen* with the 'active' female subjects preferred (via pastiche and irony) in the text.

Let me offer some examples in the case of the needle-sharing HIV story I researched.

● The writer who drew on Shakespeare's tragedies as an example of effective movement from 'hard-hitting' impact to 'comic relief', nevertheless worried that the particular commercial formula of *ACP* (of cutting very rapidly from tough AIDS message to 'the rude mechanicals' in the local club) actually weakened the impact of his health message. So, by way of both focus-group interviews and quantitative surveys (with closed and open-ended questions) I 'tested' this concern, using differently edited versions of the performed text: one with the standard *ACP* 'cutting away to comedy' formula, and two with these scenes edited out.
● The executive producer had chosen to kill off the 22-year-old daughter of one of the lead characters (a doctor) as part of his twice a year ('one marriage, one death') peak-ratings formula; but this made her too old to be the street-kid junkie whom the programme's consultant social worker advised for a 'plausible' (street-wise) story-line. Consequently, she was given a younger boyfriend who, as 'a bit of a rebel', the executive producer hoped, would appeal to the younger age group he was targeting. In this case, I used a seven-point semantic differential scale (based on focus-group audience interviews as well as the 'bit of a rebel' production intentions) to measure a range of characteristics of this character, Paul. A regression analysis was used to reveal the perceptions of Paul which prompted sympathy for him among viewers. The more sympathetic viewers were those who saw Paul as having a *set* of characteristics ('victim', 'good', 'thinks of others' and 'warm'), not including the producer's 'a bit of a rebel'. Here a statistical measure that *matched the TV industry's own daily ritualized liturgies* (that is for naturalistic, plausible, psychologically dense characterization) but was more complex in its methodology (than the producer's single-characteristic formula) was used to test their own 'audiencing' narratives.

• The script editor, whose job it is, in a ruthlessly commercial industry, to time to within 30 seconds the length of each episode, found that one of the 'AIDS' episodes was running short, and wrote an extra scene. This drew on his memory of the executive producer's comment at an earlier story conference that it would be 'nice to do a legalize heroin story'. This new scene was, however, 'read' as redundant *both* by the actor who was performing the lines (so that he did not prepare these with the kind of naturalistic attention to mood change he had used everywhere else in the four-episode story) *and* by the director (until the middle of studio recording, when he changed his camera angles to 'give it more point'). Here I used 'before' and 'after' quantitative measures to see whether there was any short-term 'effect' of this 'legalize heroin' scene (in the pre-screening questionnaire 29 per cent of the boys and 21 per cent of the girls out of a sample of 1,000 agreed that heroin should be legalized; after the screening 50 per cent of the boys and 39 per cent of the girls agreed). In addition open-ended questions asked the school students why they gave the response they did, and their reasons for legalizing heroin in the post-screening questionnaires were compared with those given by the character in the text (73 per cent of the respondents gave one or more of the lead character's reasons for legalizing heroin). At the same time, familiar *qualitative* techniques (long interviews, non-participant observation, triangulation) were used to explain *why* the director (who, as a 'BBC-trained' professional, rarely changed his shots once plotted prior to rehearsal) in fact did so, having heard a radio programme which 'made the scene real' for him. Consequently, qualitative, quantitative and 'intertextual' analysis could all be combined.

There were many other quantitative measures relating to formal performance frames of 'audiencing' in this study. The point I am making here is that these audience measures were not researcher-driven so much as *situated* by the dialogic rhetorics-in-use by way of which production was diversely performed within the micro-politics and micro-economies of commercial/ institutional practice.

In an industry driven by quantitative 'audiencing' preoccupations, I was trying to unpack the various professional rhetorics-in-practice (embodied by executive producer, writer, script editor, etc) of the 'semiotically thick' television text, and to put those to the 'test' of quantification. This was using 'data' not so much to adjudicate between 'expert' and 'lay' performance accounts, but rather in terms of the situated context in which professional ('expert') accounts are performed.

In this case, the survey questions were 'situated' in the context of the television industry's multi-layered 'audiencing' strategies. In other research – for example a project on 'School-based HIV/AIDS education in the context of media education' which I conducted with Deborah Lupton – quantitative survey questions used direct quotations from the school students which had seemed strongly held in the dynamics of focus-group interviews. So a particular feature of qualitative methodology (the situated dynamic of interpersonal negotiation which is a major advantage of focus-group interviews, but which also needs to be read as a *performance* in everyday social life) was also being 'tested' here: that is whether what one or two (perhaps dominant) members of various focus groups asserted held for the larger group. For example, when students vociferously said they were sick to death about hearing (from school *or* media) about how to avoid contracting HIV, but rather,

> 'We really need to learn about the symptoms of other STDs; what to look for and that kind of thing',

how far was this a view of a *generational* cohort (across gender, ethnic and class differences)? In fact our survey revealed that *95 per cent of girls and 89 per cent of boys* agreed with that statement.

We could also assess whether what some girls in focus groups said about using different media forms in particular, situated ways (talk-back radio for personal, anonymous feedback of information that 'you are embarrassed not to know, and so can't ask your friends about'; teenage magazines as a private library about STDs and HIV that 'you can keep under your bed') applied over the whole sample of girls (or applied to boys as well), whether the focus-group preference that television should give detailed depictions of what STDs and AIDS 'do to your body', or for school instruction by sexual health counsellors rather than teachers held with the overall sample, boys or girls, different ethnic groups (Asian or southern European), and so on.

The use of actual statements from focus-group interviews in our quantitative survey was in fact of two kinds:

- a series of statements by the students about what they perceived as effective and ineffective HIV education, either in school or in the media, or, frequently, comparing one with the other. Each statement made a single point (for 'precision'), and contained the logic-in-use for that particular preference (for 'situated meaning'): 'Magazines are good sources of information about HIV/STD because you can look things up again if you need to'; 'I like radio personally. If you want to ring up and ask questions about sex or HIV, they don't ask your name. . . . So it's a really confidential way of learning more about AIDS and other STDs.'
- a statement from students about failure to use condoms in an actual sexual performance situation. Here we followed Brenda Dervin's 'sensemaking' strategy. Dervin, who is one of the few scholars to have attempted to bring together cultural studies and quantitative approaches, works according to a number of basic principles, including: (a) taking the subject's rather than the observer's perspective; (b) anchoring the data collection in everyday life situations and real moments of behaviour; (c) positing for the purpose of data collection that individual meanings are constructions bound up in real constrained moments of time–space; (d) making the bridging of gaps (that is making movement through time–space) and the taking of steps

to bridge those gaps the central focus. Dervin's work indicates that information-seeking and use is predicted more significantly by user than observer constructions of situations. Hence the students' description of a specific situation of non-condom use during sexual performance was followed by the question: 'How can we best deal with this situation?: abstinence; better safe sex campaigns in the media; better safe sex education at school; other.' Those who agreed with either/or 'better safe sex campaigns in the media' and 'better safe sex education at school' were then asked what *kind* of campaign these should be. Here again we used specific statements by students from the focus-group interviews as a series of ranked options.

In this particular research study, after the focus-group stage, two of the groups (which had shown particular ease with the interviewer, Sue Venables) were then asked to read, comment on and redesign if necessary the questionnaire. They had the final choice as to which statements were included in the first part of the questionnaire (no statements from their own focus groups were included in the first-draft questionnaire). They were also asked advice as to a reasonable length for the questionnaire, which of course determined the number of statements included.

Finally, this draft questionnaire was trialled at another school which had taken part in the focus-group discussions. Here further modifications were made on the advice of the students. We had, for example, avoided a strongly agree to strongly disagree five-point Likert scale in this trial questionnaire because a few students both in focus groups and in personal conversation had complained about school HIV education which made them tick 'strongly agree, agree, disagree' boxes. However, the trial school students were adamant after completing the questionnaire that a two-point agree/disagree response to the statements gave them too little scope for gradations of opinion. On their advice, the five-point Likert scale was restored for the final questionnaire. Also at *their* request, three questions were added to the survey: 'What one thing do you think would be most effective in improving the "safe sex" situation?' (this question was motivated by student union pressure for installing condom machines in schools); 'Do you think HIV/ AIDS and STD education should be compulsory in schools?' (there was a strong feeling in the trial school that it should be compulsory); and 'If it were to be compulsory, at what year level should it start?'

In the final questionnaire it was made clear that the major statements which students were responding to came in fact from other students of their age. These various measures of 'below-up' input were taken to meet the kind of criticism raised about survey questionnaires by cultural/audience theorists like Justin Lewis, when he argues that 'Regardless of the conversation respondents would like to have, they are forced to follow the remorseless inner logic of the pre-designed questionnaire. . . . Our answers will then be squeezed into the appropriate box so that they can be counted and evaluated' (Lewis, 1991: 78). It is interesting that Lewis's criticism is so similar to that of some of the students themselves about the surveys they were asked to fill

in during school health classes. In this case, however, the questionnaire did
in the end represent the conversation respondents 'seemed to like to have':
(a) to the extent that we chose about 40 of their statements from the focus
groups; and (b) because this collection of statements and the scale itself had
been both approved and augmented by the students in constructing the
questionnaire.

Quantitative and qualitative methods in high-cultural research

Canonical (liberal-humanist) experts in high-cultural research resist 'numbers' fervently. How can abstracted and generalized statistics, one can hear
them say, possibly tell you anything about an artist as subtle, complex,
multi-faceted and polyphonic as Chekhov? My answer is 'not a lot, unless
you remember that Chekhov's readers are also complex, diverse and multi-
faceted' – and that 'numbers' might just release some of their situated 'lay'
knowledge of Chekhov from the monological and canonical limits of the
'expert' critics who want to tell them 'this is so, is it not?'
    In an Australian Research-Council-funded project on 'Chekhov: In Criti-
cism, Performance and Reading', Tom Burvill, Andrew Hood and I read all
refereed journal articles in English on Chekhov between 1980 and 1995 (in
itself a somewhat exhaustive 'quantitative' project!) in order to trace
dominant critical paradigms in the field. The vast majority of these many
hundreds of articles were 'liberal-humanist' (as defined in Chapter 3).
    The liberal-humanist's 'This is so, is it not?' is an 'expert' and mono-
logical reading. In contrast, Bakhtin (as read at least within current cultural
theory) argues for an approach based on the *heteroglossia* of people's
voices. So Bakhtin, like Chekhov, is *also* all about 'polyphony' in 'its
carnivalesque irreverence towards all kinds of authoritarian, repressive,
monologic ideologies' (Lodge, 1990: 21).
    The dialogues that we have looked at in this book have, in fact, accessed
and interwoven a range of types of speech, discourse, embodiments,
intertexts and reading formations (consider again our very first 'lay' voice –
Julie in the streets of Seattle). They have certainly represented 'discursive
polyphony', while trying (reflexively) to see where those different voices are
coming from. As David Lodge (whom I am drawing on here as both an
'academic' and 'creative' high-cultural voice) says about Bakhtin, this is a
theory of interactive social action, of performance.

> The words we use come to us already imprinted with the meanings, intentions and
> accents of previous users, and any utterance we make is directed towards some
> real or hypothetical Other. 'The word in living conversation is directly, blatantly,
> oriented towards a future answer word', says Bakhtin. 'It provokes an answer,
> anticipates it and structures itself in the answer's direction'. (Lodge, 1990: 21)

This dialogic relationship is fundamental to the performance of everyday
life. In Julie's case in Seattle, not only her 'inner' words (of reflexivity), but
also her 'outer' body language were 'directly, blatantly oriented' towards

both 'real and hypothetical' black Others. It is that **situational** context of discourse and the interactive nature of embodiment – the minute-by-minute negotiation of *both* real and hypothetical Others as a white woman encounters two black men in the night streets of Seattle, or as David Troughton's Lopakhin encounters Sean Murray's Trofimov before an audience at the Swan Theatre in Stratford – which makes qualitative analysis so necessary. So in the case of Chekhov as much as in the case of Julie a cultural, *performative* emphasis is important – for example, to explain why his characters do *not* (in most but not all cases) use words 'directly, blatantly, oriented towards a future answer word'.

The valuable shift from Saussure to Bakhtin in cultural studies approaches to literary (or any other) language has at the same time shifted the focus from scientific analyses of 'langue' to situated analysis of 'talk' – and at least one 'expert' theatre semiotician has described the effect this had on him *as* an academic as he moved from a 'top-down' and 'scientific' semiotics to a 'processual poetics' of theatre that required him to *listen to* and *watch* theatre practitioners, and to let them share in his analysis (Elam, 1989).

Yet even here in high-cultural research – or I am tempted to say, *because* of liberal-humanism's anathema with quantitative analysis for 'reducing' the impermeable, organic relationship between form and content – quantitative work may be useful. No less in ethnographies of high-cultural daily practice than anywhere else is David Silverman's caution valid that the 'critical reader is forced to ponder whether the researcher has selected only those fragments of data which support his [*sic*] argument' (Silverman, 1993: 162).

There are a number of ways of trying to face this problem which have already been incorporated in earlier chapters. The major one is to draw 'metamethodological' attention to 'the researcher/writer as a producer of descriptions' (Ang, 1996: 76). Throughout the book I have been trying to draw attention reflexively to the way in which the researcher/interviewers' own 'kind of representational order' has interceded dialogically in the 'fieldwork' to give order and coherence to the 'data'. A second way has been to quote as much of an actual interview's voices as possible (as in the case of the Sydney building workers) so that readers can use their own intensive criteria for assessing the internal 'textual' coherence of the argument (does the writer, for example, concentrate on the 'exotic' at the expense of the 'less dramatic'?).

Despite these two emphases, however, this leaves us a long way short of Silverman's criterion of demonstrating that 'the qualitative analysis was reasonably representative of the data as a whole' (Silverman, 1993: 163). How can we, then, avoid Bryman's critique of qualitative research, where,

> there is a tendency towards an anecdotal approach to the use of 'data' in relation to conclusions or explanations. . . . Brief conversations, snippets from unstructured interviews, or examples of a particular activity are used to provide evidence for a particular contention. There are grounds for disquiet that the representativeness or generality of these fragments is rarely addressed (Bryman, 1988: 77).

Silverman offers a number of useful guidelines to get us a bit closer to meeting this methodological problem of qualitative and ethnographic research, drawing attention to a number of specific problems that need to be addressed.

• Attention to the *categories* used to represent and analyse an interview text: for example, in quantitative audience analysis with Royal Shakespeare Company subscribers and also in my school-based HIV education research, I used *respondents'* (not researcher/interviewers') categories as direct quotations in fixed-choice surveys. By linking focus groups with quantitative methods it was possible to separate the 'exotic' which might well have fitted with the researchers' interests (for example, one RSC subscriber's comment about Lopakhin as representative of Thatcher's Britain) from the 'less dramatic' (for example the Swan subscribers' interest in the minimalist use of sets at the Swan: in fact, 61 per cent of the RSC Friends that we surveyed disagreed with the 'Thatcher' reading, while only 23 per cent agreed).

• The inadequacy of standard ethnographic approaches to validate data via *triangulation*. The problem here, as Silverman says, is the methodological eclecticism of this approach to the **situated**: 'by counterposing different contexts, it ignores the context-bound and skilful character of social interaction and assumes that members are "cultural dopes", who need a sociologist to dispel their illusions' (Silverman, 1993: 158). This is the problem of objectivist 'expert knowledgeability' that has been emphasized from the start of this book. I have already given one example of triangulation embedded in television industry rhetorics and performances. In the Chekhov research, rather than draw on different methodologies from different theories, I have focused on using triangulation to address the situated nature of accounts positioned in a production/text/audience *process*, rather than to 'adjudicate between competing versions' – for example, Trevor Griffiths' lectures at Birmingham University about Raymond Williams's 'Chekhov', his interview with me about 'rediscovering Chekhov', his studio difficulties with the set design for Act 2 of the television *The Cherry Orchard*.

Further, Griffiths' concern about the 'BBC naturalism' of his Act 2 of *The Cherry Orchard* could be 'tested' in both quantitative and qualitative audience contexts. As we saw, Griffiths' emphasis here was on a Brechtian alienation effect and subtext, requiring a two-dimensional, schematic, 'expressionist' and 'threatening' (rather than lyrical) space in contrast to the 'real depth' detail and naturalism that the set designer preferred. In addition, there were Richard Eyre's interest in a set emphasizing 'ownership' which was 'dry, arid', and also the cameraman's attempt to make Act 2 'dream-like'. In our quantitative after-screening surveys administered to 200 university students, a semantic differential question on 'staging Act 2' included the following pairs (based on various performance rhetorics-in-practice): detailed/schematic; expressionistic/naturalistic; dry, arid/green, opulent; emphasizing rootlessness/emphasizing ownership; natural/alienating; threatening atmosphere/lyrical atmosphere; historically specific/'any time or place'; two dimensional/real depth; lifelike/dreamlike.

The quantitative results showed that the students found the set 'dry, arid', 'dreamlike' *and* alienating; but then the use of open-ended survey questions and focus-group interviews could tie down the particular **rhetorics-in-use** here – for example, students of Russian at Columbia University (who fully subscribed to the liberal-humanist Chekhov) wanted to see a naturalistic, beautiful, Russian cherry orchard to justify their empathetic 'feeling of loss' with Ranevskaya's family, hence their translation of Griffiths' 'radical disjuncture' of Act 2 into a 'jarring transition', and their 'alienating' reading of the set. In contrast, students of theatre studies at Loughborough University, who had studied both Griffiths and Brecht, enjoyed what few 'alienating devices' they felt were left in the production (such as the acting of Yepikhodov) which, they agreed with Griffiths, had been lost under a surfeit of 'BBC costume drama'. Again, here 'triangulation' is used in the context of *performance rhetorics*.

● The problem of linking generalizability to entire populations rather than to *theoretical propositions*. Choosing 'RSC subscribers' as the major audience targeted by the RSC marketing office, we used statements about *The Cherry Orchard* from focus groups we ran with subscribers as a basis for a survey questionnaire to see whether they were reasonably representative of *this particular high-cultural 'fan' group*, rather than the production's 'audience as a whole'.

● The issue of *testing explanations*: Silverman, for example, speaks of the search for deviant cases in linking qualitative and quantitative research to see whether an explanation stands, whether it needs reformulating, or whether the phenomenon is redefined to exclude the deviant case. Cultural theorists and qualitative researchers tend to be extremely hesitant about 'formulating hypotheses', seeing this as a basic feature of objectivist, quantitative research. Yet, we nevertheless do very often construct implicit hypotheses in our situated narratives – so it is probably better to make them explicit.

In Chapter 5, for example, there is my explanation that David Troughton found it more difficult to play Chekhov's Lopakhin as a 'decentred' character at the RSC than Shakespeare's Caliban. My explanation there was based on the following kinds of reasoning. Because of widely circulating political/theoretical propositions (relating to new historicist and/or post-colonial discourse *vis-à-vis* Shakespeare's *The Tempest*) it is perfectly possible for both an actor and a Sydney audience to instantly 'read' an Aboriginal Caliban, so that his poetic lines can be related generally to an 'other' language masked by colonialism, and more particularly to a local 'Dreamtime' reading. Thus Caliban's 'environmental' statement can be taken as an alternative future to that of white exploitation of the land, and the 'contradiction' of a 'brute' who speaks poetry readily resolved. In the case of Lopakhin, however, the lack of an equivalent 'alternative', forward-looking discourse means that even his lines about changing the environment to achieve 'rich, active lives' are effaced in a conventional, humanist interpretation where any identity struggle he has is a matter of *past* socialization: as the son of a serf, and as a child befriended by the much more 'aesthetic' cherry orchard gentry. My explanation here tried to account for Troughton's greater difficulty, in his two 'brutes who speak poetry' parts, with preparing the part of Lopakhin, even though he said he 'feels beauty' in those lines. We would not, according to the same interpretation, expect an audience to feel the forward-looking beauty of those lines either.

Would my quantitative survey of RSC subscribers support this argument? I asked the RSC subscribers 42 questions based on direct statements from a focus group of the RSC Friends executive (and on long interviews with production personnel, including David Troughton) about the Noble *Cherry Orchard*. I will limit my brief 'counting' summary to statements about Lopakhin which relate to issues discussed conceptually in Chapter 5. (In Table 1, SA = strongly agree; A = agree; DK = don't know; D = disagree; SD = strongly disagree.) [see Table 1]

Overall, as we expected after the focus-group interview with the RSC subscribers, evaluation of Troughton himself was positive: as many as 95 per cent felt that he 'has enormous physical presence', which equates well with Troughton's own emphasis (Chapter 5) on his bodily preparation in an acting part. Also 90 per cent agreed with the focus-group respondent who felt Troughton conveyed Lopakhin's frustration well; and only 15 per cent agreed with the executive member who felt he played Lopakhin as a 'vulgar upstart'. There was about half-and-half agreement with the idea that, used to seeing Troughton playing 'larger than life characters', the RSC subscribers *expected* him to play Lopakhin that way. This disagreement also matched the discussion in the focus group.

There was very heavy agreement (82 per cent), too, with the reviewer's comment about Lopakhin as 'double-edged' (both vulgar millionaire and half-conscious perceiver of the beauty he is destroying), and with David Troughton's own comment about Lopakhin not being a 'bulldozer who doesn't see beauty in anything' (83 per cent). This was not unexpected, since this still includes the unitary 'socialized serf' Lopakhin whose 'double-edged' quality adheres to his serf mentality on the one hand, and his love for his betters on the other (Chapter 5). It is from *them* that he has acquired his 'half-conscious recognition of the beauty he is destroying and . . . is incapable of replacing'. This is a 'history' – as Barry (1995) says of humanist criticism – based entirely on the 'words on the page' (according to this tradition, what other Lopakhin, outside his textual relations as a child with his father/grandfather and with the young Ranevskaya, *could* there possibly be?). These data are not, then, necessarily inconsistent with the 72 per cent agreement with the focus-group subscriber who believed that Lopakhin's 'progress' was equivalent to today's builder of executive homes.

Table 1

	SA (%)	A (%)	DK (%)	D (%)	SD (%)
'David Troughton played Lopakhin as a vulgar upstart.':	5	13	2	63	18
'Lopakhin represents progress – like nowadays taking a lovely wild field and building executive homes on it.':	7	65	9	18	2
'It seemed to me very much a contemporary production – this is what is happening when everyone is grabbing for themselves – the worst that is brought out in people by Thatcherism.':	4	20	16	54	7
'Poignantly double-edged is David Troughton's brilliant portrayal of the self-made man born to serfdom, who has become a millionaire. Yet his triumphant ownership of the estate is still plagued by a half-conscious recognition of the beauty he is destroying and is incapable of replacing.':	34	48	5	7	5
'I was very aware of the sheer frustration of Lopakhin that he could not get them to *see*.':	22	67	9	2	0
'It's moments when Lopakhin says "we should be giants living here" that makes us realize that Lopakhin is not necessarily a bulldozer who doesn't see the beauty in things.':	6	77	11	6	0
'When Lopahkin says "I can see a time when they will start cultivating their land and your cherry orchard will have made way for rich prosperous active lives" we should believe in this possibility.':	13	63	4	19	2
'The poppy field line (Act IV) is Lopakhin's *feeling* beauty.':	2	40	56	2	0
'David Troughton has an enormous physical presence.':	27	65	6	2	0
'I think we are used to seeing David Troughton playing these big, larger than life characters. So we expected him to play Lopakhin that way.':	7	39	6	44	4

Unexpected, **however, was the 76 per cent support for the 'cultivating their lands . . . rich, prosperous, active lives' Lopakhin.** As a statement suggesting commitment to positive environmental change, this had not been prepared for anywhere, *either* in the focus-group discussion with subscribers *or* in my own analysis so far – except perhaps in my description of David Troughton's passionate emphasis on this in his part. Maybe (hidden from my analysis of the focus group, but similar to the impact of Sean Murray's playing of Trofimov for the Cumbrian 'A-level' students), David Troughton *had* achieved his own multiple-identitied ambition with Lopakhin? Perhaps it is significant here that only 2 per cent of the respondents were prepared to say they *disagreed* with Troughton's statement about the 'poppy field' line representing Lopakhin's *'feeling* of beauty'.

Whether this is the case or not, in my analysis so far this particular bit of quantitative data is unexpected, requiring perhaps some reformulating of my explanation of Chapter 5. It is a caution, I think, against relying *only* on situated analysis.

CONCLUSION: UNDERSTANDING SITUATED PERFORMANCE

> I am centrally interested in reaching an understanding of television narratives but conceived in terms of their likely 'realisations' by viewers viewing in determinate settings. (Sparks, 1992: 49)

> It's all right when you've got someone near. . . . But . . . when you're on your own, every little creak and you think somebody's getting in. You get frightened, you see. That's what it is, it's the fear, the fear. I think it builds up. You . . . see these things and think that could happen to me. . . . Being on your own, it's a big thing. . . . If you've got somebody to talk to, it gets it out of your system. You bottle it up when you're on your own. ('Mae')

We live, Clifford Geertz has said, in an era of 'blurred genres', and within, Denzin and Lincoln argue, 'the double crisis of representation and legitimation [which] confronts qualitative researchers in the social sciences' (Denzin and Lincoln, 1998: 21). Issues of reliability, validity and generalizability have been thrown into crisis, after decades of 'grounded' qualitative research seemed successfully to have established these criteria. Reflexivity has become crucially important as 'writing and fieldwork blur into one another' (Denzin and Lincoln, 1998: 21). In the absence of the 'master' narratives of modernity (and consequently of an 'objective', 'neutral' and 'detached' methodology), 'each one of us has to engage with the fluid ambiguities and uncertainties of tentative, "local" stories or accounts' (Adam and Allan, 1995: xv).

And yet, Adam and Allan say, little of a genuinely radical potential is currently being realized in the name of postmodern cultural theory. 'The rich diversity of cultural forms, practices and identities is being celebrated at the expense of a critical analysis of their implication in the daily renewal of the pernicious logics of class, sexism, racism, homophobia, ageism, nationalism, amongst others, that are all too indicative of "postmodern" societies' (1995: xv). Talk to Mae (above) about the 'rich diversity' of her life and she will laugh at you; and it is precisely because of the daily renewal of the pernicious logics of – in Mae's case – sexism and ageism that issues of generalizability and reliability of one's analysis still do matter (hence my previous chapter). It is for this reason that Terry Threadgold's call, on my opening page, for performing gender (and age) in different ways still stands. Mae does not celebrate diversity, she fears crime; and it is to re-emphasize *that* substantive element of so many of the 'pernicious logics' that Adam and Allan describe that I will make this the focus of my final chapter.

At the same time, Adam and Allan are also right about the need for a new emphasis on the inescapably local, partial and fragmentary in the context of the interconnected and globalizing. Much of the emphasis of this book has been on 'the need to reflexively examine how we are temporally and spatially situated within the institutional dynamics of theoretical production' (Adam and Allan, 1995: xvi) at the level of both 'expert' and 'lay knowledgeability'. It is this relationship between time/space co-ordinates and our reflexivity about them which in the end is – as in the case of Julie in night-time Seattle – what we mean by 'situated'.

So, despite my caution at the end of Chapter 6 about relying only on situated analysis, I want – for political and theoretical reasons – to end this book with 'stories of the everyday'. I want to reverse the order of the previous chapter, which was from situated to quantitative methodologies. Instead, ending where I began (with stories of fear of crime), I will try to show that methodological rigour, the testing of hypotheses, and the explanation of 'deviant cases' can work the other way, from the quantitatively imprecise to the qualitatively precise and situated. At the same time, I want to review the overall trend of this book which is (to repeat some comments from the Introduction) that:

- 'performativity has emerged to focus attention on the subject's (compulsory) performance of gender and the possibilities for performing gender differently', but also that we should beware the 'seductions involved in allowing oneself to be positioned totally by the discourses and genres of rewriting and refusal of metalanguages' (Threadgold, 1997: 2, 1);
- by focusing on an 'ethnography of storytelling' (Ang) we see how 'the media event is decontextualised, disconnected, diffused, re-diffused . . . rais[ing] questions about methodological procedures for understanding it' (Hughes-Freeland, 1998: 10);
- 'one never actually leaves the local. . . . Rather it is the system of local contexts, their distributions and linkages, that creates a global field' (Hirsch, 1998: 223).

There is also a polemical reason for my reversal of the 'methodological order' of Chapter 6. Whereas, arguably in dominant paradigms of high-cultural research, use of mixed qualitative and quantitative data together can give us more access to the 'lay' voices that liberal-humanist critics prefer to suppress, in 'risk' policy research the dominant expert paradigm is, as Lash, Szerszynski and Wynne argue, strongly wedded to 'an objectivist, physicalist and fully naive realism' (1996: 6). Challenging 'expert knowledgeability' here *requires* (following Wynne et al.) a commitment to the situated.

In the fear of crime field, for example, the objectivist 'disparity' between 'expert' and 'lay' knowledgeability has been the driving force behind an explosion of quantitative research. As Marian Tulloch has put it:

The risk–victimisation paradox which describes the apparent discrepancy between 'objective' measures of risk of criminal victimisation and 'subjective' measures of individuals' fear became the impetus for the development of an extensive quantitative fear of crime literature. . . . At the most general level people are seen to overestimate the prevalence of crime in the community, often believing crime in their city or state is much higher than in their local neighbourhood . . . or perceiving increases in crime that are not supported by official statistics. . . . More specifically, the risk–victimisation paradox refers to the claim that certain groups, such as women and the elderly, who are at less risk according to crime statistics, have higher levels of fear than their male and younger counterparts. (M. Tulloch, 1998: 8)

Tulloch points in these quantitative studies to the over-dependence on what for respondents may well be hypothetical questions. For example, 'How safe do you feel walking alone in your neighbourhood at night?' may not be very meaningful for an older woman who has chosen not to go out to enter-tainment at night since her partner died; or may seem ambivalent to an old person who is more fearful of walking at night because of her poor eyesight and uneven pavements than because of crime. As Tulloch says, what is less understood is the ways in which situated decisions to alter, avoid or limit at-risk behaviours impact on people's lifestyle – and underlying these 'control' strategies there are likely to be a range of both personal and social vulnerabilities which need exploring in localized ways.

Discourses of power and vulnerability about certain types of victims (eg women, the elderly, children) or certain types of offence (eg stranger danger) circulate in the public domain both through informal contact and via the media. Quantitative work has only *touched* on the central issue of how fear of crime interrelates with everyday practices. (M. Tulloch, 1998: 9)

At the other end of the fear of crime spectrum is the important qualitative work of Richard Sparks who points directly to the importance of inter-relating the analysis of media texts and everyday practice. Sparks specifi-cally calls for criminological work that is 'attentive to the ways in which images of crime, law enforcement and punishment are caught up in the fine grain of cultural and personal experience' (Sparks, 1992: 5). However, Sparks concentrates on the more formal/ideological analysis of crime drama texts and never 'approaches the audience'. By way of Sparks's analysis, I want to go further than he does, or than I have done in the book so far in examining the 'mediated' audience.

The difference between theatre and media audiences pertains to the 'mass' characteristics of the latter. As Thompson (1995) says, the characteristics of mass communication are: its technical and institutional means of production; its commodification of symbolic forms; its 'structured' break between the production of symbolic forms and their reception; its extension of the availability of symbolic forms in space and time; and its public circulation of symbolic forms (1995: 27–30). Only some of these distinguish media audiences from theatre audiences, of course, but they are significant because, as Thompson says, while television reception is always a situated activity, it is also an activity which enables individuals to take some distance from the practical contexts of their daily life. By receiving materials which involve a substantial degree of spatial (and perhaps also temporal) distanciation, individuals can lift themselves out of their life contexts and, for a moment, lose themselves in another world. The reception of media products should be seen, furthermore, as a *routine* activity, in the sense that it is an integral part of the regularized activities that constitute everyday life. (1995: 39)

It is especially this routine daily activity that distinguishes the self-constituting TV audience from even the most dedicated of theatre subscribers; and it is this relationship between the 'another world' of television *and* the very localized iconography of some its genres, as this is negotiated via audiences' situated fears and anxieties, that is the focus of Sparks's analysis. So in this chapter, by 'not leaving the local', I want to show how 'the media event is decontextualised, disconnected, diffused, re-diffused' (Ang), and thus how people, via its 'mediated visibility' (Thompson), 'perform gender [and age] differently'. It is here that 'appropriation' (much discussed in cultural and media studies: see Chapter 1) takes on the particular representational order of this book. I am using it here, in Thompson's sense of the

extended process of understanding and self-understanding. To appropriate [a text] is to take hold of its meaningful content and make it one's own. . . . In appropriating . . . we adapt it to our own lives and life contexts. We apply it to a set of circumstances which, in the case of media products, are generally different from the circumstances in which [it] was produced. (Thompson, 1995: 42)

Sparks, crime narratives and iconography

How can we, Sparks asks, get past the standard 'expert' criminological accounts of fear of crime which rely (at least implicitly) on a notional rational agent, and thus give very little insight into the nature of fear of crime *as a dimension of experience*? If 'what we mean by fear of crime is not so much a [rationalistic] calculation of probabilities as a set of "intuitions"' (Sparks, 1992: 11), and if in addition, fear of crime, far from being simply the result of direct experience of crime cannot 'be separated out from other experiences and hazards and troubles' (Sparks, 1992: 12), then what methodological procedures for understanding this global/local relationship might we adopt?

Because of his emphasis on the intuitive rather than rationalistic, and on 'fear of crime' as simply part of a web of current anxieties, Sparks focuses on television crime drama. Television, he argues, is one of the most important and routine purveyors of the 'paleo-symbolic dynamic of fear'. The paleo-symbolic (following Gouldner) is the 'emotional underpinning' (Sparks, 1992: 41) on which any successfully 'rational' transmission of ideological or discursive knowledge depends. In particular, as the police series has replaced the Western as the most popular television genre, so its particular 'command' iconography (relating especially to fears of the modern city) becomes the underpinning of 'ideological' performance frames.

Sparks argues that the routine, daily scheduling of popular police series narratives produce, reproduce, and reiterate what Bourdieu calls the 'doxic': where 'the established cosmological and political order is perceived not as arbitrary – i.e. as one possible order among others – but as a self-evident and natural order which goes without saying and therefore goes unquestioned' (Bourdieu, 1977: 166; cited in Sparks, 1992: 50–1). But it is important in Sparks's argument that this 'ideological' performance frame is based on non-rational, deep-emotional responses to television as an iconic, participatory and profoundly familiar form (as in its repeated imagery of the city). Emotionally-charged images connoting 'deep' (but not necessarily fear-specific) anxiety, then, interact, Sparks suggests, with routinized ('good guy defeats bad guy') police narratives in a ritual/performance relationship which ensures an emotional 'resolution' (rather than a rational, 'intellectual clarification').

It is in this popular genre, he argues, that people are offered – for their pleasure – troubling and dangerous issues which, in other media genres, are likely to cause fear and concern. In particular, the city offers the public's main 'landscapes of fear'. In our own Australian survey, it was indeed places in the city – usually Sydney – that respondents consistently nominated as Australia's most dangerous places: Kings Cross because of the crime around the red light district (in which some people believed the police are involved); Cabramatta because of the Asian drug gangs said to be operating from there; Redfern because of the reputation it has for 'rough' and 'bludging' Aborigines living there. Other media genres also help constitute these as 'landscapes of fear': 'hidden video' footage on the news of corrupt cops taking packets of money from sleaze kings, regular 'doco' images of the 'incivility' (graffiti, drunks, run-down houses) of Redfern, newspaper and TV news headlines of the slaying (supposedly by an Asian gang) of Cabramatta's anti-corruption member of parliament.

Thus the television city is *both* Thompson's 'another world' (most of the respondents who nominate Cabramatta, Kings Cross and Redfern as 'landscapes of fear' live far from there) *and* 'the local' (in so far as these city streets become icons of the 'local Australian', are places one catches the train 'through', are places where one works close to, and – even more importantly – become signifiers of the shape and 'cause' of crime as it spreads to one's *own* local area). Further, since the city, as Stuart Hall has argued, is 'above all the concrete embodiment of the achievement of industrial civilization' (Hall et al., 1978: 145), the media's emphasis on the breakdown and dislocation of social order in the city helps engender, Hall argues, a crisis of authority – not least, at some intuitive and local level, a crisis in the belief of our 'master narratives' of civilization altogether.

Sparks thus elaborates on the *ambivalent but central* television performances of the city as the police genre takes over from the Western as its most popular action genre, and as the emphasis on police integrity in the face of urban anomie replaces the Western's rather different focus on the rule of law at the heart of white expansion and nation building. Violence now inheres in the actions of law enforcers who themselves often find social organization too extensive to control or even comprehend, while their violent actions are played out in public city spaces that are all too recognizable to viewers, both as places of everyday work and leisure, and as ritualized 'landscapes of fear'.

The same ambivalence and tension which beset the agents of law is found therefore, Sparks argues, in the audience's response to the city images that they inhabit. The emotive power of these 'local' words and images are central to any broader 'ideological' acceptability of ideas. Television's nature as a familiarly iconic medium requires that 'such ideologies as the television watchers accept must be successful in integrating and resonating with the residual iconic imagery' (Gouldner, cited in Sparks, 1992: 42). One simple way in which this can happen, Sparks suggests, is for the local, 'known' and ambiguous images of the city to be embedded in a police series narrative which begins in a familiar locale (a police station, office or home), moves outward into the dangerously ambivalent scenes of the city to encompass its crime, violence and police pursuit, and then finally returns again to a place of safety (the police station again). 'Most crimes take place either outdoors or in public and non-domestic buildings. . . . "Indoors", on the other hand is usually a space of reflection, planning, discussion but also banter and intimacy' (Sparks, 1992: 127). It is for that reason that images of armed 'home invasion' are, Sparks says, so shocking as 'especially personal affronts' (1992: 127).

The analytical and methodological task, then, for Sparks becomes the examination of these paleo-symbolic and narrative-ideological relations of television crime in the context of people's other daily practices and discourses. Television brings the public 'other world' of power, threat, and ideological resolution into the private world of emotions and fear. But here it becomes part of our 'mutuality of interaction' (1992: 47): it is part of our talk, gossip, and so on.

> For these reasons I consider that the interpretation of television viewing, the study of the transactions which take place between institutions, programmes and audiences, is in certain important respects more akin to the study of talk than to the study of texts. I am centrally interested in reaching an understanding of television narratives but conceived in terms of their likely 'realisations' by viewers viewing in determinate settings. (Sparks, 1992: 49)

Here, then, is a potential methodological move from the quantitative (increasing numbers of TV police series, audience viewing statistics) to the qualitative. But Sparks does not, as I said, undertake this analysis of situated 'talk' about television and crime. This omission became a central emphasis of our fear of crime research. Via long interviews and focus-groups, we 'talked' with viewers about their pleasures in, and fears of, crime and media in relation to city iconicity ('landscapes of fear'), narrative (good guy/bad guy), series repetition, scheduling, place and time. We also revisited in this qualitative way the major quantitative studies of television and fear of crime, such as Gerbner's 'mean world' thesis, and Gunter's selective perception thesis (Tulloch et al., 1998: vol. 1, ch. 5). How would all of these hypotheses shape up at the level of local, situated 'talk'?

The people and their places

Sparks has argued that 'different senses of the term "fear" may be operative for different circumstances and groups of people, so that women's fear might differ from men's, or the fears of the elderly from those of the young, not just in "quantity but in kind" ' (1992: 11). I will turn now to analyses of just four people – two male, two female; two young, two much older – to look at their different senses of 'fear' as they interact, locally, with the media.

Mae is nearly 70 years old, a resident of Bathurst, a small town in country New South Wales. She is the recent widow of a farmer and now lives on a new housing estate. She will not, she emphatically told us, watch anything on television to do with 'home invasions', because this normally profiles attacks on older people, people who are on their own, and 'people who can't defend themselves. . . . It makes you wonder why they have to attack *old people*. That's what frightens me. When you're on your own, you wonder if you might be the next one.' Mae's home has become a fortified enclave since her husband's death. She ensures that everything is multiply locked up at night, and in the daytime keeps her front and back door locked as well. She feels her caution is necessary 'because of what you see on the TV and what you read in the papers.' Even police series which we found many older respondents enjoyed, like *Heartbeat* or *The Bill*, have 'got violence in, it frightens me'. Despite her fears, Mae has only contacted the police once; when a neighbour threw a 'sparkler' on to her roof.

Bill, an older man in his 80s lives with his wife in a retirement village in Sydney. Although in a heavily populated and commercial suburb of the city, the village has walls, making Bill and his wife feel safe and 'isolated rather. . . . [We feel] more secure [here].' Bill has few of the anxieties of Mae, just taking some 'sensible precautions' like locking up at night. On the occasions when they go out together in the evening, 'we don't stop anywhere, just come straight back, straight in'. Like most older people we interviewed, he was changing his view of the police in the wake of the Wood Royal Commission (into police corruption in New South Wales). But this did not make him much more anxious. As a 'youngster I played sport against policemen who were as straight as a string', and you can't blame the 90 per cent – the sins of the old ones on to the young ones. I think that they'll be all the better for [the Royal Commission].'

Lisa is a 16-year-old living now in the fashionable harbour suburb of Sydney's Rose Bay, and, prior to her mother's re-marriage, lived in the also middle-class (but 'tougher') beach suburb of Bondi. Lisa has cause to fear her home city. She has been mugged in Bondi for her Reeboks, as have a number of her friends. Her Bondi home has been burgled, and the family car broken into or stolen several times. As a young teenager, she was present when a girlfriend's mother's boyfriend attempted to molest her friend sexually. She has also been harassed sexually in the school toilets by a man posing as a doctor. In addition, her father's first wife was a drug addict. Lisa has not found the police helpful in relation to her city fears. On the contrary, she says that she and a girlfriend have been harassed by police in the streets of Bondi for the clothes they wore; another girlfriend has told her that her policeman-husband regularly beats her up; yet another girlfriend has described the inadequate police response when she was attacked and robbed on Bondi beach; and Lisa speaks of her own experience of police harassing busker friends at Sydney's Circular Quay.

Rob is a 16-year-old boy living with his lawyer mother and younger sister in the inner-western Sydney suburb of Enmore. He has not been subject to the same degree of violence, harassment or family trouble as Lisa. But the bank across the road from his home has been held up, and there was a recent stabbing death at the local ice-rink. Rob's attitude to the police is much less negative than Lisa's, and he feels safe in his own suburb walking home at night because of the police presence there. He is aware, though (through his lawyer mother) of police corruption in the south-coast town where he lived prior to moving to Sydney. Rob is not especially fearful about his own home location, though he occasionally thinks about 'home invasions' when he sees them on the media.

Images of the city: 'landscapes of fear'

When her children were young, Mae used to take them to the public parks. But now she stays at home most of the time, never visiting the park. But Sydney, she says, would be even more dangerous to walk about the streets. She believes that television would not keep reporting all these things about drugs and burglaries there if it wasn't happening. In contrast, as a *resident* of Sydney, Bill feels that the media represent only the bad news not the good because 'young people take notice of it'. But he feels that he doesn't let the media image of Sydney affect him too much. He doesn't, for example, allow the media's accounts of one of its major 'landscapes of fear', Cabramatta, put him off visiting the Vietnamese restaurants there when a friend from the country who likes Asian food comes to Sydney. So, despite being in his 80s, Bill gets out and about, taking 'sensible precautions' for someone who is an 'old bloke . . . on his way out'. Meanwhile, the much younger Mae hides away inside her home walls.

Both Lisa and Rob *locally differentiate* their city images. In her present home in Rose Bay, Lisa is much less fearful because, even though the windows do not lock properly, it is a 'much safer' suburb than Bondi (where even 'the police are evil'). She also does not go to the city centre alone. Rob derives some of his city 'landscapes of fear' from the media. 'Kings Cross – sometimes they talk about that and occasionally I go there to see friends or something. I worry about people there. Like you get bad news on a certain area, and when you go there you worry about what's going to happen to you. . . . Occasionally I hear something about a stabbing or a mugging. I walk down the street with nice clothes on, good target. I get worried about that.' Because of media influence, he says he would never go to Cabramatta. 'Different gangs or drugs. See images of lots of syringes. Just the images and interviews about it.'

However, as well as the media's 'landscapes of fear', Rob constructs his own through his talk with other young people. Recently he was staying at a YMCA in the city centre, and heard from 'students who lived in the area' not to walk in Hyde Park at night. Now he believes that this will become a trouble spot during the Sydney 2000 Olympics because tourists who are 'loaded with money' will not realize that this central park is a dangerous site at night. As with Lisa, this makes him feel that the media do not adequately deal with some of the local contexts he knows about. 'You hear bits and pieces, but there is no real focus that I know of. You don't hear them talking about certain open areas like Hyde Park – I've never heard that one on the news. The only way I hear about it is that people told me not to go there at night.' He also criticizes the local media for this. He notes that the local newspaper did not report significant events which have happened within a few metres of his house, like the bank robbery and the ice-rink knifing, because 'the local paper tries to give a good view of the community not the bad.'

Narrative good guys and bad guys

Mae and Bill: the seniors

Both Mae and Bill prefer the 'good guys' to win in cop series, but their responses are very differently situated. Mae says 'You don't like to see evil triumph'; but with her much greater personal fear she tries not to watch evil on TV at all.

> That's the trouble, they're getting too much like what's happening out on the streets . . . like what you read in the paper, the knifings. I watched the shorts last night and they had a big stick . . . that I don't know whether they used or not. But those sort of things frighten me. I didn't watch [the programme] to know how it happened.

Bill's relationship with the media is less solipsistic and intensive than Mae's. He can achieve the reflexive distance from newspapers to say that they *choose* to print the bad news to gain a market of younger people; and he equally both enjoys and distances himself from various TV police series. He regularly watches *The Bill*: 'I like the reality of it. The others . . . sort of like to be . . . a little over the top, you know, fellows jumping off 50-foot towers and landing on one foot.' Still, he does like the 'good guys' to win, so in this case it is *not* the more anxious Mae (as Sparks and Gunter would predict) but the much more secure Bill who enjoys the 'feel-good thing. . . . You don't like to see evil triumph.' But Bill's sense of security, as we will see, resides more centrally in other circuits of communication than cop shows, which he says he can easily do without.

In juxtaposition with Sparks's notion of police narratives, we were interested in asking questions relating to Gerbner's thesis about heavy television viewing and a 'mean world' belief; and also to Gunter's critique of Gerbner, following his own hypothesis that anxious people turn to television to cultivate crime prevention competence. In our long interviews, we asked a couple of questions relating to how acutely respondents were concerned about crime (via the media). One question asked whether they could remember any particular crime news story in the last couple of weeks; the second was the question: 'Overall, do you think you are nearer to the "private" end of the spectrum (worrying about things you see on TV but not talking much about them or able to do much about them) or at the more "active" end (in a community group, or through the work you do, or through letters to the media, etc)?'

Mae admitted to being at the privatized end of the spectrum, not even talking with her family about her fears. She certainly has a 'mean world' view of her environment, yet she does not watch a lot of television (unlike Gerbner's 'mean world' heavy viewers). Nor does Mae use television crime shows instrumentally to cultivate crime prevention competence, as Gunter suggests. In fact, Gunter's (and Sparks's) suggestion that 'the anxious viewer should find comfort and relief in drama because it ultimately *reduces* their anxieties by projecting a just world . . . [via] the ultimate triumph of justice' (Gunter, 1987: 92) does not work for Mae at all! I am not, of course, trying to 'disprove' a quantitative thesis with one example here. Rather, I am pointing to the way in which we need to embed our understanding of how anxiety works in any one individual's use (or non-use) of a variety of circuits of communication. In Mae's case this included not only television, but newspapers – and not only national newspapers but also local ones – in addition to talk, local gossip and so on. It seems that in the short period since her husband died Mae has in fact begun to re-'read' more fearfully the *same* police series (like *The Bill* and *Australia's Most Wanted*) that she once watched with him, replacing their 'talk' with a ritualized attention to local and national newspapers, and with an occasional anxious communing with her neighbours. As a result of this new contextualization of her television watching, Mae argues that these police series are getting more mean and cynical: 'That's the trouble, they're getting too much like what's happening out on the streets.' Mae is a victim of what Thompson describes as the 'monological character and the separation of contexts' of 'televisual quasi-interaction', where producers of crime series are 'severed from the reflexive monitoring of others' responses which is a routine and constant feature of face-to-face interaction' (Thompson, 1995: 96). Like many older people, Mae feels that crime series are portraying too mean and frightening a world, and that she cannot tell them so. So, unlike Gerbner's 'mean world' heavy viewer, Mae actually turns her TV off (especially avoiding police shows); yet her world gets meaner still!

Though Mae's case does not support Gunter's selective perception thesis either (vis-à-vis the relationship between anxious viewers and the instrumental use of crime series), in other respects she does support his theory; in particular Gunter's:

- general finding that personal confidence in competence to defend oneself relates most closely to risk evaluation (as in Mae's major fear about criminals who attack older people 'who can't defend themselves');
- suggestion that viewers' interpretations of the television programmes depends on whether they find the content realistic or relevant (Mae's 'home invasion' fear);
- emphasis on situation-specific factors (in this case Mae's recent bereavement and isolation in her privatized home) in relation to feelings of personal vulnerability when viewing television.

Although much older than Mae, Bill is, of course, male (Gunter notes that women more frequently perceive a strong likelihood of being violently assaulted than men), feels more secure in his 'village' environment, engages far more in 'talk' when upset by media reports of major crimes, and is far less anxious about wandering the streets of Sydney (even 'landscapes of fear' like Cabramatta), provided it is in the daytime. Furthermore, Bill's understanding of 'realism' in TV police series does not change according to a privatized alteration of personal history, as it has in Mae's case, but rather according to changes in the broader history 'out there', as revealed in the New South Wales police inquiries. As Thompson has argued, the new kind of 'mediated visibility' embedded in modernity is neither the type of 'theatrical' spectacle that Foucault and Greenblatt found in the early modern period, nor simply Foucault's 'Panopticon' visibility of the many by the few.

The very strong influence that we found among our respondents (especially among older people) of television coverage of the Wood Royal Commission is a very good example of Thompson's point that modernity's 'mediated visibility' includes a new kind of visibility of the few by the many. Here television audiences are faced with the accentuating of symbolic materials (like police corruption) that are distanced from the spatio-temporal contexts of everyday life, and which can become a source of discordance and tension with traditionally held values, but at the same time also a source of new audience knowledge and empowerment. It is in this spirit that Bill does not turn police shows off instantly, as Mae does, but instead now enjoys the new, 'meaner', more 'graphic' and 'true-to-life' series like Phoenix. Bill is appropriating, in Thompson's sense, mediated experience to inform and refashion – even in his 80s – his own self-project.

Lisa and Rob: the teenagers

Lisa and Rob do appropriate the various media crime genres to negotiate their crime fears. For Lisa, it is the 'real life' crime incidents shown on the TV news that really frighten her, because they indicate that violence is 'normal' and always around the corner. She prefers not to watch the news alone; and tries to talk with her family about worrying events afterwards, in order 'to write them off '. But for Lisa *no* television crime genre works to reduce her fears (which were sufficiently intense for a while in Bondi for her to sleep with a knife in her bed because of her fear of rape or murder by an intruder). Though Lisa fears items on the news, she doesn't believe this genre helps with her own local experiences of mugging, sexual molestation, harassment and drugs. This is because TV 'goes for the ratings'; and so her own 'ordinary events' do not get shown in the context she experienced them in.

> With child molesting what they show is on a bigger scale – paedophilia, old men or something, rather than just like in a family situation. . . . Muggings get shown heaps on cop shows, but don't really get shown on the news very much. And the same with like family abuse or whatever, it gets shown on shows but doesn't really get on the news so much. And drug addict mothers get shown on cop shows but not really on the news. More would happen on cop shows because they're not believable.

Police series do deal with these 'ordinary events', but 'not believably'. Her own more intimate local contexts and mental maps – of *her* situations of mugging, sexual harassment and robbery – are not portrayed adequately by either of these television crime genres.

In Rob's case, television, as we have seen, helps construct his city 'landscapes of fear'. But his response to various TV crime genres is very specifically situated. On the one hand, as a male, Rob is a little more confident that he can learn about physical strategies 'like walk, side swipe and duck easily' from the television interviews. On the other hand, as a young man into raves and their attendant drugs, he – like Julie, but in his own differently situated way – is dismissive of television's way of dealing with his own experiences.

> The way they tell it, they don't have an understanding of what actually goes on. . . . The reality is very open. TV shows just one point of view. It shows the bad things that are happening [at raves]. But there is a lot more good things. . . . You meet real nice people. It is like nobody is crazy or anything. But they're the kind of things they show on TV – where somebody comes up to talk . . . just gives them drugs . . . takes them home, videotapes them, and kills them. It is just one point [of view]. For starters, you would not take anything off somebody unless you paid for it.

Like many of our other teenager respondents, Rob was annoyed by the media's coverage of the Anna Woods affair (the case of a middle-class teenager who died at a rave party after too much water consumption with her ecstasy experimentation). Now, at least, he says, things are much safer. 'From my experience now, people tell you not to drink too much water – that's how she died, I believe, she drowned. And . . . your friends control how much water you drink, and you decide to buy one bottle, and you only drink that. So it's a lot more safer. It is rarely that people go out of control.' None of this 'lay knowledge' has been reproduced, Rob complains, by popular television. He instances a recent episode of the TV programme *Millennium* which presented the 'evil pusher-takes-home-and-murders-young person scenario'. Similarly, in *Renegade* 'this person was operating illegal raves, and they would spike the punch and drink whatever with certain drugs. The way they imitated the rave scene at the time was unrealistic.'

Unlike the seniors Mae and Bill, Lisa and Rob do *not* like police series where the 'good guys' win – even though an Australian series they both regularly watch is called *Good Guys, Bad Guys*. For Lisa the 'good guys' in this series '*are* bad guys, but not *the* bad guys. . . . Elvis is OK but his whole family are crooks.' The 'nice crooks' win, so 'it's funny. . . . The police in *Good Guys, Bad Guys* are all evil, sort of. . . . They're all corrupt. But in *The Bill* they're all sweet, lovely . . . which is not like real life.' So *Good Guys, Bad Guys* for Lisa is 'just TV stories, TV characters, not real'. What *is* real for Lisa is her actual experience of police and her friends' 'talk' about police. In this context of local 'knowledge', the reiterated quality of television *increases* Lisa's fears. Police series are not 'doxic', in Bourdieu's sense of calming her terror within the ideological narrative of the 'good police' always winning. Rather, weekly 'real life' crime reconstruction series like *Australia's Most Wanted* actually have added to her fears because they have confirmed her view about how 'dumb' the police are in not being able to solve most crimes. 'It's brought the little hidden thought at the back of my mind right to the front. . . . It shows how much is actually happening in our community . . . like passes by without us kinda even knowing or being able to stop it. So it makes it worse.'

It is within this situated and dialogic mix of her own life experiences of crime and friends' stories about the police that *Good Guys, Bad Guys* performs for Lisa. 'Cop shows like *Good Guys, Bad Guys* . . . kind of lighten [my fears about crime] so it's not as bad in some ways. But not on the news because they show you how much of it is actually happening, and so you've got a bigger chance of it happening to you.'

Like Lisa, Rob likes *Good Guys, Bad Guys* because it is 'funny' and because the 'good guys don't always win. . . . Elvis's . . . not good. Like he'll still be devious in his actions. But in the end, he will always beat the bad guys. But he is not truly good. That's what I like about that.' Despite this similarity, there is a significant difference in Lisa's and Rob's liking of this series, which became apparent when we asked them about 'good role models' in the media. As her best example, Lisa actually chose the fictional Elvis from *Good Guys, Bad Guys* because 'he wouldn't hurt anybody, without being a goody-goody'. She rejected Arnold Schwarzenegger as a role model: his films were 'funny because stupid', with so much violence 'that you don't take it in'. Rob also juxtaposed his discussion of *Good Guys, Bad Guys* with Arnold Schwarzenegger, but he said he enjoyed the latter 'for the violence I guess. I have seen basically every one of his movies. . . . I like the storyline of the violence. . . . It's the way people get hurt. Seeing people in pain. That's fun.' Rob said similar things about his enjoyment of computer games. '*Diablo, Doom, Quake*, different war games like *Command and Conquer*. Just different games, different degrees of violence.'

As for *Good Guys, Bad Guys*, although both Rob and Lisa liked it because the 'good guys don't always win', they *read* this in different ways. Whereas Lisa argued this was because 'Good doesn't always win in real life' (as she felt she knew from experience), Rob's response was more overtly performative. He said he 'would rather see a dramatic ending – like the good guys getting hurt at the end. Adds more spirit to it.'

In her analysis of ritual, Susanna Rostas argues that ritualization is constrained, whereas performativity is what 'gives an enactment its zest' (Hughes-Freeland, 1998: 17); and this is certainly Rob's definition of his pleasure in *Good Guys, Bad Guys* compared to the ritualized police series. For Rob, 'it's good when a cop gets killed because you know it's one for the bad guys, finally. . . . It's the same with computer games, like *Command and Conquer*. It's a war game where you can either be the good guys or the bad guys. I always like to be the bad guys so that I can beat the good guys.'

As Sparks suggests, the 'realisations' of TV crime by viewers 'in determinate settings' depend on a play between different generic forms. But, despite his emphasis on determinate settings and the need for situated analysis, Sparks's analysis is in fact too formalistic, even essentialist. It is not the case that either Lisa or Rob turn to police series' 'good guy' narratives and scheduling to restore the 'doxic' in the face of the terrors of other city crime genres. Rather, they appropriate crime genres in their different, localized ways. Whereas Lisa shifts her discussion from the 'unreal' police series to the other more frightening and 'real' crime genres (where she tries to contain her fear by way of talk), Rob compares the 'unreal' standard cop series with the more 'real' world of *Renegade*, a bounty hunter series that emphasizes police corruption, and other 'true stories about death, murder.'

At one level, the difference between Lisa's emphasis on her fear of rape and sexual abuse (via the news and personal experience) and Rob's pleasure in violence is a familiar, gendered one. Rob, with his enjoyment of violent computer games and 'cop gets killed' television is very much the kind of young male as 'Other' that Mae and many older respondents we interviewed said they most worried about. But on the other hand, it is important to take Rob's own localized performance of the media and his situated 'talk' seriously. Speaking about his pleasure in computer games, he says: 'I would not say that it reflects on the personality. I'm not a violent person. It doesn't really influence me.' Nothing that we know of Rob suggests that he is 'affected' by media violence. In fact, he gives an entirely plausible reason for his pleasure which is based on his distinction between formal and everyday performance:

> it could be fun if it doesn't seem real. . . . Like if somebody was in pain on the ground I wouldn't *know what to do*. But people on TV, because they are actors, they mightn't have the experience about what pain's like. It might seem funny. I just like seeing the good guy lose for once.

Hearing Rob say, with considerable feeling, that he would hate to experience real-life pain on the ground in front of him, I certainly believed him. It was clear, too, that a major part of his 'fun' in violence was a performative one. He did *not* get his comfort and pleasure in the 'landscapes of fear' of Sydney by watching the 'good guy' always winning in television police series; so he enjoyed the symbolic violence that he knew was 'only acting'.

Turning to 'talk', and other circuits of communication

As Hirsch says, we never actually leave the local, but rather it is 'the system of local contexts . . . and linkages' that creates the global (Hirsch, 1998: 223). And it is these which, in Hughes-Freeland's words, disconnect, diffuse and recontextualize the 'fixed site' of a globalizing media. Mae, Bill, Lisa and Rob re-work Sparks's 'paleo-symbolic' city images and 'doxic' police narratives in their own situated ways; and they do so by actively *performing* different circuits of communication, some more face-to-face, others more 'mediated'.

While avoiding all television police series, Mae assiduously reads about crime in the newspapers. She has recently begun to worry about her grandchildren and drugs. Reading the local Bathurst *Advocate* and the Sydney *Telegraph*, she compares the two newspapers, and fears that the drug problem has spread from the city to her previously safe country area. In the local paper, she always reads the court cases section: and nine out of ten items, she says. are about drugs. Local newspaper reports of drug-taking also fuel Mae's main fear: home invasion. It is her belief that unemployment and drug-taking are the main reason for young people increasingly breaking into homes nowadays; and to confirm this she reads her local paper in detail. It is here that she 'proves' the causal relation between Sydney's dangerous city streets and her threatened country-town home. It is very noticeable how exclusively the home invasion and drug stories in the paper catch her attention. Recently there had been a front page news item in *The Advocate* about an armed robbery at a betting shop only two blocks away from her home, yet she could not recall it. In contrast, she vividly remembered a television item on the bashing of an old man in his front garden in Sydney. The assault on an older, isolated and vulnerable victim was much closer to her, even though it occurred 200 kilometres away.

Bill, in contrast, is more relaxed about his local newspaper. In his view, there are few reports of crime in the local paper (the only one that worried him was the report of a robbery at a local National Bank, because his daughter works at another branch). The local paper mainly appears to report petty crime or driving under the influence; and he says it was the same when he lived in the country. However, like Mae, Bill does use another circuit of communication to offset his television viewing. Much more significant than TV police series in Bill's tactic for managing fear of crime is a discussion group every Friday night at the Returned Soldiers' League Club with other men in 'the village'. As an example, he described how it was here, talking with his mates, that he dealt with the shock of the television coverage of the Port Arthur and Dunblane massacres (where lone killers, one in the 'heritage' convict site in Tasmania, the other in a small Scottish country town, shot many people, including children). 'That Port Arthur business was shocking and so was the Dunblane. . . . We talked about gun control and the necessity for it. We thought that the Government did the right thing immediately putting it on.' While there was some debate in the discussion group about whether people in rifle and pistol clubs should have been able to keep their guns 'under lock and key in a vault somewhere, perhaps in a police station', there was overall agreement about gun laws. So it made them feel better talking about it, especially as some government action on gun laws followed. Bill's sense of reasonable empowerment as a result of his 'village' security and being surrounded there by others with whom he could talk, was very different from Mae's situation. She did talk with neighbours about Port Arthur, but they all felt less threatened by that one event than by 'home invasions', since these 'are happening every day'. Unlike Bill, Mae feels she has no one near her to talk to about her fears. She says that even her children never talk with her about her anxiety, even though they must notice the multiple locks on the doors when they visit.

Bill's and Mae's responses to the police 'real life' series, *Australia's Most Wanted* is symptomatic of their difference in this sense of security through talk. Mae watched it when her husband was alive, but now she doesn't because it would play on her mind that those things could happen to her. In contrast, Bill watched the series for a time, but didn't feel affected by it, one way or another. Again he was able to be more reflexive about it than Mae. 'We know crime's going on. But you don't have to have it shoved in front of you. Somebody's making money out of something, so it's another one I switch off.'

Lisa, as we have seen already, turns to talk with her parents to try to help her anxieties after watching television news reports of crime. Lisa tends also to rely on talk with her girlfriends about the way that violent events like the Perth serial killings or the shootings at Port Arthur seem to be committed by 'ordinary' people, which makes them more scary. The Perth serial killings made Lisa more fearful 'of everything, everywhere. . . . I guess it does make me heaps more fearful because they are presumed normal people.' She talks with her girlfriends about how everything seems normal but it is not, how you are not really safe anywhere you go, and cannot fully protect yourself. This kind of talk may or may not calm Lisa, but talk with friends did help her deal with the earlier sexual harassment incident. 'It was pretty bad in some ways. But it was OK because we like talked to each other heaps about it. But it was a bit bad not being able to tell anyone [else].' Lisa also turned to talk to her neighbours who were also 'always being robbed' to help her manage other Bondi fears. 'It does help because you kind of know that you're not the only person thinking that's pretty scary. . . . So it does help to talk.'

Rob does not talk with friends much about fear of crime, and nor does he feel that the local newspapers help him deal with it. But, as we have seen, Rob has his own performative way of dealing with violent crime. He controls it by making it 'funny', challenging Sparks's 'doxic' narrative by his choice of television 'cop' series and violent computer games. In his own local environment, where Rob feels fairly safe, he also uses television police series in specifically situated ways. Whereas Lisa found *Australia's Most Wanted* disturbing because it confirmed her experience of the police and the 'normalcy' of crime, Rob watches it more regularly, applying it to his work as a supermarket 'checkout chick' (till operator) where 'you see a lot of people, I watch just in case I see somebody'. These are all ways in which, as Sparks says, 'stories' and 'talk' that circulate about crime and justice beyond this or that specific risk are appropriated and become important.

We can see very clearly, by way of Mae's, Bill's, Lisa's and Rob's stories, how the 'focus on performance allows us to understand situations interactively, not in terms of communication models, but as participatory ones' (Hughes-Freeland, 1998: 15). In other words, as we hear of their participatory and dialogic use of different communication forms, we can see how these four differently situated people are neither the 'effect' nor the 'inscribed readers' of one or other communication model (as in American 'effects' or 'screen theory' models). But nor are they simply the 'subject-effect' of structuralism's symbolic systems, nor of poststructuralism's 'citations'. As I said in the Introduction, the understanding of performance as 'technologies of the self/selves' takes our attention away from 'texts' to embodied, situational performances. Thus, as she sits alone in her home turning her television on and off, Mae is no less interactive and 'dialogic' than she was before her husband died. It is just that she is now on a different (more isolated) stage, and her performance relies on a different set of communication voices than when she talked with her partner.

In this chapter I have used everyday stories to 'test' (and situate in different age, gender and time/space co-ordinates) both quantitative *and* qualitative work on fear of crime and the media. This includes objectivist accounts of fear of crime (which rely all too often on a single 'fear of crime walking at night in your neighbourhood' question in a general survey), Gerbner's 'mean world thesis', and Gunter's 'selective perception thesis'. But it also includes Sparks's textualist approach to the 'paleo-symbolic' and the 'doxic' in TV police series.

In particular, I have indicated some very different ways in which 'those who perceive their neighbourhood as out of control and lacking a sense of community cohesion, those who have a lack of confidence in their ability to cope with attack or have a high perceived level of physical or social vulnerability, are more fearful' (Tulloch et al., 1998: vol. 1, 27). But I have also tried to show how, in more situated ways than Sparks's 'doxic' hypothesis suggests, people devise tactics to help with (or in some cases increase) their fear via a 'dialogic' interaction with a range of different circuits of communication. Thus, as Rapport says, they agentively construct and reconstruct themselves via their mix of narrational performances, and these are co-present and co-dependent with their 'liturgical' understandings of 'good guy/bad guy' narratives and their city's 'landscapes of fear'.

This is the kind of appropriation of 'crime' that Thompson describes as 'a narrative of self-identity'. In this understanding of 'appropriation',

> the self is a symbolic project that the individual actively constructs . . . out of the symbolic materials which are available to . . . weave . . . into a coherent account of who he or she is, a narrative of self-identity. This is a narrative which for most people will change over time as they draw on new symbolic materials, encounter new experiences and gradually refine their identity in the course of a life trajectory. To recount to ourselves or others who we are is to retell the narratives – which are continuously modified in the process of retelling. . . . We are the unofficial biographers of ourselves, for it is only by constructing a story, however loosely strung together, that we are able to form a sense of who we are and of what our future might be. (Thompson, 1995: 210)

If we compare my first 'everyday story' of this book with my last ones, Julie with Lisa and Mae, we may note that all these women talk about recognizing fear in 'everything, everywhere'. And yet we might ponder also the remarkably different senses of personal control that these three women have. Julie is of course older than Lisa, younger and less vulnerable than Mae. But she is also a lesbian feminist. When we make this kind of comparison of three women's fears, the practical politics of changing the *possibilities* of everyday stories certainly seems more important than changing the 'expert systems' which analyse them. To return to Terry Threadgold's point, the material limitations on performing gender differently as between Mae and Lisa and Julie become insistently and practically apparent.

Yet, if we think so, we should also remember the importance to Julie of her feminist narrative: 'there is no safety anywhere, anytime, so you may as well live your life and not let the fear control you'. Then we should note again Threadgold's gloss on Foucault's 'archive', as:

> the network of everyday and expert knowledges, of official and unofficial narratives and events, of official and everyday writings and rewritings, which made it possible to say things in certain ways, to tell certain stories, to go on doing these things, to remember some of them and not others, and at certain times to suddenly, but under very particular kinds of contextual and intertextual constraints, begin to tell them and perform them again. (Threadgold, 1997: 197)

If we are going to perform our cultural stories again, we will need always to remember that it is this *network* of everyday and expert knowledges that 'makes it possible to say things in certain ways', and, 'in certain circumstances' (as in Julie's case), to begin to tell them again, differently. Performing culture is always going to be a matter of stories told – dialogically – of expertise *and* the everyday.

REFERENCES

Adam, Barbara and Allan, Stuart (1995) *Theorizing Culture: an Interdisciplinary Critique after Postmodernism*. London: UCL Press.

AGB McNair (1993) 'Evaluation Summary', in S. Venables and J. Tulloch *Your Little Head Thinking Instead of Your Big Head: the Heterosexual Men's Project*. Sydney: Family Planning New South Wales. pp. 46–7.

Alasuutari, Pertti (ed.) (1999) *Rethinking the Media Audience*. London: Sage.

Ang, Ien (1985) *Watching Dallas: Soap Opera and the Melodramatic Imagination*. London: Methuen.

Ang, Ien (1996) *Living Room Wars: Rethinking Media Audiences for a Postmodern World*. London: Routledge.

Australian Department of the Prime Minister and Cabinet (1992) *Access and Equity*. Canberra.

Australian Vice-Chancellors' Committee (1994) *Academic Standards in Higher Education*. Canberra: AVCC.

Bacon-Smith, Camille (1992) *Enterprising Women: Television Fandom and the Creation of Popular Myth*. Philadelphia: University of Pennsylvania Press.

Bakhtin, M.M. (1981) *The Dialogical Imagination*. Ed. M. Holquist, trans. by C. Emerson and M. Holquist. Austin: University of Texas Press.

Bakhtin, M.M. (1984) *Problems of Dostoevsky's Poetics*. Ed. and trans. by Caryl Emerson. Minnesota: University of Minnesota Press.

Bakhtin, M.M. (1986) *Speech Genres and Other Late Essays*. Trans. by V.W. McGee. Austin: University of Texas Press.

Barry, Peter (1995) *Beginning Theory: an Introduction to Literary and Cultural Theory*. Manchester: Manchester University Press.

Beck, U., Giddens, A. and Lash, S. (1994) *Reflexive Modernization: Politics, Tradition and Aesthetics in the Modern Social Order*. Cambridge: Polity Press.

Bennett, Tony and Woollacott, Janet (1987) *Bond and Beyond: the Political Career of a Popular Hero*. Basingstoke: Macmillan.

Billig, Michael (1987) *Arguing and Thinking: a Rhetorical Approach to Social Psychology*. Cambridge: Cambridge University Press.

Bourdieu, Pierre (1977) *Outline of a Theory of Practice*. Trans. by R. Nice. Cambridge: Cambridge University Press.

Brown, Keith (1998) 'Macedonian culture and its audiences: an analysis of *Before the Rain*', in Felicia Hughes-Freeland (ed.), *Ritual, Performance, Media*. London: Routledge. pp. 160–76.

Bryman, A. (1988) *Quantity and Quality in Social Research*. London: Unwin Hyman.

Butler, Judith (1993) *Bodies That Matter: On the Discursive Limits of 'Sex'*. New York: Routledge.

Butler, Judith (1995) 'Burning acts – injurious speech', in A. Parker and E. Sedgwick (eds), *Performativity and Performance*. New York: Routledge. pp. 197–227.

Carlson, Marvin (1996) *Performance: a Critical Introduction*. London: Routledge.

Certeau, Michel de (1984) *The Practice of Everyday Life*. Trans. by S. Randall. Berkeley: University of California Press.

Coleman, Simon and Eisner, John (1998) 'Performing pilgrimage: Walsingham and the ritual construction of irony', in Felicia Hughes-Freeland (ed.), *Ritual, Performance, Media*. London: Routledge. pp. 46–65.

Conquergood, Dwight (1985) 'Performing as a moral act: ethical dimensions of the ethnography of performance', *Literature in Performance*, 5: 1–13.

Crawford, June, Kippax, Susan and Tulloch, John (1992) *Review of Issues and Methodologies in National AIDS Education Campaigns*. Canberra: Commonwealth Department of Community Services and Health.

Davies, Bronwyn (1991) 'The concept of agency: a feminist poststructuralist analysis', in A. Yeatman (ed.), *Postmodern Critical Theorising*, special issue of *Social Analysis* 30 (December): 42–53.

Davies, Charlotte A. (1998) ' "A oes heddwch?" Contesting meanings and identities in the Welsh National Eisteddfod', in Felicia Hughes-Freeland (ed.), *Ritual, Performance, Media*. London: Routledge. pp. 141–59.

Denzin, Norman K. and Lincoln, Yvonna S. (1998) *Collecting and Interpreting Qualitative Materials*. Thousand Oaks, CA: Sage.

Dollimore, Jonathan and Sinfield, Alan (1994) *Political Shakespeare: Essays in Cultural Materialism*, second edn. Ithaca, NY: Cornell University Press.

Douglas, Mary (1992) *Risk and Blame: Essays in Cultural Theory*. London: Routledge.

Editorial (1994) 'Sensitization and training for health promotion on HIV/AIDS and STDs', *AIDS Health Promotion Exchange*, 2: 1–2.

Elam, Keir (1989) 'Text appeal and the analysis paralysis: towards a processual poetics of dramatic production', in T. Fitzpatrick (ed.), *Altro Polo. Performance: from Product to Process*. Sydney: University of Sydney, Frederick May Foundation for Italian Studies. pp. 1–26.

Fortier, Mark (1997) *Theory/Theatre: an Introduction*. London: Routledge.

Foucault, Michel (1978) *The History of Sexuality: Volume 1, An Introduction*. London: Allen Lane.

Frow, John (1993) 'Regimes of value', in P. Mead and M. Campbell (eds), *Shakespeare's Books: Contemporary Cultural Politics and the Persistence of Empire*. Melbourne: University of Melbourne. pp. 207–18.

Giddens, Tony (1984) *The Constitution of Society*. Cambridge: Polity Press.

Gore, Charles (1998) 'Ritual, performance and media in urban contemporary shrine configurations in Benin City, Nigeria', in Felicia Hughes-Freeland (ed.), *Ritual, Performance, Media*. London: Routledge. pp. 66–84.

Greenblatt, Stephen (1992) 'Invisible bullets: Renaissance authority and its subversion, *Henry IV* and *Henry V*', in R. Wilson and R. Dutton (eds), *New Historicism and Renaissance Drama*. Harlow: Longman. pp. 83–108.

Griffiths, Trevor (1978) *The Cherry Orchard* in a new English version by Trevor Griffiths, from a translation by Helen Rappaport.

Gunter, B. (1987) *Television and the Fear of Crime*. London: John Libby & Co.

Hall, S. (1987) 'Minimal selves', *ICA Documents 6. Identity*. (London: Institute of Contemporary Arts.

Hall, S. (1989) 'Politics and letters' in T. Eagleton (ed.), *Raymond Williams: Critical Perspectives*. Cambridge: Polity.

Hall, S., Clarke, J., Jefferson, T., Critcher, C. and Roberts, B. (1978) *Policing the Crisis: Mugging, Law and Order and the State*. London: Macmillan.

Handmer, John (1996) 'Communicating uncertainty: perspectives and themes', in T.W. Norton, T. Beer and S.R. Dovers (eds), *Risk and Uncertainty in Environmental Management*. Canberra: Australian National University. pp. 86–97.

Hastrup, Kirsten (1998) 'Theatre as a site of passage: some reflections on the magic of acting', in Felicia Hughes-Freeland (ed.), *Ritual, Performance, Media*. London: Routledge. pp. 29–45.

Hirsch, Eric (1998) 'Bound and unbound entities: reflections on the ethnographic perspectives of anthropology *vis-à-vis* media and cultural studies', in Felicia Hughes-Freeland (ed.), *Ritual, Performance, Media*. London: Routledge. pp. 208–28.

Hobson, Dorothy (1982) *Crossroads: the Drama of a Soap Opera*. London: Methuen.

Holland, Peter (1982) 'Chekhov and the resistant symbol', in J. Redmond (ed.), *Drama and Symbolism*. Cambridge: Cambridge University Press. pp. 227–58.

Hollway, W. (1984) 'Gender difference and the production of subjectivity', in J. Henriques, (ed.), *Changing the Subject*. New York: Methuen.

Hughes-Freeland, Felicia (ed.) (1998) *Ritual, Performance, Media*. London: Routledge.

Jenkins, Henry (1992) *Textual Poachers: Fans and Participatory Culture*. London: Routledge.

Kruger, Loren (1993) 'Placing the occasion: Raymond Williams and performing culture', in D.L. Dworkin and L.G. Roman (eds), *Views Beyond the Border Country: Raymond Williams and Cultural Politics*. London: Routledge. pp. 55–71.

Lash, Scott, Szerszynski, Bronislaw and Wynne, Brian (eds) (1996) *Risk, Environment and Modernity*. London: Sage.

Lawson, Sylvia (1977) 'Good taste at Hanging Rock', in J. Tulloch (ed.), *Conflict and Control in the Cinema: Readings in the Sociology of Film*. Melbourne: Macmillan. pp. 201–12.

Lawson, Sylvia (1979) 'Towards decolonizing film history in Australia', in S. Dermody, J. Docker and D. Modjeska (eds), *Nellie Melba, Ginger Meggs and Friends: Essays in Cultural History*. Malmsbury: Kibble Books. pp. 19–32.

Lewis, Justin (1991) *The Ideological Octopus: an Exploration of Television and its Audience*. London: Routledge.

Lodge, David (1990) *After Bakhtin: Essays on Fiction and Criticism*. London: Routledge.

Lupton, Deborah and Tulloch, John (1997) *Social Marketing: Its Place in Public Health*. Report to Australian Federation of AIDS Organisations, Sydney.

McRobbie, Angela (1996) 'All the world's a stage, screen or magazine: when culture is the logic of late capitalism', *Media, Culture & Society*, 18: 335–42.

Metchnikoff, Elie (Metchnikov, I.I.) (1910) *The Prolongation of Life*, trans. by P. Chalmers Mitchell. London: Heinemann.

Metchnikoff, O. (1921) *Life of Elie Metchnikoff, 1845–1916*. Boston: Houghton-Mifflin.

Moeran, Brian (1996) 'The orient strikes back: advertising and imagining Japan', *Theory, Culture and Society*, 13 (3): 77–112.

Morgan, M. Granger (1993) 'Assessing risk', *Scientific American*, July: 24–5.

Morris, Meaghan (1988) 'Tooth and claw: tales of survival, and *Crocodile Dundee*', in *The Pirate's Fiancee: Feminism, Reading, Postmodernism*. London: Verso. pp. 241–87.

Murdock, Graham and Golding, Peter (1989) 'Information poverty and political inequality: citizenship in the age of privatised communications', *Journal of Communication*, 39 (3): 180–95.

Murry, John Middleton (1920) 'Thoughts on Chekhov', in *Aspects of Literature*. London: Collins., re-printed in V. Emeljanow, *Chekhov: the Critical Heritage*. London: Routledge and Kegan Paul. p. 204.

Osipov, E. (Ossipow), Popov, I. (Popow) and Kurkin, P. (Kourkine) (1900) *La Médicine du Zemstvo en Russie*. Moscow.

Parker, Andrew and Sedgwick, Eve K. (eds) (1995) *Performativity and Performance*. New York: Routledge.

Patton, Cindy (1995) 'Performativity and spatial distinction: the end of AIDS epidemiology', in A. Parker and E. Sedgwick (eds) *Performativity and Performance*. New York: Routledge. pp. 173–96.

Penley, Constance (1991) 'Feminism, psychoanalysis and the study of popular culture', in L. Grossberg, C. Nelson and P. Treichler (eds), *Cultural Studies*. New York: Routledge. pp. 45–63.

Pickering, Michael (1997) *History, Experience and Cultural Studies*. Basingstoke: Macmillan.

Pink, Sarah (1998) 'From ritual sacrifice to media commodity: anthropological and media constructions of the Spanish bullfight and the rise of women performers', in Felicia Hughes-Freeland (ed.), *Ritual, Performance, Media*. London: Routledge. pp. 121–40.

Popkin, Cathy (forthcoming) *Bodies of Knowledge: Chekhov's Corpus.* Stanford, CA: Stanford University Press.

Radway, Janice (1984) *Reading the Romance: Women, Patriarchy, and Popular Literature.* Chapel Hill: University of North Carolina Press.

Rapport, Nigel (1998) 'Hard sell: commercial performance and the narration of the self ', in Felicia Hughes-Freeland (ed.), *Ritual, Performance, Media.* London: Routledge. pp. 177–93.

Roach, Joseph (1995) 'Culture and performance in the circum-Atlantic world', in A. Parker and E. Sedgwick (eds), *Performativity and Performance.* New York: Routledge. pp. 45–63.

Rostas, Susanna (1998) 'From ritualization to performativity: the Concheros of Mexico', in Felicia Hughes-Freeland (ed.), *Ritual, Performance, Media.* London: Routledge. pp. 85–103.

Schieffelin, Edward L. (1998) 'Problematizing performance', in Felicia Hughes-Freeland (ed.), *Ritual, Performance, Media.* London: Routledge. pp. 194–207.

Shotter, John (1993) *Cultural Politics of Everyday Life.* Buckingham: Open University Press.

Silverman, David (1993) *Interpreting Qualitative Data: Methods of Analysing Talk, Text and Interaction.* London: Sage.

Sparks, Richard (1992) *Television Drama and the Drama of Crime: Moral Tales and the Place of Crime in Public Life.* Buckingham: Open University Press.

Strathern, M. (1987) *Out of Context: the Persuasive Fictions of Anthropology.* Hemel Hempstead: Harvester Wheatsheaf.

Taylor, Ian, Evans, Karen and Fraser, Penny (1996) *A Tale of Two Cities: Global Change, Local Feeling and Everyday Life in the North of England. A Study in Manchester and Sheffield.* London: Routledge.

Thompson, John B. (1995) *The Media and Modernity: a Social Theory of the Media.* Cambridge: Polity Press.

Threadgold, Terry (1997) *Feminist Poetics: Poiesis, Performance, Histories.* London: Routledge.

Tulloch, John (ed) (1977) *Conflict and Control in the Cinema: A Reader in Film and Society.* Melbourne: Macmillan.

Tulloch, John (1980) *Chekhov: a Structuralist Study.* Basingstoke: Macmillan.

Tulloch, John (1981) *Legends On The Screen: The Narrative Film in Australia 1919–1929.* Sydney: Currency.

Tulloch, John (1990) *Television Drama: Agency, Audience and Myth.* London: Routledge.

Tulloch, John (forthcoming) 'Approaching theatre audiences: active school students and commoditised high culture', *Contemporary Theatre Review.*

Tulloch, John and Burvill, Tom (1999) ' "Going to Chekhov": cultural studies and theatre studies', *Journal of Dramatic Theory and Criticism,* 13(2): 23–55.

Tulloch, John and Jenkins, Henry (1995) *Science Fiction Audiences: Watching Doctor Who and Star Trek.* London: Routledge.

Tulloch, John and Lupton, Deborah (1997) *Television, AIDS and Risk: a Cultural Studies Approach to Health Communication.* Sydney: Allen & Unwin.

Tulloch, John, Burvill, Tom and Hood, Andrew (1997) 'Reinhabiting "The Cherry Orchard": class and history in performing Chekhov', *New Theatre Quarterly,* 13 (52): 318–28.

Tulloch, John, Lupton, Deborah, Blood, Warwick, Tulloch, Marian, Jennett, Christine, Enders, Michael (1998) *Fear of Crime* (2 vols). Canberra: National Campaign Against Violence and Crime Publications.

Tulloch, Marian (1998) 'Quantitative review', in J. Tulloch, D. Lupton, W. Blood, M. Tulloch, C. Jennett and M. Enders, *Fear of Crime* (vol. 1). Canberra: National Campaign Against Violence and Crime Publications. 9–28.

Vaughan, Alden T. and Vaughan, Virginia M. (1991) *Shakespeare's Caliban: a Cultural History.* Cambridge: Cambridge University Press.

Venables, Susan and Tulloch, John (1993) *Your Little Head Thinking Instead of Your Big Head: the Heterosexual Men's Project.* Sydney: Family Planning New South Wales; includes Venables, S. 'Background to the project', 4–26; and Tulloch, J. 'Your little head thinking instead of your big head', 27–45.

WHO (1992) World Health Organization Global Programme on AIDS, Editorial and 'Intervention Planning', *AIDS Health Promotion Exchange*, 3: 1–3 and 12–15.

WHO (1994) World Health Organization Global Programme on AIDS, Editorial, *AIDS Health Promotion Exchange*, 2: 1–2.

Williams, Raymond (1977) *Marxism and Literature*. Oxford: Oxford University Press.

Williams, Raymond (1989) *The Politics of Modernism*. London: Verso.

Williams, Raymond (1991) *Drama in Performance*. Milton Keynes: Open University Press.

Williams, Raymond (1993) *Drama from Ibsen to Brecht*. Hogarth: London. pp. 101–11.

Willis, P. (1980) 'Notes on method' in S. Hall et al. (eds), *Culture, Media, Language*. London: Hutchinson.

Wilson, Richard and Dutton, Richard (eds) (1992) *New Historicism and Renaissance Drama*. Harlow: Longman.

Wilson, Scott (1995) *Cultural Materialism: Theory and Practice*. Oxford: Blackwell.

Worthen, W.B. (1989) 'Deeper meanings and theatrical technique: the rhetoric of performance criticism', *Shakespeare Quarterly*, 40: 441–55.

Worthen, W.B. (1996) 'Invisible bullets, violet beards: reading actors reading', in *Textual and Theatrical Shakespeare: Questions of Evidence*. Iowa: University of Iowa Press. pp. 210–29.

Wynne, Brian (1996) 'May the sheep safely graze? A reflexive view of the expert–lay knowledge divide', in S. Lash, B. Szerszynski and B. Wynne (eds), *Risk, Environment and Modernity*. London: Sage. pp. 44–83.

Index

active audience theory, *see* audience
actors, 33, 70; double agency, 8, 85, 126;
    interaction with, 18, 117–36
advertisements, 42–6, 65–6, 68
age/ageism, 15, 159, 162
agency, 5–6, 9, 16, 40–1, 66, 84, 116;
    intentionality and, 7–8, 17, 84;
    structure and, 4, 20–1, 86, 121, 140
alien voices, *see* voices
alienation, 30, 40, 154–5
anthropology, 3, 4–5, 6–11, 106, 139
appropriation, 6, 162, 176; resistance and,
    27–32, 38, 84
arbitrary closures, 60–5, 138, 145
archive, 10, 20–1, 26, 176
art (intertextual use), 104, 105
audience, 1, 3, 6, 8–10, 34; active, 34,
    60–1, 66, 107, 112–13, 119, 128, 139,
    143; actor interaction, 18, 117–36;
    constituted, 129–36; cultural reading,
    106–37; disciplined, 11, 22, 60; lost
    voices, 21, 23–6, 30–2, 38, 106, 114;
    popular culture, 146–52; third
    generation theory, 18, 106–8, 117–19,
    128, 134, 147
Australia: film theory, 21, 22, 23–32

Belvoir Street Theatre, 107–8
bricolage, 3, 29, 83, 86, 116
Brief and True Report (Harriot), 89–93

canonical performance, 8, 10, 11, 18, 20,
    66–9, 72, 85–7, 105, 144, 147, 152
carnival, 3, 136, 152
Chekhov, Anton, 10–11, 18, 152; cultural
    materialism, 97–105; high-cultural
    framing, 70–83; new historicism and,
    86–8, 93–6; on television, 103–5, 108,
    154–5; *see also Cherry Orchard, The*
    (Chekhov)
Cherry Orchard, The (Chekhov), 73, 75,
    93–5; Griffiths' text, 97–102, 108; 'In
    Conversation', 113–17; Lopakhin,
    100–2, 111, 114, 117–29, 131–3, 136,

Cherry Orchard, The (Chekhov) *cont.*
    155–8; RSC marketing, 108–13, 155;
    RSC performance, 79–83, 129–33, 136
citations, 3–4, 10, 14, 16–17, 35, 145, 175
cities, 13, 31–2, 163–4, 166–7, 172
citizenship, 17, 39–69
co-texts, 93–5, 97–9, 102, 110
commodification, 30, 71, 102–5, 108–13,
    128–30
community, 38, 141–4, 176
condoms (health campaigns), 17–18, 42–69,
    150–1
consciousness, 14, 116, 117, 121
constraint, creativity and, 7, 8, 17, 39, 84,
    86, 140, 144
consumption, 1, 8, 17, 29, 30, 42–5
contextual constraints, 20, 21, 176
control, 32, 40, 41, 161
corporate-raider chic, 29–32, 38
creativity, 36; constraint and, 7, 8, 17, 39,
    84, 86, 140, 144
crime: attitudes to police, 167–73; fear of,
    31–8, 159–61; media reports, 167–8,
    170–1, 173–7; narratives, 12–17, 162–5
Crocodile Dundee (film), 21, 26–32
cultural archive, 1, 20–1, 26, 176
cultural capital, 16, 30, 77, 111–13
cultural imperialism, 21, 23–4, 26, 141
cultural materialism, 18, 76, 88–9, 92, 96,
    106, 114; Griffiths and, 97–105
cultural methods, 138–58
cultural policy, 39–69, 106, 140
cultural production, 30, 112–13, 140
cultural reading, 18, 106–37
cultural strategies/tactics, 3, 4, 14, 38, 86
cultural studies, 8, 153; project and
    formation, 20–2; in sites of high
    culture, 18, 70–84, 85–105; third
    generation, 18, 106–8, 117
cultural theory, 20–38, 138, 159; positioned
    truths of, 58, 106

disciplinary society, 89, 93
disciplined audiences, 11, 22, 60
doxic narratives, 171–3, 175–6

economic capital, 16, 30
effects theory, 128, 175
empiricism, 33–4, 114, 140, 141
enterprise culture, 140, 147
epidemiology, 4, 66–7, 91, 142
epistemology, 2, 6, 10, 15, 40–1, 77
equity, citizenship and, 42, 43
ethnography, 5, 9, 31, 61, 107, 128, 134, 141, 154; storytelling, 1, 24, 34, 39, 96, 113, 117–18, 138–40, 145–7, 160
everyday life, 5–6, 8, 119, 128, 147; experience, 2, 117, 140; performance, 2–3, 7, 11–17, 47–8; in risk society, 20, 32–8
experience, 2, 117, 140, 141
expert, 35–8, 117; expertise, 2, 11, 15–16, 20, 83; model (health), 143–4; narratives, 17–18, 39, 47–55; system, 32, 34, 91–3, 96, 176; voices, 26–7, 30, 65–6
expert knowledge, 22–3, 25, 30, 58, 67, 94, 114, 154; lay and, 17, 20, 39–42, 91–3, 144–5, 149, 160; reflexivity within, 17, 32, 40
expressionism, 98, 99, 154

fantasy of modernism, 18, 75–80
fear: of crime, see crime; landscapes of, 31, 34–5, 163–4, 166–7, 170, 173, 176; narratives, 12–17; news media and, 167–8, 170–1, 173–7
feminism, 1, 12, 15–17, 26, 88, 134, 140, 176
film theory (Australia), 21, 22, 23–32
flâneur, 31
formal performance, 2–3, 6–7, 60, 147; high-cultural framing, 70–84; high- cultural re-framing, 85–105; reading, 108–36
formalism, 21, 77, 88

gender, 1, 4, 12–17, 135–6, 140, 159–60, 162, 176
global contexts, 9, 12–13, 15, 25, 86, 140, 160, 162, 163
government, 12–13, 141–4
grand narratives, 26, 73–5, 95–6, 121
Greenblatt, Stephen, 89–93
Griffiths, Trevor, 97–105, 108
Grim Reaper advertisement, 42–5, 46

habitus, 8, 83, 112–13
health campaigns: Grim Reaper, 42–6; Heterosexual Men's Project, 17–18, 45–69, 114, 118, 144–6; social marketing, 141–4

Heterosexual Men's Project, 17–18, 45–69, 114, 118, 144–6
hidden voices, 98–9, 101, 106, 108
high culture, 5, 8, 11; framing, 70–84; marketing, 108–13; re-framing, 85–105; research (qualitative methods), 152–8
history: construction, 18, 74–8, 83–4; new historicism, 18, 86–98, 102, 106, 140
HIV/AIDS campaigns, 10, 11, 17–18, 39, 41–69, 114, 118, 143–6, 149–52
Holland, Peter, 113–17
humanism, 1, 70, 76, 121–2, 128, 156; see also liberal humanism; literary

iconography, 162–5
identity, 6, 8, 39–40, 176
ideology, 75–80, 98, 120, 122–3
illocutionary, 3, 8
illusion, 7, 9–10, 17, 71, 84
'In Conversation' interview, 113–17
instrumentalism, 40, 120, 122, 123, 125
intentionality, 7–8, 17, 84
interpellation, 4, 16, 66, 68
intertexts, 11, 26, 104–5, 116, 126, 149, 176; multiple, 58–60
interviewers, 17, 47–58
ironic performance, 8, 85
iterability, 3, 17, 30

knowledge, 5, 16, 17, 20; see also expert knowledge; lay knowledge; scientific knowledge

landscapes of fear, 31, 34–5, 163–4, 166–7, 170, 173, 176
language, 3, 7, 86; games, 11; meta-language, 1, 160; see also linguistics
langue, 3, 153
Lawson, Sylvia, 22–6, 114
lay knowledge, 25–6, 29, 53–5, 67; and expert, 17, 20, 39–42, 91–3, 144–5, 160; risk and, 32–8
lay narratives, 17, 55–8
lay voices, 30, 160
legitimacy/legitimation, 2, 159
liberal humanism, 72–3, 77, 79, 83–4, 86, 94, 105, 117, 133, 152, 155, 160
liminality/liminoid, 2, 3, 6–7, 86, 135
linguistics, 3, 8, 21–3, 27
literary humanism, 71, 83–4, 140
liturgy, 8, 10–11, 18, 36, 51, 84–6, 105, 113, 139, 144, 147, 176
local contexts, 9, 12–13, 15, 86, 140, 160, 162–3; case studies, 21–38

Lopakhin: on stage performances 100–2,
    111, 114, 117–29, 131–3, 136; in the
    text, 119–23; Troughton, 123–9, 155–8
lost voices, *see* voices
ludic excess, 8, 10, 103

magazines, 140, 147, 148, 150
marketing high culture, 108–13
master narrative, 17, 22–3, 30, 138, 159,
    163
material capital, 111, 112
material reality, 17, 30, 38
materialism, 25, 114, 116; *see also* cultural
    materialism
materiality, 16–17, 26, 30, 38, 144
mean world thesis, 165, 168–9, 175
media: crime narratives, 12–17, 167–75;
    HIV/AIDS campaign, 10, 11, 17–18,
    39, 41–69, 143–6, 149–52; news,
    167–8, 170–1, 173–7; radio, 150; and
    risk society, 32–8; *see also* television
mediated: audience, 161; modernity 96, 103;
    narratives, 82; visibility, 103, 162, 169
memory, 4, 23, 31
mental maps, 13, 31, 98, 170
meta-narratives, 31
metalanguages, 1, 160
metamethodology, 19, 138, 152–8
metaphysics, 2, 9, 117, 139
metatheory, 16, 69
micro-economies of culture, 140, 147, 149
micro-narratives, 134
micropolitics, 11, 140, 149
modernism, 27, 31: fantasies of, 18, 75–80;
    high-cultural framing, 70–80, 105;
    ideologies of, 18, 75–80, 83; naturalist,
    76–7, 98, 99
modernity, 8, 27, 32, 159; fixing, 18, 80–3;
    grand narrative of, 73–5, 121; high-
    cultural framing, 70–80, 105
Morris, Meaghan, 21, 26–32
multiple intertexts, 58–60
multiple subjectivities, 58–60, 116, 117, 122
myth, 25, 28, 31, 78

narrative(s), 1, 139; attitudes to police,
    167–73; closures, 60–5, 138, 145;
    crime, 162–5; doxic, 171, 172–3,
    175–6; expert, 17–18, 39, 47–55;
    grand, 26, 73–5, 95–6, 121; lay, 17,
    55–8; master, 17, 22–3, 30, 138, 159,
    163; situated, 34, 140
nationalism, 16, 22, 23
naturalism, 78–9, 98–9, 102–3, 114–16,
    122, 154–5

naturalist modernism, 76–7, 98, 99
new formalism, 77, 88
new historicism, 18, 86–98, 102, 106, 140
news media, 167–8, 170–1, 173–7
Noble, Adrian, 113–17
Nottingham Playhouse, 97, 99–102

ontology, 9, 10
other, 6, 30, 37, 42–4, 49, 61, 82, 139,
    152–3, 155, 172; voices, 93, 96

paintings (intertextual use), 104, 105
paleo-symbolic, 162, 173, 175
paradigm theory, 33, 77
parody, 8, 10, 27
parole, 3
performance: cultural reading, 18, 106–37;
    everyday life, 20–69; formal, *see*
    formal performance; high culture,
    70–84, 85–105; on the street, 11–17;
    situated, 154, 159–77; in theory, 3–11;
    transformative, 4, 10, 18, 85–105, 139
performativity, 1–6, 11, 39, 66–70, 86,
    139–40, 160, 172; being/becoming, 8,
    120; cultural materialism, 97–105;
    discourse as, 15–16; new historicism,
    18, 86–96; power and, 85–6, 89, 91–2;
    situational interaction, 7–10; of subject-
    effect, 17, 95
phenomenology, 77–8
police series, 35–7, 162–4, 166–76
political intervention, 9, 10, 14, 39
politics, 83; cultural/political, 29–30, 34, 38;
    micropolitics, 11, 140, 149;
    representational orders, 18, 30, 33, 115
popular culture, 8, 11, 83–4, 146–52
positioned truths, 58, 106, 113, 114
postcolonial culture, 1, 21, 27, 34–8
postindustrial society, 1, 22, 27, 31
postmodernism, 1, 19, 27–32, 42, 88, 117,
    138–40, 159
postmodernity, 8, 30, 42
power, 1, 14–16, 92–3, 97, 139

Q-Theatre, 129, 133–7
qualitative methods, 2, 31, 160, 164–5;
    metamethodology, 19, 138, 152–8
quantitative methods, 144–51, 160–1, 164;
    metamethodology, 19, 138, 152–8

race, 4, 13–17, 34–8, 140
rational choice theory, 32
rational self, 121, 122
reading formations, 11, 58–60, 71, 108, 114,
    116

reality, 1, 15, 115–16; framing of, 7, 9–10, 17, 71, 84; material, 17, 30, 38; social, 8, 10, 70, 85
reflexivity, 8, 13–14, 62, 83, 159–60; cultural methods, 140, 152–3; cultural reading, 106, 113–16, 119; of risk society, 17, 31–8, 40; storytelling, 2, 15, 21, 113
regimes of value, 18, 70–1, 80, 84, 87, 88, 94, 130
representation, 2, 18, 30–2, 72, 159
representational order, 20, 27, 30, 33, 106, 113, 115, 145, 153, 162
resignification, 16, 20, 30
resistance, 15, 42, 84, 97–8, 136; colonial, 21–32; risk society, 32–8
rhetoric, 11, 17, 78, 147–9, 155
risk: groups, 4, 66–7, 91; society, 20, 31–40, 42–5, 91, 106, 143; theory, 17, 160–1
ritual, 4, 7–10, 85, 139–40, 147, 172
Royal Shakespeare Company, 18, 106, 154; audience strategy, 79–83, 129–33, 136; marketing policy, 108–14, 130, 155–6

science, 17, 22–3, 91–3, 95–6
scientific knowledge, 33–4, 39–40, 51, 54, 94
screen theory, 21, 23, 175
script, 3, 7, 8, 86
selective perception, 165, 169, 175
self, 6–7, 9, 72, 116–17, 121–2, 175–6
semiotic institutions, 70–1, 96, 105, 130, 153
semiotic labours, 16, 17, 26
sexual behaviour: alcohol and, 55, 61, 65, 68; Grim Reaper campaign, 42–6; Heterosexual Men's Project, 17–18, 45–69, 114, 118, 144–6
Shakespeare, William: cultural materialism 97, 101; Henry IV/Henry V, 89–92; A Midsummer Night's Dream, 82, 129, 133–6; new historicism, 86–93
social class, 15, 79, 80, 140
social control, 40, 41

social constructionism, 3, 10, 19, 138
social marketing, 141–4
social reality, 8, 10, 70, 85
sociology, 3, 9, 22, 32
Sparks, Richard, 162–5
spectatorship: cultural reading, 18, 106–37; cultural theory, 20–38; as participation, 7–9, 17, 84, 86, 139; see also audience
storytelling, 2, 9, 11–17, 47–8; see also ethnography
structuralism, 21
structuration, 5
structure/agency, 4, 20–1, 86, 121, 140
structure of feeling, 25, 31, 97–8
subject-effect, 17, 95
subjectivities, 15–16, 58–60, 116, 122
survival stories, 26–32
symbolic system, 8, 34, 100, 161, 175–6

television, 9, 12; high-culture on, 85–6, 89, 102–5, 108, 154–5; police series, 35–7, 162–4, 166–76; soaps, 146–9
text/textualism, 10, 15, 87, 93–5, 108, 119–23, 162, 173, 175
theatre, 3–6, 70–105, 153, 161–2
third generation theory, see audience transformative process, 4, 10, 18, 85–105, 139
triangulation, 154, 155
Trofimov (in The Cherry Orchard), 100, 120–1, 12–5, 128–9, 133, 136, 158
Troughton, David, 123–9, 155–8

utterances, 3, 14, 17, 59–60, 78, 80, 83–4, 86, 91, 94–5, 97–100, 105, 116

violence, 12–17, 32–8, 159–73
voices, 11; alien, 91–2, 94, 96, 99, 101–2; 106; expert, 26–7, 30, 65–6; hidden, 98–9, 101, 106, 108; lay, 30, 160; local, 22–38; lost, 21, 23–6, 30–2, 38, 106, 114

Wynne, Brian, 91